Journal of Brand Management:
Advanced Collections

**Series Editors**
Tim Oliver Brexendorf
Henkel Center for Consumer Goods
WHU-Otto Beisheim School of Management
Düsseldorf, Germany

Joachim Kernstock
Centre of Competence for Brand Management
University of St. Gallen
St. Gallen, Switzerland

Shaun M. Powell
School of Management and Marketing
University of Wollongong
Wollongong, New South Wales, Australia

The Journal of Brand Management (JBM) has established itself as a leading journal in the field. Published by Palgrave it encompasses contributions from both academics and practitioners and covers topics such as luxury branding, research methods and corporate branding to name a few. The *Journal of Brand Management: Advanced Collections* series provides definitive and comprehensive coverage of broad subject areas. Books in the series are ideally used on PhD programmes or by upper level students looking for rigorous academic material on a popular subject area, and for scholars and discerning practitioners, acting as 'advanced introductions.'

Organised thematically the series covers historically popular topics along with new and burgeoning areas that the journal has been instrumental in developing, showcasing the incremental and substantial contributions that the journal has provided. Each book is guest edited by a leading figure in the field alongside the Journal Editors who will provide a new leading article that will cover the current state of research in the specific area.

More information about this series at
http://www.springer.com/series/15099

Jean-Noël Kapferer • Joachim Kernstock • Tim Oliver Brexendorf • Shaun M. Powell
Editors

# Advances in Luxury Brand Management

*Editors*
Jean-Noël Kapferer
Inseec Business School
Paris, France

Tim Oliver Brexendorf
Henkel Center for Consumer Goods
WHU-Otto Beisheim School of
Management
Düsseldorf, Germany

Joachim Kernstock
Centre of Competence for Brand
Management, University of St. Gallen
St. Gallen, Switzerland

Shaun M. Powell
School of Management and Marketing
University of Wollongong
Wollongong, New South Wales, Australia

Journal of Brand Management: Advanced Collections
ISBN 978-3-319-51126-9      ISBN 978-3-319-51127-6 (eBook)
DOI 10.1007/978-3-319-51127-6

Library of Congress Control Number: 2017935420

© The Editor(s) (if applicable) and The Author(s) 2017
This work is subject to copyright. All rights are solely and exclusively licensed by the Publisher, whether the whole or part of the material is concerned, specifically the rights of translation, reprinting, reuse of illustrations, recitation, broadcasting, reproduction on microfilms or in any other physical way, and transmission or information storage and retrieval, electronic adaptation, computer software, or by similar or dissimilar methodology now known or hereafter developed.
The use of general descriptive names, registered names, trademarks, service marks, etc. in this publication does not imply, even in the absence of a specific statement, that such names are exempt from the relevant protective laws and regulations and therefore free for general use.
The publisher, the authors and the editors are safe to assume that the advice and information in this book are believed to be true and accurate at the date of publication. Neither the publisher nor the authors or the editors give a warranty, express or implied, with respect to the material contained herein or for any errors or omissions that may have been made. The publisher remains neutral with regard to jurisdictional claims in published maps and institutional affiliations.

Cover illustration © Mmdi, Stone/Getty images

Printed on acid-free paper

This Palgrave Macmillan imprint is published by Springer Nature
The registered company is Springer International Publishing AG
The registered company address is: Gewerbestrasse 11, 6330 Cham, Switzerland

# Contents

**Introduction: Luxury Brand Management Insights and Opportunities**     1
*Joachim Kernstock, Tim Oliver Brexendorf and Shaun M. Powell*

**The End of Luxury as We Knew It?**     25
*Jean-Noël Kapferer*

**Luxury Brand Marketing – The Experience Is Everything!**     43
*Glyn Atwal and Alistair Williams*

**The Luxury Brand Strategy Challenge**     59
*Uché Okonkwo-Pézard*

**The Specificity of Luxury Management: Turning Marketing Upside Down**     65
*Jean-Noël Kapferer and Vincent Bastien*

**Luxury Consumption in the Trade-Off Between Genuine and Counterfeit Goods: What Are the Consumers' Underlying Motives and Value-Based Drivers?**     85
*Klaus-Peter Wiedmann, Nadine Hennigs and Christiane Klarmann*

**Is Luxury Compatible with Sustainability? Luxury Consumers' Viewpoint** 123
*Jean-Noël Kapferer and Anne Michaut-Denizeau*

**Probing Brand Luxury: A Multiple Lens Approach** 157
*Karen W. Miller and Michael K. Mills*

**Managing the Growth Tradeoff: Challenges and Opportunities in Luxury Branding** 179
*Kevin Lane Keller*

**Measuring Perceptions of Brand Luxury** 199
*Franck Vigneron and Lester W. Johnson*

**Managing Luxury Brands** 235
*Jean-Noël Kapferer*

**Index** 251

# List of Figures

| | | |
|---|---|---|
| Fig. 1 | Beyond rarity, how do luxury megabrands sustain their desirability? | 36 |
| Fig. 2 | Experiential zones | 50 |
| Fig. 3 | The scope of the luxury goods and services industry | 60 |
| Fig. 4 | The conceptual model | 90 |
| Fig. 5 | The effect of anti-counterfeiting countermeasures | 98 |
| Fig. 6 | Shocking news about luxury brands' misbehaviour – Euclidian Distances. INDSCAL (stress = 0.10462, RSQ = 0.96) | 142 |
| Fig. 7 | Proposed framework of brand luxury index | 204 |
| Fig. 8 | Results from the mulitrait-multimethod matrix of correlations | 223 |
| Fig. 9 | The luxury industry according to McKinsey | 237 |
| Fig. 10 | The luxury and brand system | 241 |
| Fig. 11 | Luxury brands' attraction power in Europe | 246 |

# List of Tables

| | | |
|---|---|---|
| Table 1 | Analysis of prominent corporate brands in the luxury industry | 4 |
| Table A1 | Literature review – consumer value perception of luxury counterfeits | 103 |
| Table 2 | Shocking news about luxury brands' misbehaviour | 137 |
| Table 3 | Sample description: Demographics | 138 |
| Table 4 | Sample description: Sustainable development sensitivity and behaviour | 138 |
| Table 5 | Consumers' opinions on luxury and standard deviation (N = 966) | 140 |
| Table 6 | Explaining the perceived contradiction between luxury and sustainability | 143 |
| Table 7 | Explanatory variables and relationships with perceived contradiction between luxury and sustainability | 146 |
| Table A2 | Construction of explanatory variables | 149 |
| Table 8 | Competing definitions, depictions of brand luxury | 159 |
| Table 9 | Competing typologies and depictions of brand luxury | 166 |
| Table 10 | Antecedents and consequences of brand luxury | 169 |
| Table 11 | Management strategy and/or benefits of brand luxury | 170 |
| Table 12 | Lexical items delineating brand luxury from prestigious (premium) brands | 171 |
| Table 13 | Ten defining characteristics of luxury brands | 180 |
| Table 14 | Some brand marketing tradeoffs | 185 |

# List of Tables

| | | |
|---|---|---|
| Table 15 | Review of factors describing luxury brands across three studies | 206 |
| Table 16 | Summary of the scale development process | 211 |
| Table 17 | Reliability coefficients for each brand and each dimension | 213 |
| Table 18 | Varimax rotated factor structure: full data set. Original 30 items used for scale development | 214 |
| Table 19 | Dimensions of original 30-item scale | 216 |
| Table 20 | Results from the different models | 216 |
| Table 21 | Correlations between BLI scale and criterion-related scale | 219 |
| Table 22 | Correlations between BLI scale and related attitude scales | 220 |
| Table 23 | Percentage of respondents sorted among each scale category | 222 |
| Table 24 | Twenty items in the BLI scale | 227 |

# Introduction: Luxury Brand Management Insights and Opportunities

## Joachim Kernstock, Tim Oliver Brexendorf and Shaun M. Powell

The luxury industry is large, complex and very competitive and one that has flourished significantly in the past couple of decades (Okonkwo, 2009a; Ko et al., 2016). Luxury was once known as a quiet industry that was driven by product excellence and managed by families. Its value

---

J. Kernstock (✉)
Centre of Competence for Brand Management, University of St. Gallen, St. Gallen, Switzerland
e-mail: joachim.kernstock@km-sg.ch

T.O. Brexendorf
Henkel Center for Consumer Goods, WHU-Otto Beisheim School of Management, Dusseldorf, Germany
e-mail: tim.brexendorf@whu.edu

S.M. Powell
School of Management and Marketing, University of Wollongong, Wollongong, New South Wales, Australia
e-mail: spowell@uow.edu.au

© The Author(s) 2017
J.-N. Kapferer et al. (eds.), *Advances in Luxury Brand Management*, Journal of Brand Management: Advanced Collections,
DOI 10.1007/978-3-319-51127-6_1

proposition was made up of a mix of high-quality products, brand heritage, unique knowledge, exclusivity, personalisation of services, and bespoke communications fused with long-term relationships with selected clientele and categorised by high prices and prestigious physical stores (Kapferer, 2014). Most of the above is still relevant and true for the luxury industry, but nowadays much of the industry is driven by large conglomerates. The economic concentration is increasing with the top ten of the largest companies accounting for more than 50 percent of all revenues in the luxury industry (Deloitte, 2016). From a research perspective manuscripts on luxury brand management have proven to be historically popular amongst the readership of the *Journal of Brand Management* (Powell, 2014), and the areas continuing importance further reinforced in recent years (Brexendorf et al., 2014; Kapferer, 2014).

We start our introduction by taking the corporate brand management perspective and provide insights into the largest luxury corporates. We then present an overview of some of the very latest research coming to the fore in luxury brand management and conclude by providing an orientation for the remainder of this book and chapters.

## The Luxury Industry

First we will give an overview of what is considered as the luxury industry. We follow the corporate brand perspective by analysing the largest brand conglomerates within the luxury industry. Different rankings are used by selecting the top ten corporates. Sometimes 'luxury' corporates are mixed with fashion companies. Ralph Lauren Corporation, for example, is often included in the luxury industry rankings. We excluded corporates focussing on fashion only and are following the more exclusive definition provided by Kapferer (2014, p. 717) who discusses luxury as 'a concept, an industry and a very specific strategy'. The manuscripts in this advanced collection book each conform to this view on the luxury industry and their brands (see also Chapter 'The End of Luxury as We Knew It' in this book).

# Introduction: Luxury Brand Management Insights and Opportunities

While analysing the corporate brands of the most prominent in the luxury industry we present a description of the corporate self, the mission and vision statement, if existing, and the corporate brand values (see Table 1). Summarising some of the lessons learned from our analysis, the major corporates of the luxury brand industry identify themselves as 'leaders' and acting 'globally'. The aspiration of 'innovation' (Rolex) and 'craftsmanship' (Hèrmes) are still there but not in the centre core of all top ten luxury corporates.

Missions and visions reflect as generally acting within the spirit of entrepreneurs (LVMH) or in the footprint of the founder (Estée Lauder). More importantly, reflecting the relationship to the customer, all top ten luxury corporates are emphasising a specific relationship to their clients, which provides the purchase of a luxury product. As LVMH points out the ambition to refine *art de vivre*, as centre to the mission of luxury.

The corporate brand values are composed of 'craftsmanship', 'innovative aspiration', and 'entrepreneurial spirit and creativity' as typical for the luxury industry. Additionally, we also find more corporate-oriented values like 'learning culture', 'responsibility' or 'quest for excellence', 'trustworthiness', 'long-term success', and 'authenticity'. Most of the top luxury conglomerates are operating several luxury brands or a luxury brand portfolio, acting independently from each other. Please find the most popular luxury brands delineated in Table 1.

The overview provided in Table 1 serves as an industry snapshot in 2016. Comparing this list of brands with previous year's, readers might perceive that there has not been much change occurring in the luxury industry. Nonetheless, luxury brands are facing challenges on the product brand level.

## Consumer Luxury Brand Perceptions

There is a limited understanding of consumer perceptions toward luxury brands. Gaining a better understanding of the consumer behaviour towards luxury brands is of tremendous importance for building, managing and sustaining luxury brands. Several major trends have changed

Table 1 Analysis of prominent corporate brands in the luxury industry

| Rank | Company | USDm* | Description | Mission | Vision | Corporate brand values | Major luxury brands | Source |
|---|---|---|---|---|---|---|---|---|
| 1 | LVMH Moët Hennessy-Louis Vuitton SA | 23,297 | The world leader in luxury, LVMH has deployed a business model marked by dynamic growth since its creation in 1987. The LVMH group comprises 70 exceptional Houses that create high-quality products. It is the only group present in all five major sectors of the luxury market. | LVMH brings together truly exceptional Houses. Each of them creates products that embody unique savoir-faire, a carefully preserved heritage and a dynamic engagement with modernity. These creations make our Houses ambassadors of a distinctively refined art de vivre. | 'Our business model is anchored in a long term vision that builds on the heritage of our Houses and stimulates creativity and excellence. This model drives the success of our Group and ensures its promising future'. – Bernard Arnault, Chairman and CEO of LVMH | The three fundamental values are shared by every member of LVMH. The three imperatives 'be creative and innovative, deliver excellence and cultivate an entrepreneurial spirit' inspire excellence and constitute the pillars of our performance and long-term success. | Moët & Chandon, Dom Pérignon, Louis Vuitton, Christian Dior, Acqua di Parma, Benefit Cosmetics, TAG Heuer, Hublot, La Grande Epicerie de Paris | (LVMH, 2016a, b) |

| | | | | | | | |
|---|---|---|---|---|---|---|---|
| 2 | Compagnie Financiere Richemont SA | 13,217 | Richemont owns several of the world's leading companies in the field of luxury goods, with particular strengths in jewellery, luxury watches and premium accessories. | Not available | As a responsible luxury goods company, our vision is to create long-term value for our business and wider society, while preserving our heritage in quality, craftsmanship, and innovation. | The five group values are entrepreneurship, creativity and innovation, customer focused, learning culture, and craftsmanship. | Cartier, Van Cleef & Arpels, Piaget, Vacheron Constantin, Jaeger-LeCoultre, IWC Schaffhausen, Panerai, Montblanc | (Richemont, 2016a, b, c) |
| 3 | The Estée Lauder Companies Inc. | 10,780 | We are the global leader in prestige beauty – delighting consumers with transformative products and experiences, inspiring them to express their individual beauty. We are the only company focused solely on prestige makeup, skin care, fragrance, and hair care with a diverse portfolio of 25+ brands sold in 150 countries. | Bringing the best to everyone we touch and being the best in everything we do. | Infused throughout our organisation is a passion for creativity and innovation – a desire to push the boundaries and invent the unexpected – as we continue the bold work of our founder Estée Lauder. | We are a values-driven organisation. Our actions are rooted in the Lauder family values of respect for the individual, uncompromising ethics and integrity, generosity of spirit, and fearless persistence. | Estée Lauder, M.A.C., Aramis, Clinique, Aveda, Tom Ford Beauty, Bobbi Brown | (Estée Lauder, 2016a, b, c) |

*(continued)*

Table 1 (continued)

| Rank | Company | USDm* | Description | Mission | Vision | Corporate brand values | Major luxury brands | Source |
|---|---|---|---|---|---|---|---|---|
| 4 | Luxottica Group SpA | 10,172 | Luxottica is a global leader in the design, manufacture and distribution of fashion, luxury and sports eyewear with high technical and stylistic quality. | Luxottica's mission is to protect the eyes and enhance the look of women and men in the world, creating the best possible eyewear to satisfy its clients and interpret consumer tastes and aspirations. | Luxottica's long-term strategy is to continue to expand in the eyewear and eye care sectors by growing its various businesses, whether organically or through acquisitions. | The company will continue to focus on the following strategic pillars: vertical integration, design and technological innovation, brand portfolio management, market expansion, financial discipline and the development of talented and committed employees. | Ray-Ban, Oakley, Vogue Eyewear, Persol, Oliver Peoples and Alain Mikli, Giorgio Armani, Burberry, Bulgari, Chanel, Dolce&Gabbana, Michael Kors, Prada, Ralph Lauren, Tiffany & Co., Versace, Valentino** | (Luxottica, 2016) |

| | | | | | | |
|---|---|---|---|---|---|---|
| 5 | The Swatch Group Ltd. | 9,223 | Swatch Group is an international group active in the design, manufacture, and sale of finished watches, jewellery, watch movements and components. | The Swatch Group has a very special emotional culture. We produce beauty, sensuality, emotionality in watches – and we also produce high-tech on your wrists. Both, emotionality or poetry and high-tech are part of what we feel towards our customers. We love them genuinely. We want them to be happy – we want YOU to be happy. | You will discover a fascinating world of diversity, beauty and quality with our brands and a high level of craftsmanship and industrial know-how with our production companies. | Breguet, Blancpain, Omega, Longines, Rado, Tissot, Balmain | (Swatch Group, 2016a, b, c) |
| 6 | Kering SA | 8,984 | Kering is a world leader in luxury apparel and accessories with sport and lifestyle activities. We develop a well-balanced ensemble of 20 brands. | Our mission is to enable our customers to express their personality and to fulfil their dreams, while making a positive contribution to people and the planet. Imagination – the ability to conceive something that does not yet exist – is what drives us at Kering. It fuels the creativity of our brands and makes us more resourceful as a business. | Diversity – of gender, nationality, age, background, talent and aspiration – is part of the Kering experience. Across our brands, we invest in the preservation of traditional craftsmanship through training and technical programmes. | Gucci, Bottega Veneta, Alexander McQueen, Pomellato, Boucheron, Saint Laurent | (Kering, 2016a, b) |

*(continued)*

**Table 1** (continued)

| Rank | Company | USDm* | Description | Mission | Vision | Corporate brand values | Major luxury brands | Source |
|---|---|---|---|---|---|---|---|---|
| 7 | Chow Tai Fook Jewellery Group Limited | 8,285 | Chow Tai Fook Jewellery Group Limited is a world-class leading jeweller. The acquisition of Hearts On Fire in 2014 has further underpinned the Group's stature as a diamond expert in the industry. | Sincerity – Eternity – the brand's philosophy and value originates from over 80 years' heritage. We combine sophisticated design and exquisite craftsmanship to create precious jewellery pieces that last from generation to generation. | | At Chow Tai Fook our core values are "sincerity – eternity". Our products symbolise trustworthiness, authenticity, and quality. | Chow Tai Fook, Hearts on Fire | (Chow Tai Fook, 2016) |
| 8 | L'Oréal Luxe | 8,239[e] | L'Oréal Luxe opens a unique world of beauty. Its international brands incarnate all the facets of elegance and refinement in three major specialisations: skin care, make-up, and perfume. | L'Oréal Group has set itself the mission of offering all women and men worldwide the best of cosmetics innovation in terms of quality, efficacy, and safety. By meeting the infinite diversity of beauty needs and desires all over the world. | Our ambition for the coming years is to win over another one billion consumers around the world by creating the cosmetic products that meet the infinite diversity of their beauty needs and desires. | Our values are embedded in L'Oréal's genetic code. The Group's six founding values are passion, innovation, entrepreneurial spirit, open-mindedness, quest for excellence, and responsibility. | Lancôme, Biotherm, Helena Rubinstein, Urban Decay, Paloma Picasso, Giorgio Armani | (L'Oréal, 2016a, b, c, d) |

| | | | | | | | |
|---|---|---|---|---|---|---|---|
| 9 | Rolex SA | 5,581[e] | Pioneer of the wristwatch since 1905, Rolex is at the origin of landmark innovations in watchmaking. For over a century, Rolex watches have accompanied explorers and achievers around the world, from the top of the highest mountains to the deepest reaches of the ocean. | Their mission is to make watches, and they do everything possible to make mechanical watches that are as good as possible (Adams, 2013). | To be the world-recognised leader and benchmark in service (Bilanz, 2004). | Rolex, Tudor (Deloitte, 2016, S.18) | (Rolex, 2016) |
| 10 | Hermès International SCA | 5,475 | For over 175 years, Hermès has been creating, inventing, and innovating. Although it has achieved international stature, Hermès has never lost its human touch and continues its tradition of fine craftsmanship. | Serving Hermès' ambition for excellence and its human-centric project – both founded on a bedrock of strong, shared values – while supporting the group's growth. | Sustainable development is a notion that echoes the house's founding values, in particular its long-term vision and the importance it attaches to its employees and to its culture of excellence and expertise, as well as its respect for nature, from which its materials are sourced. | International in scope, Hermès is characterised by superlative manufacturing inspired by the values of traditional craftsmanship, and remains a family firm with a uniquely creative spirit that is continuously renewed. | Hermès, John Lobb, Puiforcat, Saint Louis | (Hermès, 2016) |

[*]Only luxury goods sales FY2014 (result can defer from total revenues of the companies); [**]License portfolio
[e]Estimation
Deloitte, 2016, S.18

the landscape for luxury brands. Recently emerging issues relate to luxury, uniqueness and rarity. As highlighted by Kapferer and Bastien (2009, p. 316) for luxury brands 'being unique is what counts, not any comparison with a competitor'. Luxury brand managers also 'want to know what are the levers of the desire today for their brands, beyond rarity, on which they need to capitalize. How to compensate the loss of rarity and the diluting effects of the higher penetration resulting from their growth made through sales of accessories and second lines, more accessible' (Kapferer and Valette-Florence, 2016, p. 121).

*Individual luxury perceptions.* Cristini et al. (2017) have further discussed that the meaning of luxury is complex with more than one meaning depending on the context. Additionally, Kapferer and Laurent (2016) have identified a high diversity of luxury consumers and therefore 'luxury is in the eye of the consumer' (p. 339). Hence future research needs to investigate consumers' own perceptions based on their own definition of luxury to help luxury managers better decide which segment to target.

*Luxury vs. non-luxury brands.* Despite its growing importance, little is known about how consumers perceive luxury brands versus non-luxury brands. What are the similarities and differences to non-luxury brands? Especially important is the distinction between luxury brands and premium brands and what influences their perception and motivates their consumption. More conceptual research is needed to delineate luxury from non-luxury and to differentiate different forms or levels of luxury. For example, De Barnier et al. (2012) distinguish between accessible, intermediate and inaccessible luxury.

*Functional, symbolic, and experiential benefits.* How do consumers of luxury brands evaluate the functional, symbolic, and experiential benefits of luxury brands? What are expected features? What is the interplay between utilitarian and hedonic aspects of the luxury brand? How does this interplay influence the attitude and the purchase intention towards the luxury brand? Early research results indicate that a small utilitarian feature to a luxury product can serve as a 'functional alibi' justifying the indulgent purchase and reducing guilt (Keinan et al., 2016).

*Gender and age.* Initial research on luxury brands indicates that gender plays an important role, for example that women have a more positive attitude toward and a higher purchase intention of luxury brands versus non-luxury brands than men. Some research indicates that men may also be less responsive to the uniqueness, hedonic, and status value of luxury brands than women (Stokburger-Sauer and Teichmann, 2013). Another study on gender influence of luxury goods proposes that men use conspicuous luxury products to attract mates whereas women use such products to deter female rivals and to tacitly signal them that their partners are loyal to them (Wang and Griskevicius, 2014). Further research is needed to understand the relevance of gender differences for luxury brands. This understanding has large implications for the industry on how to develop and market their luxury brands and products based on gender.

## Ingredient Branding

Additionally within marketing an ingredient branding strategy is often used when introducing new products to a market, via a host brand integrating with another brand to produce a new product (Desai and Keller, 2002). Recent research has started to consider how luxury brands might best integrate, perhaps out of necessity, with non-luxury brands. For example, TAG Heuer (luxury host brand) integrating with Intel and Google to produce a luxury smartwatch (Moon and Sprott, 2016). However, potential clashes also exist in terms of fit between the luxury brand and the technology orientated brands, which may be dissimilar in a number of dimensions from a consumer perspective (Moon and Sprott, 2016). With an increasing trend, or at least opportunities for the use of wearable technologies integrated into some luxury items, we foresee the need for further investigation into the use of ingredient brand strategies in the context of luxury branding, to help identify the potential positives and pitfalls.

## Luxury Brand Experience and Journey

Luxury brands need to provide and sustain unique, exclusive and differentiating brand experiences. Delivering strong and positive experiences is more than ever of tremendous importance for luxury brand's success (Atwal and Williams, 2009; see Chapter 'The End of Luxury as We Knew It?' of this book). Luxury brand marketers must try to carefully control all aspects of the marketing program to ensure the aspiration, quality, and the consumption experience is positive with the brand (Keller, 2009). Customers interact with luxury brands through a myriad of touch points where each of them can shape the brand experience. Several authors argue that luxury brands should include a hedonistic and personal component (Atwal and Williams, 2009; Kapferer and Bastien, 2009). Designing, managing, and monitoring the total customer experience with the luxury brand and enabling customers to optimise and customise the experience is an important task for luxury brand marketers. Concurrently, it has become increasingly complex for brands to create, manage, and attempt to control the experience and journey of each customer, and different touch points can be identified and differentiated between brand owned, partner owned, customer owned and social external touch points (Lemon and Verhoef, 2016). Store environment for example is a specific touch point that could be categorised as brand owned (own stores) or partner owned (retailer). Each touch point could have further distinct sub-dimensions – like design, social, and ambient factors for store environment (Baker et al., 2002). Most existing research focuses on parts or specific touch points of the customer journey in isolation, providing granular insights into these touch points. Nevertheless, for luxury brand marketers a holistic view of touch points is of particularly importance (Baxendale et al., 2015). Granular as well as holistic journey studies would help to gain deeper understanding of the luxury brand experience and journey. One interesting and important granular key touch point for many luxury brands and interesting research area is the sales and the service encounter. Salesperson and service provider can play a crucial role for the customer's experience with and evaluation of the luxury brand. The employees of the brand epitomise, represent, and define the brand to the customer and by this they transform and implement a company's brand strategy (Brexendorf et al., 2010). Here many important research questions can be posed including: Which skills and capabilities do luxury brand salespeople need to represent the luxury brand consistently? Researchers have paid little attention to this important topic of luxury brand management to date.

## Luxury Brand Co-creation in a Digitally Connected World

It has been observed that in the past luxury brands appeared to have been reticent, for various reasons, to engage with and integrate internet and digital technologies (Okonkwo, 2009b). Indeed some continue to argue that 'luxury lags other consumer sectors when it comes to understanding and applying digital technologies... the speed of technology development is endangering their current business models' (Boston Consulting Group, 2016).

We believe that today the question is not if luxury brands should be present online and use online media, the question is more about how to most effectively incorporate and use digital media. According to a study by the Boston Consulting Group (2016) digital offers an opportunity for a transformative difference in how to reach and retain luxury customers, with six out of ten luxury purchases being influenced by digital channels. The use of online channels allows sales growth, differentiation and worldwide presence. Hence luxury brands require a presence in the physical but also digital world. An omnichannel presence is inevitable for most luxury brands. However, luxury brand marketers should look for new ways on how to assert exclusivity and uniqueness of their brand in the digital world. Possible ways are exclusive collections, exclusive platforms, and exclusive services. Although online media allow people to decrease distances, it also allows to increase the distance between consumers.

For example, in recent years the implications of social media and the facilitation of interaction for brand building, plus the support of online brand communities, have come to the fore. One early line of inquiry has been how social media may facilitate the sharing of brand stories between customers and/or help develop relationship quality, along with the challenges and opportunities these bring (Gallaugher and Ransbotham, 2010; Hajli et al., 2017; Tsai and Men, 2013). Accordingly we observe that one tension of particular interest moving forward will be the continuing challenges faced by luxury brands to further embrace and facilitate consumer empowerment due to the co-creation nature of social media, while also needing to maintain (and not dilute) their exclusive brand identity and image (Hughes et al., 2016). For example, the influence of YouTube vloggers on consumer luxury brand perceptions and intentions has started to be investigated (Lee and Watkins, 2016), with implications relating to whom to choose as a vlogger in their capacity as a luxury brand ambassador. Also the use of narrative-transportation storylines and/or storygiving may offer potential utility in such contexts (Hughes et al., 2016; Kim et al., 2016).

Hence it is clear to us that additional research is needed on applying digital technologies in the luxury sector, and on understanding their use and impact, and to also focus on social media across multiple platforms as a socio-commercial activity within the luxury sector a (Godey et al., 2016; Hughes et al., 2016).

## Luxury and Sustainability

In both, practice and theory of luxury brand management, there is a vivid debate about the relationship between luxury and sustainability. Can luxury be sustainable and can sustainability be luxurious? Many luxury brand consumers expect sustainability and environmental responsibility to be an integral part of luxury brands – especially within production processes and use of materials or ingredients. However, luxury is often more associated with unsustainability than with sustainability. Many consumers often see both concepts as contradictorily especially with regard to the social and economic facet of sustainability. Early research shows that this contradiction is lower for customers who define luxury as very high quality and much higher for those who define luxury as expensive or rare (Kapferer and Michaut-Denizeau, 2014). Chapter 'Luxury Consumption in the Trade-Off Between Genuine and Counterfeit Goods: What Are the Consumers' Underlying Motives and Value-Based Drivers?' in this book gives deeper insights into the results of this study. Several other studies demonstrate that consumers are less likely to take ethical criteria into account when they bought luxury products than when they bought FMCG products or commoditised products (Davies et al., 2012; Achabou and Dekhili, 2013).

One study also reveals an incompatibility between recycling and luxury products (Achabou and Dekhili, 2013). Although early empirical results have gained new insights into this important relationship, much more research is needed to understand the detailed interplay between these two important concepts. Another important area for further research is luxury brand counterfeits.

## Luxury Brand Counterfeits

A growing number of organisations are counterfeiting luxury goods, which fuel or satisfy an ever increasing parallel market (Nia and Zaichkowsky, 2000; Romani et al., 2012; Valette-Florence, 2012; Kapferer and Michaut, 2014; Randhawa et al., 2015; Wilson and Sullivan, 2016; Wilson et al., 2016). As noted by Wilson and Sullivan (2016) brand owners operating internationally or globally face various difficulties in measuring product counterfeiting, due to multiple legal systems, customs agencies and practices, alongside complicated and frequently changing supply chains. The use of the Internet and/or digital channels by counterfeiters to promote or even distribute counterfeit products across various platforms adds to this complexity. Nonetheless, the research by Wilson and Sullivan (2016) and Wilson et al. (2016) indicates that many organisations attempt to monitor and address counterfeiting, using whatever resources and mechanisms that may be available to them, although some have more experience/ resources, and are more proactive (than reactive) than others.

Therefore, we are in agreement that more research is needed to better understand and address this ever-changing landscape, particularly within the luxury brand domain.

## Outline of Chapters

In the remainder of this introduction we provide a brief outline of the different chapters. All chapters address a variety of topics within luxury brand management and are multifaceted in terms of methodologies involved, the type of contributions they make, and the authors' affiliations, which are international in scope.

In Chapter 'The End of Luxury as We Knew It?' Jean-Noël Kapferer provides a thought-provoking and challenging insight of industry challenges, which represent the current issues of the luxury brand industry. He contests historically developed common sense of research and rules of the industry. This chapter opens new avenues of research needed on luxury brand management and encourages the eagerness of the reader to delve deeper into the emergence of knowledge on luxury brand management as also represented in this book via the following chapters.

In Chapter 'Luxury Brand Marketing – The Experience Is Everything' Glyn Atwal and Alistair Williams discuss the relevance of experiential marketing in luxury branding, while explaining that experiences are central to luxury consumption activity. In so doing they highlight that in experiential marketing it is customer experiences and lifestyles which provide sensory, emotional, cognitive, and relational values to the consumer. Hence it is likely that innovative experience design will become an increasingly important component of luxury marketing.

In Chapter 'The Luxury Brand Strategy Challenge' Uché Okonkwo outlines the increased interest in luxury brand management through to 2009, due to a number of reasons which have also driven a shift from the 'top-down' relationship that has existed for centuries with luxury brands to a bottom-up affiliation. Factors discussed as driving the shift include: globalisation, wealth-creation opportunities, new luxury markets (China, Russia, India, the Middle East, Brazil, and Mexico), new market segments, digital communications, international travel, and culture convergence.

In Chapter 'The Specificity of Luxury Management – Turning Marketing Upside Down' Jean-Noël Kapferer and Vincent Bastien consider some of the counter-intuitive rules for successfully marketing luxury goods and services, which from a marketing perspective may also appear somewhat provocative. Taking a historical, sociological, and anthropological perspective they further consider the functions of luxury, and how to implement them.

### Introduction: Luxury Brand Management Insights and Opportunities 17

In Chapter 'Luxury Consumption in the Trade-Off Between Genuine and Counterfeit Goods: What Are the Consumers' Underlying Motives and Value-Based Drivers' Klaus-Peter Wiedmann, Nadine Hennigs, and Christiane Klarmann take a holistic view of the phenomenon of counterfeit consumption, undertaking a review of the research on counterfeiting in the luxury domain, leading to a model to help reduce some of the complexity faced.

In Chapter 'Is Luxury Compatible with Sustainability? Luxury Consumers' Viewpoint' Jean-Noël Kapferer and Anne Michaut-Denizeau investigate the level of sensitivity of luxury buyers to the cause of sustainable development and test whether luxury consumers perceive a contradiction between their luxury consumption and sustainability. They also discuss specific drivers of any perceived contradiction.

In Chapter 'Probing Brand Luxury: A Multiple Lens Approach' Karen Miller and Michael Mills probes brand luxury through seven lenses in order to provide greater clarity and to delineate brand luxury from other similar terms and concepts. They argue that many of the terms used in the luxury domain are not part of the construct of brand luxury and hence should not be confused with the construct of brand luxury.

In Chapter 'Managing the Growth Tradeoff: Challenges and Opportunities in Luxury Branding' Kevin Lane Keller outline ten characteristics that help to define luxury branding and identifies and discusses some of the challenges and opportunities in managing their growth trade-offs, in order to attract new customers without alienating existing customers.

In Chapter 'Measuring Perceptions of Brand Luxury' Franck Vigneron and Lester Johnson consider high-luxury brands from those that are low on luxury, via the development of a theoretical framework of the brand-luxury construct that leads to a specification of the dimensions of luxury as applied to brands, via the Brand Luxury Index scale.

In Chapter 'Managing Luxury Brands' Jean-Noël Kapferer concludes with his pioneering piece on luxury branding within the *Journal of Brand Management* from 1996, discussing how luxury brands differ from the 'up-market' brand or the ordinary brand, and whether the differences are simply those of degree or if they are inherent in the luxury brand's nature. In so doing he insightfully highlights that despite pressure for change and discontinuity exerted via numerous parties involved in a brand's international diffusion, the identity concept remains crucial to luxury brand management – and brands should never compromise on the brand's set of values or its deeply rooted identity traits.

## Conclusion

This introduction has provided an up-to-date snapshot of the luxury industry and discussed various avenues of topical luxury brand management research including issues relating to: luxury, uniqueness and rarity; consumer luxury brand perceptions; ingredient branding; luxury brand experience and journey; luxury brand co-creation in a digitally connected world; luxury and sustainability; and luxury brand counterfeits.

While the topics and research avenues as presented are not exhaustive, they do indicate that these are challenging and exciting times for the luxury industry with much still to learn about and to contribute to luxury brand management. We therefore encourage further innovative and rigorous research in the various pillars of luxury brand management. The discussion above and the chapters that follow will help by providing advanced insights, perspectives, and inspiration for luxury brand students, academics, and practitioners alike within one collection. It is our hope that you enjoy reading this compendium as much as we have enjoyed compiling it, written by renowned researchers and colleagues in the field.

## References

Achabou, M. A., & Dekhili, S. (2013). Luxury and sustainable development: Is there a match? *Journal of Business Research*, 66(10), 1896–1903.

Adams, A. (2013, December 5). Inside Rolex: Understanding the world's most impressive watch maker. *Forbes Magazine*. Retrieved on the 22.09.2016 at 22:20 from, http://www.forbes.com/sites/arieladams/2013/12/05/inside-rolex-understanding-the-worlds-most-impressive-watch-maker/#6c2ac93c34ad

Atwal, G., & Williams, A. (2009). Luxury brand marketing – The experience is everything! *Journal of Brand Management*, *16*(5–6), 338–346.

Baker, J., Parasuraman, A., Grewal, D., & Voss, G. B. (2002). The influence of multiple store environment cues on perceived merchandise value and patronage intentions. *Journal of Marketing*, *66*(2), 120–141.

Baxendale, S., Macdonald, E. K., & Wilson, H. N. (2015). The impact of different touchpoints on brand consideration. *Journal of Retailing*, *91*(2), 235–253.

Bilanz. (2004, October 27). Die Rolex-story: Die Legende Rolex. *Bilanz – das Schweizer Wirtschaftsmagazin*. Retrieved on the 22.09.2016 at 22:10 from, http://www.bilanz.ch/unternehmen/die-rolex-story-die-legende-rolex

Boston Consulting Group. (2016). Digital or die. The choice for luxury brands, https://www.bcgperspectives.com/content/articles/technology-digital-consumer-insight-digital-or-die-choice-for-luxury-brands/#chapter1. Accessed 25 October 2016.

Brexendorf, T. O., Mühlmeier, S., Tomczak, T., & Eisend, M. (2010). The impact of sales encounters on brand loyalty. *Journal of Business Research*, *63*(11), 1148–1155.

Brexendorf, T. O., Kernstock, J., & Powell, S. M. (2014). Future challenges and opportunities in brand management: An introduction to a commemorative special issue. *Journal of Brand Management*, *21*(9), 685–688.

Cristini, H., Kauppinen-Räisänen, H., Barthod-Prothade, M., & Woodside, A. (2017). Toward a general theory of luxury: Advancing from workbench definitions and theoretical transformations. *Journal of Business Research*, *70*(1), 101–107.

Davies, I. A., Lee, Z., & Ahonkhai, I. (2012). Do consumers care about ethical luxury? *Journal of Business Ethics*, *106*(1), 37–51.

De Barnier, V., Falcy, S., & Valette-Florence, P. (2012). Do consumers perceive three levels of luxury? A comparison of accessible, intermediate and inaccessible luxury brands. *Journal of Brand Management*, *19*(7), 623–636.

Deloitte. (2016). *Global powers of Luxury goods 2016. Disciplined innovation*. Diegern, Belgium: Deloitte University EMEA CVBA. Retrieved from, http://www2.deloitte.com/content/dam/Deloitte/global/Documents/Consumer-Business/gx-cip-gplg-2016.pdf

Desai, K. K., & Keller, K. L. (2002). The effects of ingredient branding strategies on host brand extendibility. *Journal of Marketing*, *66*(1), 73–93.

Fook, C. T. (2016). Our story. Retrieved on the 19.09.2016 at 17:50 from, http://www.chowtaifook.com/en/ourstory

Gallaugher, J., & Ransbotham, S. (2010). Social media and customer dialog management at Starbucks. *MIS Quarterly Executive, 9*(4), 197–212.

Godey, B., Manthiou, A., Pederzoli, D., Rokka, J., & Aiello, G. (2016). Social media marketing efforts of luxury brands: Influence on brand equity and consumer behaviour. *Journal of Business Research, 69*(12), 5833–5841.

Hajli, N., Shanmugam, M., Papagiannidis, S., Zahay, D., & Richard, M. O. (2017). Branding co-creation with members of online brand communities. *Journal of Business Research, 70*(1), 136–144.

Hermès. (2016). Annual report. Retrieved on the 19.09.2016 at 19:10 from, http://finance.hermes.com/var/finances/storage/original/application/630394b9a95603bf81b399744dbbf044.pdf

Hughes, M. U., Bendoni, W. K., & Pehlivan, E. (2016). Storygiving as a co-creation tool for luxury brands in the age of the internet: A love story by Tiffany and thousands of lovers. *Journal of Product and Brand Management, 25*(4), 357–364.

Kapferer, J. N. (2014). The future of luxury: Challenges and opportunities. *Journal of Brand Management, 21*(9), 716–726.

Kapferer, J. N., & Bastien, V. (2009). The specificity of luxury management: Turning marketing upside down. *Journal of Brand Management, 16*(5–6), 311–322.

Kapferer, J. N., & Laurent, G. (2016). Where do consumers think luxury begins? A study of perceived minimum price for 21 luxury goods in 7 countries. *Journal of Business Research, 69*, 332–340.

Kapferer, J. N., & Michaut, A. (2014). Luxury counterfeit purchasing: The collateral of luxury brands' trading down policy. *Journal of Brand Strategy, 3*(1), 59–70.

Kapferer, J. N., & Michaut-Denizeau, A. (2014). Is luxury compatible with sustainability? Luxury consumers' viewpoint. *Journal of Brand Management, 21*(1), 1–22.

Kapferer, J. N., & Valette-Florence, P. (2016). Beyond rarity: The paths of luxury desire. How luxury brands grow yet remain desirable. *Journal of Product and Brand Management, 25*(2), 120–133.

Keinan, A., Kivetz, R., & Netzer, O. (2016). The functional alibi. *Journal of the Association for Consumer Research, 1*(4), 479–496.

Keller, K. L. (2009). Managing the growth tradeoff: Challenges and opportunities in luxury branding. *Journal of Brand Management, 16*(5/6), 290–301.

Kering. (2016a). Group. About Kering. Retrieved on the 19.09.2016 at 17:35 from, http://www.kering.com/en/group/about-kering

Kering. (2016b). Brands. Retrieved on the 19.09.2016 at 21:00 from, http://www.kering.com/en/brands

Kim, J. E., Lloyd, S., & Cervellon, M. C. (2016). Narrative-transportation storylines in luxury brand advertising: Motivating consumer engagement. *Journal of Business Research*, 69(1), 304–313.

Ko, E., Phau, I., & Aiello, G. (2016). Luxury brand strategies and consumer experiences: Contributions to theory and practice. *Journal of Business Research*, 69(12), 5749–5752.

L'Oréal. (2016a). Brand l'oréal luxe. Retrieved on the 19.09.2016 at 18:10 from, http://www.loreal.com/brand/l'oréal-luxe

L'Oréal. (2016b). Group. Who we are. Our ambition. Retrieved on the 19.09.2016 at 18:25 from, http://www.loreal.com/group/who-we-are/our-ambition

L'Oréal. (2016c). Group. Our mission. Retrieved on the 22.09.2016 at 21:20 from, http://www.loreal.com/group/who-we-are/our-mission

L'Oréal. (2016d). Group. Who we are. Our values and ethical principles. Retrieved on the 19.09.2016 at 18:30 from, http://www.loreal.com/group/who-we-are/our-values-and-ethical-principles

Lauder, E. (2016a). Who we are. Retrieved on the 22.09.2016 at 20:15 from, http://www.elcompanies.com/who-we-are

Lauder, E. (2016b). Who we are. Culture and values. Retrieved on the 22.09.2016 at 20:10 from, http://www.elcompanies.com/who-we-are/culture-and-values

Lauder, E. (2016c). Our brands. Retrieved on the 22.09.2016 at 20:15 from, http://www.elcompanies.com/our-brands

Lee, J. E., & Watkins, B. (2016). YouTube vloggers' influence on consumer luxury brand perceptions and intentions. *Journal of Business Research*, 69(12), 5753–5760.

Lemon, K. N., & Verhoef, P. C. (2016). Understanding customer experience throughout the customer journey. *Journal of Marketing*. http://dx.doi.org/10.1509/jm.15.0420

Luxottica. (2016). About us. Company profile. Retrieved on the 17.09.2016 at 14:40 from, http://www.luxottica.com/en/about-us/company-profile

LVMH. (2016a). About LVMH. The LVMH model. Retrieved on the 17.09.2016 at 13:10 from, https://www.lvmh.com/group/about-lvmh/the-lvmh-model/

LVMH. (2016b). About LVMH. The LVMH spirit. Retrieved on the 17.09.2016 at 13:15 from, https://www.lvmh.com/group/about-lvmh/the-lvmh-spirit/

Moon, H., & Sprott, D. E. (2016). Ingredient branding for a luxury brand: The role of brand and product fit. *Journal of Business Research*. http://dx.doi.org/10.1016/j.jbusres.2016.04.173

Nia, A., & Zaichkowsky, J. L. (2000). Do counterfeits devalue the ownership of luxury brands? *Journal of Product and Brand Management*, 9(7), 485–497.

Okonkwo, U. (2009a). The luxury brand strategy challenge. *Journal of Brand Management*, 16(5/6), 287–289.

Okonkwo, U. (2009b). Sustaining the luxury brand on the Internet. *Journal of Brand Management*, 16(5/6), 302–310.

Powell, S. M. (2014). Twenty-one years of the journal of brand management: A commemorative review. *Journal of Brand Management*, 21(9), 689–701.

Randhawa, P., Calantone, R. J., & Voorhees, C. M. (2015). The pursuit of counterfeited luxury: An examination of the negative side effects of close consumer–brand connections. *Journal of Business Research*, 68(11), 2395–2403.

Richemont. (2016a). Corporate social responsibility. Vision. Retrieved on the 17.09.2016 at 13:40 from, https://www.richemont.com/corporate-social-responsibility/vision/introduction.html

Richemont. (2016b). About Richemont. Retrieved on the 17.09.2016 at 13:45 from, https://www.richemont.com/about-richemont.html

Richemont. (2016c). Corporate social responsibility. Richemont as an employer. Retrieved on the 17.09.2016 at 13:50 from, https://www.richemont.com/corporate-social-responsibility/richemont-as-an-employer/your-journey-with-us.html

Rolex. (2016). Rolex history. Retrieved on the 19.09.2016 at 18:40 from, https://www.rolex.com/rolex-history.html

Romani, S., Gistri, G., & Pace, S. (2012). When counterfeits raise the appeal of luxury brands. *Marketing Letters*, 23(3), 807–824.

Stokburger-Sauer, N. E., & Teichmann, K. (2013). Is luxury just a female thing? The role of gender in luxury brand consumption. *Journal of Business Research*, 66(7), 889–896.

Swatch Group. (2016a). Group profile. Retrieved on the 22.09.2016 at 20:40 from, http://www.swatchgroup.com/en/group_profile

Swatch Group. (2016b). Group profile. Nicholas G. Hayek – message from the founder. Retrieved on the 17.09.2016 at 14:55 from, http://www.swatchgroup.com/en/group_profile/nicolas_g_hayek_message_from_the_founder

Swatch Group. (2016c). Brands and companies. Retrieved on the 17.09.2016 at 15:00 from, http://www.swatchgroup.com/en/brands_and_companies

Tsai, W. H. S., & Men, L. R. (2013). Motivations and antecedents of consumer engagement with brand pages on social networking sites. *Journal of Interactive Advertising, 13*(2), 76–87.

Valette-Florence, P. (2012). Luxury and counterfeiting: issues, challenges and prospects. *Journal of Brand Management, 19*(7), 541–543.

Wang, Y., & Griskevicius, V. (2014). Conspicuous consumption, relationships, and rivals: Women's luxury products as signals to other women. *Journal of Consumer Research, 40*(5), 834–854.

Wilson, J. M., & Sullivan, B. A. (2016). Brand owner approaches to assessing the risk of product counterfeiting. *Journal of Brand Management, 23*(3), 327–344.

Wilson, J. M., Grammich, C., & Chan, F. (2016). Organizing for brand protection and responding to product counterfeit risk: An analysis of global firms. *Journal of Brand Management, 23*(3), 345–361.

**Joachim Kernstock** is Head of Centre of Competence for Brand Management (KMSG) and a lecturer of marketing at the University of St. Gallen, Switzerland. He is an experienced corporate brand strategy advisor and works with leading Swiss and European corporates as well as SMEs. He has published several books and articles in a number of internationally referred journals and is also Co-Editor-in-Chief of the *Journal of Brand Management*. He is Professor of Marketing and Director of the Henkel Center for Consumer Goods (HCCG) at WHU, Otto Beisheim School of Management, Germany, and also a permanent visiting researcher at Tuck School of Business at Dartmouth College, USA.

**Tim Oliver Brexendorf** is Professor of Marketing and Director of the Henkel Center for Consumer Goods (HCCG) at WHU, Otto Beisheim School of Management, Germany, and also a permanent visiting researcher at Tuck School of Business at Dartmouth College, US. His work has been published in a number of leading International Journals and he is the author of an edited book on brand management. He is also Co-Editor-in-Chief of the *Journal of Brand Management*.

**Shaun M. Powell** is Senior Lecturer in Marketing in the Faculty of Business at the University of Wollongong in Australia and Co-Editor-in-Chief of the *Journal of Brand Management*. Following a period in industry Shaun has worked in the higher education sector in Australia, UK, and Asia, undertaking various roles including Associate Head of School, Academic Director, and Postgraduate Course Coordinator. He undertook his PhD in the Business School at the University of Strathclyde. Shaun has published in the field of brand management via various books and international journals such as *European Journal of Marketing; Journal of Business Ethics; Journal of Brand Management; Journal of Consumer Marketing; Corporate Communications: An International Journal; Qualitative Market Research: An International Journal;* and *Young Consumers*. His past or present professional memberships include American Marketing Association, Academy of Marketing Science (AMS), Marketing Science Institute, Academy of Marketing (UK), Australian Marketing Institute (AMI), International Association of Business Communicators (IABC), and Fellow of the Higher Education Academy UK (FHEA).

# The End of Luxury as We Knew It?

Jean-Noël Kapferer

## From Niche to Mass

Luxury growth comes mainly from the newly rich, especially those in emerging economies that are enjoying great growth. These newly rich consumers are eager to enter the world of consumption and conspicuous pleasures, seeking to catch up with their Western counterparts. Unlike patricians (Han et al., 2010), who had little need to demonstrate their status, the newly rich crave love, power, and status through conspicuous consumption. The luxury business would not grow if wealthy consumers mostly saved their money and looked like everyone else, as described in the concept of the "millionaire next door" (Stanley and Danko, 1998). But the newly rich do not want to be next door; they want their success to be visible, such that

---

J.-N. Kapferer (✉)
Inseec Business School, Paris, France
e-mail: jnkapferer@inseec.com

they are frequent buyers of mansions and gorgeous flats all over the world, as well as high-end furnishings to fill these homes. The luxury business needs their conspicuous consumption: If Lamborghinis stay in garages, they cannot fuel imitation desires in society (Girard and Williams, 1966).

Another source of luxury growth is the vast number of "excursionists" (Dubois and Laurent, 1995), ordinary people from the upper middle classes who emulate their wealthy peers. They cannot buy lofts or penthouses, or even Chanel suits, but they might occasionally buy a small product from a prestigious brand for themselves, friends, or some important contact. This development drives the queues of tourists waiting outside the Louis Vuitton or Gucci flagship stores in capital cities. It also is evidenced in the immediate depressive effect on the luxury watch and spirits industries in China when President Xi Jinping decided to crack down on corruption in 2012.

More generally, luxury has gained enormous visibility. Hunger and poverty still reign globally, yet airports all over the world are transforming into luxury commercial centers, in which the luxury brand names are the same from one capital city to the next, and they appear as well in urban department stores and malls. Despite the growth of e-commerce and the Internet, such luxury stores remain destinations for travelers who spend hours walking the aisles, discovering consumption at its best and experiencing a world of privilege where everyone can dream.

From a sociological perspective, luxury is the symbol of an euphoric society, itself a product of the evolution of capitalism. For decades, the main challenge that has worried financial investors and capital markets has been finding ways to sustain economic growth. One option is sustainable development, which might create new demand and opportunities for innovation and thereby lead to growth. Another source is technology, which also produces obsolescence. More fundamentally though, stimulating purchases (and economic growth) when the consumer already has "everything," or at least all the necessities, requires moving to nonnecessities. Luxury is a business of nonnecessities. Its goal is to create value growth but de-emphasize volume growth.

## Is Luxury Brand Management a Financially Driven Strategy?

In a rare interview, Bernard Arnault (2001), the founder and CEO of the world's top luxury group LVMH, defined luxury as "items that serve little purpose in the lives of consumers except to fulfill dreams. And those dreams don't come cheap." In a later comment, he added, "Luxury is the only sector that can provide luxurious margins" (Capital, May 2010). In these rare comments, Arnault offered the benefit of clarity: The luxury industry exists because owners and financial investors dream about the available margins (Kapferer and Tabatoni, 2011). These margins are created by the dreams that brands embed in their products and the prices they demand from consumers to have the right to exhibit them and become symbolically part of the privileged group of the brand's clientele. Thus press releases about luxury brands tend to provide two main types of information: What fabulous event was staged when the brand launched its latest product or new collection, and who was invited (or not)? And which luxury brands are the most profitable? (Hermès still leads this race.) The first type of information aims to attach feelings of exclusivity to the brand and disseminate a sense of prestige. Through social media, any exclusive luxury event can be immediately shared with the masses, building their desire for something they can dream of but not access. The second type of information is the measure of greater interest to a luxury brand: luxurious margins.

Many brands today claim to be luxury brands, because the word "luxury" sells. To expand the definition to these claimants to luxury, new terms even have been invented, such as accessible luxury, popular luxury, and casual luxury, with the goal of leveraging the benefits of the "luxury" tag for non-luxury brands. But these developments also have disrupted the positioning of luxury, pushing it to the extreme spheres with terms such as "überluxury," "high luxury," or "ultra luxury." As a result of the proliferation of *luxuries*, the word also has lost some substance. Academic efforts to resolve the issue by proposing a new definition of luxury are in vain, because luxury is inherently a subjective notion, even if the criteria are generally well known and accepted (De Barnier et al., 2012). For criteria such as beauty, quality, love of craft, emotion, expense, feelings of exclusivity, and privileged service, the challenge becomes defining, for example, what expensive means. Is there a threshold of luxury according to these criteria? The horizon can never be met, because it moves constantly as the consumer gains wealth or revenues (Kapferer and Laurent, 2015). Similarly, high quality might mean various things. Consider a phrase contained on the website of a famous brand: "Artisans and innovators, we continually refine and perfect our collections to create some of the most luxurious handbags in the world." But how could a consumer identify the brand based on this claim? Is it Michael Kors? Coach? Chanel? Prada? Words have lost their discriminating power, as have images online, as luxury brands constantly feed the social media beast with new fuel for the luxury dream.

But profitability is not subjective. Operating profit ratios can indicate which brands sell a priceless dream, and which don't, according to a threshold of about 30 percent. As the CEO of a famous champagne brand once explained to us, the goal of being a luxury is to free prices from any constraint. For real luxury, prices have no relationship with the cost of the goods. In a recent, straightforward analysis, BCG compared the average prices of core luxury brands with those of mass-market segments, as well as those of ultra-luxury with core luxury segments. On average, core luxury watch brands are 163 times more expensive than mass brands. But ultra-luxury watches are 107 times more expensive than core luxury watch brands (and 17,441 times more expensive than mass brands). Can quality explain such price differences?

In some sense it can, for ultra-luxury watches, because they tend to be very rare objects, crafted by artisans over weeks or months. The collectors who buy them are connoisseurs who do not care about branding. The first Richard Mille RM-01 watch, launched in 2001 at a price of 250,000 euros, prompted immediate demand by collectors, even though the brand was totally unknown, and despite its price (or maybe because of it). The price was the signal of an extraordinary product. Brands at the top of the luxury pyramid can tell stories that apply to the whole luxury industry; they help reinforce the myth of luxury using their associations with words such as "craft," "rare," "highest quality," "painstaking work," or "priceless." Most ultra-luxury brands in turn are relatively unknown among the newly rich, much less the upper middle class. Because they are unknown, these brands cannot serve the purpose of luxury buying that seeks to display love, seduction, or power. Whereas no one would likely look twice at a person sporting a Richard Mille watch, the core luxury brands Rolex or Cartier can invoke envy and notice.

## From Bespoke Brands to World Megabrands

So how many watches does Rolex sell each year? This privately owned brand does not offer any data, but rumors suggest about 1 million, so the watches cannot be considered rarities anymore. Yet Rolex remains a global icon for watches. Noting former French President Nicolas Sarkozy's Rolex, his counselor J. Seguéla explained, "if at 50 years old, one still does not own a Rolex, one has missed one's life." Similarly, the most profitable car brand is not Bugatti, which sells a few hundred Veyrons for 1 million euros each, or Lamborghini, which sells a few thousands cars. It is Porsche, which sold 225,000 cars in 2015. Thus it appears that a niche approach can feed the luxury myth, but the sector also likes bigger numbers, especially when the analysis considers share value, which requires both growth and high margins. Financial investors have no interest in brands that limit their growth by an excess of scarcity. High margins with no growth perspective are not attractive. High growth together with high margins is the goal, as exemplified by Louis Vuitton (LV). Since its takeover and the formation of the LVMH group, this brand has grown constantly; it even offers an emblem of China's economic recovery.

Observers predicted that the massive growth of LV also signaled its imminent fall, but these critics have been proven wrong. There are enough newly rich consumers in the world, and particularly in Tier 2 Chinese cities (10 million inhabitants each) to guarantee future growth. The same promise holds for Rolex, BMW, Mercedes, Chanel, Gucci, Prada, and Hermès. The difference here is that without volume, there was no brand power. Unlike collectors, who buy new and exceptional watches even from unknown brands, newly rich consumers and their followers look for visas of distinction, proofs of good taste, signs of respect, and signals for love. To act as such signals, luxury brands must be known by a larger audience than the target market. Thus, the luxury industry needs volume.

First, volume helps amortize huge marketing and public relations costs, as well as the considerable retail costs for luxury brands that maintain highly experiential stores. Single-brand stores always run the risk of insufficient traffic, but the rental costs of a store on Nanjin Road (Shanghai) or New Bond Street require that luxury brands cover a lot of needs. Montblanc used to sell pens only; it now functions as a generalist brand of accessories and fragrances.

Second, volume with increased penetration creates visibility, and such visibility is needed to build brands' fame. Without fame, there is no high pricing; it is the price of entering the select club of brand owners.

Briefly then, today's luxury brand management is luxury megabrand management. It is striking that the same luxury brands are present in all capital cities, whether in downtown flagship stores or international airports. The story of the craftsman in his or her atelier conflicts with the reality of big business. But luxury brands still need to maintain their founding myths, just as Apple needs to sustain the myth of the garage where Steve Wozniak and Steve Jobs started it all. Yet Apple is also a megabrand; the garage is long gone, even if the myth is not. Apple's corporate goal is to remain the most highly valued brand in the world.

## Why Luxury Needs Cult Products

Cartier or Tiffany regularly announces unique pieces, sold at very high prices, that only the happy few can afford. Beyond such rare events, a sustained source of revenue requires famous, iconic products associated with the brand. For Cartier, these products might be Santos or Tank watches or Love rings. The purpose of these iconic products is primarily to harvest the benefits of fame. Financially, they are continual sources of cash.

In this sense, there is a key difference between the financial model of fashion and that of luxury: In the fragile fashion business model, products sell by being fashionable, which means capturing the spirit of the moment. Fashion brands earn profits by selling as much as possible, at full price, as soon as the season begins. With time, fashion fades away, and products need to be heavily discounted. Thus, fashion is less interested in quality; why invest in quality if the product will not be worn beyond the season? This system thereby creates an urgency to renew a wardrobe each year or more, a form of socially constructed obsolescence. In contrast, the essence of luxury brand management is time. Luxury takes time, and luxury sells time. Luxury brands need cult products that fix the dreams of clients, after which they can wait for the moment those consumers are ready to indulge (e.g., "One day I will buy a . . . Santos watch, Rolex Daytona, Jaeger Lecoultre Reverso"). There is no hurry, because the products are here to stay, and the price will remain. True luxury never offers discounts or rebates.

By appearing in the product range, year after year, these icons come to represent an antidote to fast consumption and a throw-away society. They embed heritage, craft, and myth, and over time, they acquire their own mystique and reputation. The truly wealthy might not even consider products that have diffused so far, other than as an initial watch to offer their children. But for the middle class, these products provide a focus for their dreaming. What better gift can a lover offer than a Cartier Love ring? Cult products are never revolutionary, though they can evolve, so the Porsche 911 gets slightly upgraded each year.

## Is Luxury Management a Science of Artificial Rarity?

Academics still debate the true meaning of luxury (and whether there even is a single, valid meaning for all people around the world), but luxury clearly is a thriving business, attracting investors, venture capital, and luxury groups. Kering originally was a wood company that became a conglomerate, owning department stores and mail order companies that offered products at all prices levels. But today, it specializes exclusively in luxury, a high growth sector with strong profits. Luxury has grown into a 1 trillion euro sector (Bain and Co., 2016), spanning automobiles, personal products (clothing, leather, watches, skin care, jewelry), hospitality, food and wine, and even yachts – a tiny sector that still sparks people's imagination.

For the founder of economics, Adam Smith, luxury starts as soon as a person buys something that is not necessary. For economists, luxury purchases are not rational; they demand excess spending for reasons tied to intangible, not tangible, qualities. This view highlights the irrationality of the watch prices example provided previously. What quality difference could possibly justify a price multiplier of 163 between core luxury and mass market watches? There is not one; the difference is due to intangibles, the signaling dimension of the brand, and the resulting ego benefits that purchases have for buyers. Luxury is a business of self- and social elevation; luxury brands are visas of class and good taste, as well as the access fee required to enter a restricted club of owners. Price is not the measure of value; price creates value.

Economists thus cannot understand luxury brand management easily. Classical theory identifies an economic equilibrium where supply meets demand. But for luxury brand management, the theory is inverted, so the goal is to create an excess of demand without satisfying it. Unlike any other sector, for luxury, growth creates ambivalence, because the expanded market penetration dilutes perceived exclusivity. By starving the market, managers can drive prices up and earn excess margins, which can be reinvested in creating brand prestige. Thus, luxury brand management is highly specific and turns traditional marketing principles upside down. Megabrands such as Rolex, Chanel, Gucci, Prada, Vuitton, Tiffany, and Ferrari have empirically established the rules, or what we might call the "anti-laws of marketing."

The luxury strategy also aims to create intangible value that makes luxury brands incomparable with any other brand, so they can avoid commoditization, which is the fate of most growth markets. In this consideration, we find the main difference between luxury and *premium* products. The latter mostly rely on tangible characteristics to build their attractiveness. Premium brands compete by looking for comparisons (compare-by-reason), but as soon as any reason is more important than emotion, consumers would quit buying luxury offerings. E-commerce sites that sell luxuries at discounted prices contribute to commoditization and dangerously assimilate luxuries with premium products. Instead, to build incomparability, luxury brands must inject "*time, space and blood*" in the brand.[1]

---

[1] This insightful wording comes from Professor Carlo Alberto Carnavale, Bocconi Business School (Milano, Italy).

Time refers to heritage, history (legendary, not simply a factual historical summary), and storytelling about craftsmen who need years and years to acquire their unique know-how (e.g., 21 years for Royal Salute whiskey to mature).

Space means that luxury must never delocalize its production. Most people do not understand why this anti-law of marketing is so important; most fashion and technology brands already produce in low-wage countries, so that they can build value by reducing costs. But luxury creates value by building intangibles. The skilled sewing artisans that LV employs are not the only people who can create perfect leather bags; remarkable counterfeits are produced in China. But buying fakes anxiously, with the fear that police will soon come and arrest the shopkeeper and maybe you too, does little to create a dreamed-of luxury experience through purchase. Thus, Chinese travelers continue to queue at LV's Champs Elysées flagship store, in ways they would not if they learned that the leather bags had been made in China. For them, Paris, France, means uniqueness, and the brands are endowed with the capacity to pass on benefits to buyers, such as seduction, power, elegance, respect, and love. Countries of origin offer more than credibility based on know-how or legitimacy (e.g., Switzerland for watches, Germany for cars, France for fragrances, Italy for menswear). The countries of origin even function as brands, conveying intangible values that set all their legitimate products apart from any copy by a mass prestige brand. "Made in France" means *Made of France.*" France means elegance, Italy means aesthetics and "dolce vita," the United Kingdom means aristocracy, and the United States means wealth and power. Other countries may mean nothing special though. They are not brands, just towns. Delocalization to such sites must be defended against cost-cutting managers who do not understand the luxury strategy.

The importance of "space" also explains why the luxury business still is an oligopoly and a closed club that benefits from the extra profits due to oligopolistic competition. In personal luxury goods markets, two countries dominate production and sales (Italy and France), as do two others in the automobile market (Germany and Italy). This does not mean that French champagne has nothing to fear from Australian or Californian sparkling wines; it just means that the latter are premium products, not yet luxuries.

It takes time and space to become a luxury. In a few decades, Ralph Lauren will look as if it had been created a century ago.

Finally, blood is the biological ingredient and proof of authenticity. Most luxury brands take the name of their founder, a mythical figure. Unlike recent or invented brands, this status gives the sense of dynasty. Mellerio dit Meller jewelers is managed by the fourteenth generation of the same family; the Hermès CEO represents the sixth generation. But Ralph Lifschitz changed his name to found Ralph Lauren and took on the name of his own brand; his son David Lauren appears in all the brand's advertising, to prepare for his introduction as the heir of the symbolic kingdom.

These three pillars of incomparability act as barriers to entry for the many newcomers attracted by the margins of the luxury sector. Some brands have an intrinsic production limit; the skyrocketing prices of a bottle of Romanée Conti Bourgogne wine are attributable to the legend but also to the purposely low productivity by hectare, so that each vine and grape promises magical ingredients, coming from nature and the soil. The property of Romanée Conti is very tiny, limiting its capacities to expand production, so it can offer only about 45,000 bottles some years. Demand thus is quickly exceeding production capacities.

For leather bags, it is customary to wait at least a year to get a custom Hermès Kelly bag. The company could create new ateliers, to reduce this waiting time, which would like increase sales substantially and immediately, yet it would ruin the long-term value of the brand. Family brands have an advantage over investor-owned or listed brands on this point, because they can take a long-term perspective. Capital investors instead seek revenues and results, and operational sales managers are judged by profit-and-loss figures. But CEOs and members of the board should focus instead on the value of assets, and the brand is the most important asset for a luxury firm, because its prestige commands the ability to demand high prices. Luxury brand management overlooks many issues of governance. John Idol, CEO of Michael Kors, once boasted that the brand was the fastest growing luxury brand in the world, but speed of growth is not a good performance indicator for any luxury brand. Rather, it applies to fashion brands, for which the future counts less than the present. Thus the prices for Michael Kors leather bags stop where the entry prices of LV or

Hermès start. It can deliver extra value only within the limitations of its fast growth in volume, market penetration, and distribution.

Yet all luxury brands, especially those managed by groups, aim to continue to grow. So how can they nourish feelings of rarity or privilege while increasing their volume, such that they sustain their own desirability? We propose some artificial rarity tactics:

- Multiply small collections, produced in limited quantities, so purchasing priority becomes a competitive goal among clients.
- Partner with famous, avant-garde artists to endow the limited collection with extra value and feed the aftermarket that can be created (e.g., on eBay) immediately after the last item is sold.
- Regularly introduce exceptional, unique pieces by a famous designer, sold at extraordinary prices, at auctions in which part of the price goes to a charity, which creates buzz.
- Limit distribution. As shown in Fig. 1, selective distribution is a critical lever of sustained desirability. In China, the perceived prestige of luxury brands is inversely correlated with the number of stores. E-commerce and open access through the Internet thus are major challenges to sustaining the perceived exclusivity of a luxury brand over time.
- Sustain the dream by keeping the penetration rate below the brand awareness rate. This essential difference, or the "rarity principle," stems from the dream equation, which has been validated in the West and in Asian countries. A typical equation shows that sustaining the luxury dream rests on the difference between brand awareness and brand penetration:

$$\text{Brand dream} = -7.0 + 0.312\ \text{Awareness} - 0.405\ \text{Penetration} + 0.58\ \text{Tradition}\ (R^2 = 0.64).$$

- Exhibit high-status buyers. Luxury brands need to select their buyers. They receive cash from their clients but also most of their status. When people queuing outside the flagship stores are mainstream, it is essential to compensate for the effect by diffusing images of extreme selectivity through social networks. A key role of social media is to make widely known who was present at selective events organized by

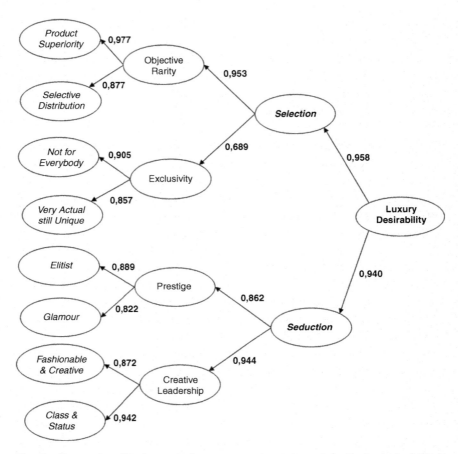

**Fig. 1** Beyond rarity, how do luxury megabrands sustain their desirability? (*Source*: Kapferer and Valette-Florence, 2016)

the luxury brand – and who was not. This information is how prestige, glamour, and eliteness can be conveyed to the brand.

- Use pricing to discriminate. Luxury exists because not everybody can access it. The sociological function of luxury (to restratify classless societies) occurs through pricing. If there were no luxuries, how would people compare themselves? This point is not to suggest that all luxury brands need to be very expensive. But they need to be expensive enough for the target to consider the purchase a sacrifice and excess spending, worth the exception, because it delivers accrued benefits for self-elevation.

## Self-elevation: Learning from Religion and Art

All societies have condemned luxury consumption. Excess spending, beyond necessities, attracts moral criticisms. Luxury is evidence of a non-equalitarian society; the Chinese government has banned luxury ads on the streets, to avoid the blatant proof of the growing distance between the rich and the poor in this communist country. A modern avatar of moral criticisms is sustainable development and its activist movements. For sustainable development advocates, as modern luxury extends its audience, its sales endanger rare species and ingredients, while also promoting disharmony in society. An alternative argument holds though that luxury promotes true sustainability values by lasting forever, unlike fashion, which will be thrown away after the season, or high-tech businesses that thrive on planned obsolescence. This debate remains open.

In any case, similar to any sector, luxury must address its own legitimacy and right to exist. Currently it uses two methods to do so: stick to a craft/atelier/heritage story (though, as we have noted, the pursuit of volume by luxury megabrands makes this story less credible) or use religious and art metaphors to reposition luxury purchase as cultural activities.

This process of "artification" is currently underway in most luxury Maisons. Artification refers to the purposeful transformation of nonart into art. Thus luxury exhibitions around the world appear in well-known museums, such as a display of Coco Chanel's life that positions her in proximity to famous artists of her epoch, to signal that she herself was an artist. Just as it is perfectly justifiable to buy a lithograph of a painting by a famous artist, there is then no harm in indulging and buying Chanel bags. Another artification takes place at the brand level, as manifested by the Louis Vuitton Foundation in Paris, which offers a monument of modern art itself.

A slightly different legitimizing process links luxury to sacredness. The importance and magnificence of luxury stores stems from their links to famous architects, reminiscent of cathedrals. The brand cult and its magnificence can be expressed through all five senses – far more so than is possible on an Internet site.

## What Are the New Purposes of Luxury Stores Today?

The preceding remarks highlight a fundamental challenge for the luxury industry today: redefining the role of retail. This industry has just shifted its focus and investments from the production side to the retail side. Alas luxury retail stores now demand a new approach. To grow, luxury brands often seek to create controlled, perfect experiences in retail locations, which call for more cash and new talents. To maintain control over their prices and each consumer's experience, the luxury industry also has favored vertical integration and directly operated stores (DOS). This retail process requires financial resources to extend the retail network, as well as talents to manage the supply chain and customer relationship management on a global scale. But brands also need to promote luxury culture in new countries. Each salesperson thus must become an experienced cast member. The associated demands have led many luxury Maisons, which had long maintained their independence and family ownership, to sell out and join luxury groups (Kering, LVMH, Richemont) or submit to be purchased by investment funds. Luxury conglomerates offer cash and human resources, as well as parenting expertise and crucial synergies at the retail level.

Also in the retail sector, e-commerce is becoming a growing channel for luxury sales, with steeply positive predicted sales forecasts. If new luxury consumers (millennials, Chinese) prefer to buy online, what goals should retail stores pursue? How should they be evaluated? What performance indicators are most important? There cannot be a cult without a place of worship; the stores exist to impress and deliver an experience, more than they do to sell. They are the temples of the luxury cult.

But the stores are often empty, especially in China (Solca, 2016) where the brands have invested heavily to take anticipatory positions in the country predicted to be a luxury "Eldorado" and soon the top luxury market. Chinese travelers represent 31 percent of all sales of personal luxury products in the world (Bain and Co., 2016). But sales in mainland China of personal luxuries are less than the sales in New York alone. In Chinese city centers and luxury malls, the luxury stores are empty, yet rents continue to climb, putting the entire business model at risk. Because modern customers often research in one channel and purchase in another, brands cannot enclose their processes within online versus offline silos; they must adopt methods to cater to the consumer seamlessly. In this context, shops are not enemies of e-commerce. They have a specific role, remaining as a destination venue that gives customers a remarkable experience on the spot.

## Luxury Challenges for the Future: Sustaining the Gap

Advanced luxury brand management must cope with new challenges that continue to emerge and that are disruptive enough to push the luxury market off balance. They even might crack the foundational pillars of luxury success thus far. Interestingly, these new challenges are largely brought about by technological and sociological revolutions. Consider six notable shifts.

1. High technology is everywhere. Do people still need Swiss luxury watches if they have connected phones and watches on their wrists? Vertu, a luxury smartphone brand, did not succeed and ultimately was sold to a Chinese group. In essence, can luxury be compatible with the obsolescence that is built in to high-technology? Can a sector that worships the past still embrace technology?
2. Services such as Uber and AirB&B make luxuries accessible to all. Anyone can hire a private chauffeur through Uber, and travelers can enjoy a beautiful flat on one of the best streets of Paris, instead of patronizing traditional hotels.
3. Amazon seeks a position as the world's top retailer, selling everything it can, including luxury products. This goal threatens a key lever of perceived exclusivity, namely, selective distribution.
4. Tesla and Google are both disrupting the automotive industry, especially for premium and luxury brands. Innovation in the new post-gas, safe driving, clean atmosphere era does not come not from Mercedes or BMW, which as a result look like twentieth-century brands, not members of the twenty-first.

5. The Internet offers open access to brands, peer-to-peer communication, evaluations of products and services, the power of communities, and bloggers. It thus marks the end of the total control and top-down communications that luxury brand management has relied on thus far. Furthermore, the Internet needs brand content, day and night. Luxury brands thus get compared with non-luxury brands in terms of the number of likes on Facebook or the number of bags sold on Weibo. Big data rules the Internet, along with big numbers. Brand comparisons focus on digital IQ – mere numbers that merge with the performance indicators used by brands that adopt classical marketing strategies. Recently hired digital managers tend to favor what is immediately measurable, which also can contribute to their own promotion.
6. On a sociological basis, how will millennials behave tomorrow? A flood of survey data highlights the new values and ideals of this generation, all echoing the same basic information. But the youth of any epoch pursue idealistic goals, some of which shift as they age and mature. Once the millennials earn a wage and gain success, will they buy traditional cars or indulge in luxuries – or will they buy a car at all? Will possession still be a critical goal, or will a sharing economy emerge? The digital natives are highly connected and fond of technology, which may have effects as well.

These are just some of the key issues that the *Journal of Brand Management* should seek to address with regard to luxury brand management.

# References

Arnault, B. (2001). The perfect paradox of star brands. *Harvard Business Review*, *79*(9), 117–123.
Bain & Co. (2016). *World luxury market report*. Milano: Italy.
De Barnier, V., Falcy, S., & Valette Florence, P. (2012). Do consumers perceive three levels of luxury? *Journal of Brand Management*, *19*(7), 623–636.

Dubois, B., & Laurent, G. (1995). Luxury possessions and practices. *European Advances in Consumer Research*, (2), 69–77.

Girard, R., & Williams, J. G. (1966). *The Girard reader*. Crossroad Herder editions.

Han, Y., Nunes, J., & Dreze, X. (2010). Signaling status with luxury goods. *Journal of Marketing*, 74(July), 15–30.

Kapferer, J.-N., & Laurent, G. (2015). Where do consumers think luxury begins: A cross cultural comparison over 21 luxury products in 7 countries. *Journal of Business Research*, 69, 332–430.

Kapferer, J.-N., & Tabatoni, O. (2011). Is luxury really a financial dream? *Journal of Strategic Management Education*, 7(4), 271–286.

Kapferer, J.-N., & Valette-Florence, P. (2016). Beyond rarity: The paths of luxury desire. *Journal of Product and Brand Management*, 25(2), 120–133.

Solca, L. (2016). Myths and realities of luxury demand. ExaneBNPParibas Reports, Paris.

Stanley, T., & Danko, W. (1998). Pocket Books (Simon & Schuster Inc.), New York, NY. *The millionaire next door*. Harper Collins Ed.

**Jean-Noël Kapferer** is a worldly renowned authority on luxury. HEC Paris Graduate and Emeritus Professor, PhD Kellogg Business School (USA), he conducts his research at INSEEC Luxury on the mutations of luxury and luxury brand management. Honorary editor of the *Luxury Research Journal*, he has widely published his articles in international journals. Co-author of the reference book *The Luxury Strategy: Break the Rules of Marketing to Build Luxury Brands*, author of *How Luxury Brands Can Grow Yet Remain Rare*, he leads executive seminars on luxury all around the world (USA, China, Korea, and Europe) and is advisor to the president of INSEEC business school. JN Kapferer enjoys travelling, skiing, and windsurfing.

# Luxury Brand Marketing – The Experience Is Everything!

Glyn Atwal and Alistair Williams

## Introduction

Experiential marketing has become a cornerstone of many recent advances in areas such as retailing, tourism and events marketing; however, marketing in the luxury goods sector does not appear to have explicitly engaged the theoretical issues involved. This raises the question, what does experiential marketing have to offer marketers within the luxury goods sector? In this chapter, we will seek to

---

This chapter was Reprinted from Atwal, G. and Williams, A. (2009) 'Luxury Brand Marketing- The experience is everything!', *Journal of Brand Management*, 16, pp. 338-346. With kind permission from the *Journal of Brand Management*. All rights reserved.

G. Atwal (✉)
Burgundy Business School, Dijon, France
e-mail: glyn.atwal@escdijon.eu

A. Williams
Department of Marketing, Johnson & Wales University, Providence, USA

© The Author(s) 2017
J.-N. Kapferer et al. (eds.), *Advances in Luxury Brand Management*,
Journal of Brand Management: Advanced Collections,
DOI 10.1007/978-3-319-51127-6_3

introduce the experiential marketing debate and will demonstrate how the questions raised by the concept are crucial to the development and implementation of effective marketing strategies within the luxury goods sector.

The marketing of luxury goods has become increasingly complex, being associated not only with conveying an image of quality, performance and authenticity but also with attempting to sell an experience by relating it to the lifestyle constructs of consumers. The characteristics of luxury goods suggest that marketing within the sector is different from many other industries. Despite the amount of literature being written on these perceived differences, there is, however, evidence to suggest that marketing in the luxury goods sector relies heavily on traditional marketing concepts, and it is often difficult to discriminate approaches to luxury goods marketing from those advocated for other consumer products.

# A New Luxury Paradigm

## Parameters of Luxury

Vickers and Renand (2003) suggest that luxury and non-luxury goods can be conceptualised according to functional, experiential and interactional symbolic dimensions. Luxury has traditionally been associated with exclusivity, status and quality. Phau and Prendergast (2001) state that luxury brands 'evoke exclusivity, have a well-known brand identity, enjoy high brand awareness and perceived quality, and retain sales levels and customer loyalty'. Changes in contemporary consumer behaviour in Western societies have led to the emergence of a new meaning and perception of luxury. 'New luxury' has been defined as 'products and services that possess higher levels of quality, taste, and aspiration than other goods in the category but are not so expensive as to be out of reach' (Silverstein and Fiske 2003). A striking example of this phenomenon, covered widely in the popular media, was the launch of Karl Lagerfeld and Stella McCartney designed products at the fashion retail chain Hennes & Mauritz. Within a broader context, observers have pointed to the trend of middle-market consumers trading up for products that meet their aspiration needs, referred to as the 'luxurification of society' (Yeoman and McMahon-Beattie 2006). This trend appears to be evident within a global context. Atwal and Khan (2008) discuss the significance of the rapid growth of the Indian middle class, who 'are no longer at a financial distance from luxury, and are trading up to meet their current aspirations'. The result is that marketers within this sector need to redefine their strategies to reflect these changes.

## Consumption of Luxury

A review of the literature reveals conceptual frameworks of luxury consumption. Vigneron and Johnson (2004) differentiate between non-personal- and personal-oriented perceptions. Non-personal-oriented perceptions refer to perceived conspicuousness, uniqueness and quality. It is generally acknowledged that Western consumption of luxury in the 1980s and 1990s was motivated primarily by status-seeking and appearance. Indeed, acquisitive luxury has been attributed to contemporary luxury consumption in emerging markets such as Russia and China. According to Dubois and Duquesne (1993) 'Motivated by a desire to impress others, with the ability to pay particularly high prices, this form of consumption is primarily concerned with the ostentatious display of wealth'. This was typified by the emergence of the so-called yuppie lifestyle segment in British society. Although the demise of the yuppie culture has been widely acknowledged, commentators have pointed to lifestyle trends that suggest that social status is still an evident motivation of contemporary Western luxury consumption. A Jaguar enthusiast describes his driving experience as follows: 'I love the way that I catch people admiring the XJ-S as I blast past them and the way that people often give me right of way in traffic and then watch the car as it goes by' (Reeves 2007). As Vigneron and Johnson (2004) argue, 'The consumption of luxury brands may be important to individuals in search of social representation and position. This means that social status associated with a brand is an important factor in conspicuous consumption'. The reality is, however, much more complex than such a scenario suggests. Contemporary consumers use consumption to make statements about themselves, to create identities and to develop a sense of belonging. According to Dubois and Duquesne (1993), luxury goods are acquired for what they symbolise, which is argued to be consistent with personal-oriented perceptions – the hedonic consumption and extended self-personality models. Atwal and Williams (2007) argue that this reflects a mindset change on how luxury is valued from a transactional relationship to a holistic experience. As Unity Marketing (2006) report, 'The baby boom generation luxury consumer has a passion for self-indulgence while maintaining an iconclastic world view, which is transforming the luxury market from its "old" conspicuous consumption model to a totally new, individualistic type of luxury consumer one driven by new needs and desires for experiences'. This is consistent with Dumoulin (2007): 'The expression of "today's luxury" is about a celebration of personal creativity, expressiveness, intelligence, fluidity, and above all, meaning'.

## Luxury and Postmodernism

Recent arguments have been sounded that aspects of contemporary luxury consumption have reflected the phenomenon of postmodernism. The definition and evolution of postmodernism has been widely discussed and debated within the literature. As Baumann (1992) suggests, 'postmodernity means very different things to many different people'. Postmodernism is essentially a Western philosophy that 'refers to a break in thinking away from the modern, functional and rational' (Williams 2006). This school of thought has been described as 'the evasion of the subconscious' (Berthon and Katsikeas 1998). Within the broad context of marketing, it is generally acknowledged that consumption has become a defining feature of postmodern societies (Holt 2002). In terms of experiential marketing, two aspects of the postmodern discourse are most relevant: hyper-reality and image.

Hyper-reality is one of the most discussed conditions of postmodernism and supports the argument that reality has collapsed and has become image, illusion, simulation and simulacra. Hyper-reality refers to 'the blurring of distinction between the real and the unreal, in which the prefix "hyper" signifies more real than real. When the real that is the environment, is no longer a given, but is reproduced by a simulated environment, it does not become unreal, but realer than real' (Atwal and Williams 2007). Atwal and Williams (2008) cite the example of Bollywood to illustrate the so-called Disneyfication of reality within the context of contemporary Indian society: 'Bollywood captures not only the imagination in the form of song, music and dance but fairy tale settings, romantic melodrama and heroic storylines immerse the viewer in "simulated reality"'. The hyper-reality phenomenon has wide-ranging implications, as reported by Berthon and Katsikeas (1998), 'Hyper-reality engenders a general loss of the sense of authenticity – ie what is genuine or real'. Visitors to the Kempinski Hotel at the Mall of the Emirates enjoy an Alpine experience that features the world's third-largest indoor ski resort and the largest covered snow park. In postmodern society, people have become fascinated by signs, and as a result, they exist in a state where signs and images have become more important than what they stand for. The result is that consumers in contemporary society consume imagery and do not focus on what the images represent or mean. As Miller and Real (1998) argue, 'we live in a world where the image or signifier of an event has replaced direct experience and knowledge of its referent or signified'.

Although it is accepted that there are problems with investigating luxury goods marketing through a postmodern orientation, it clearly encompasses a broad range of consumer experiences. In addition, it has the potential to reframe our thinking about marketing practice in an increasingly fragmented global marketplace. Traditional marketing provided a valuable set of strategies, implementation tools and methodologies. As Schmitt (1999) argued, 'traditional marketing was developed in response to the industrial age, not the information, branding and communications revolution we are facing today'. In a new age, with new consumers, we need to shift away from a features-and-benefits approach, as advocated by traditional approaches to consumer experiences. We need to consider new concepts and approaches that capitalise on the opportunities offered by these new consumers. One such approach is experiential marketing, an approach that in contrast to the rational features-and-benefits view of consumers takes a more postmodern orientation and views them as emotional beings concerned with achieving pleasurable experiences. The characteristics of the postmodern consumer demand 'an experienced-based marketing that emphasises interactivity, connectivity and creativity' (Cova 1996). As Tsai (2005) argues, 'The traditional product/service value proposition is no longer adequate for reaching consumers or creating significant differentiation. Businesses must facilitate the enhancement of a seamless total experience for consumers, which determines whether products or services maintain competitive edges'.

## Experiential Luxury Marketing

### The Experience Economy

Experiential marketing is a growing trend worldwide, evident in most sectors of the global economy. A visit to the SEB Bank in Frankfurt (Germany) does not feel like walking into an ordinary bank. Customers are greeted personally in an area of open space, dark wooden floors and subtle lighting. Against a backdrop of easy-listening music, customers can sip cappuccinos in a Starbucks-feel café, surf at one of the Internet terminals or simply catch the latest news headlines from one of the TV monitors. Penguin in the United Kingdom launched a series, My Penguin, in which books are published without front covers, allowing readers to create their own, unique and personalised designs. This phenomenon of experiential marketing is, however, not restricted to Western societies. In India, Coca-Cola introduced its experiential lounges in the summer of 2007. Coke's Red Lounges are open-air youth corners with comfortable couches, iPod stations and gaming options. As Schmitt (1999) states, 'experiential marketing is everywhere'. The question is, what has caused this evolution in the world of marketing, and what are the implications for luxury consumers?

Experiential marketing was first introduced by Pine and Gilmore (1998), as part of their work on the experience economy. Pine and Gilmore (1999) explained their view of experiential marketing in the following manner: 'when a person buys a service, he purchases a set of intangible activities carried out on his behalf. But when he buys an experience, he pays to spend time enjoying a series of memorable events that a company stages to engage him in a personal way'. Experiential marketing is thus about taking the essence of a product and amplifying it into a set of tangible, physical and interactive experiences that reinforce the offer. Holbrook and Hirschman (1982) identified the following experiential aspects of consumption: fantasies, feelings and fun. Experiential marketing essentially describes marketing initiatives that give consumers in-depth, tangible experiences in order to provide them with sufficient information to make a purchase decision. It has evolved as a response to a perceived transition from a service economy to one personified by the experiences in which consumers participate (Petkus 2002). As Tsai (2005) argues, 'Increasingly, consumers are involved in the processes of both defining and creating value, and the co-created experience of consumers through the holistic brand value structure becomes the very basis of marketing'.

Earlier, we asked what the implications of this re-orientation were for the marketing of luxury goods. The answer would appear to be significant. It is clear that the fact that many luxury goods are almost always experiential puts luxury marketers in a unique position to apply the principles of experiential marketing to their activities. The problem is that simply having an intrinsically, inherently experiential offering is very different from actively and deliberately marketing that offer in an experiential manner. To achieve this goal, frameworks through which luxury marketers can strategically identify, enhance and deliver their offers have to be introduced.

## Dimensions of the Luxury Experience

Pine and Gilmore (1998) suggest that we think about experiences across two bipolar constructs – customer participation and connection. We have adapted this framework, based on customer involvement and intensity, to identify four 'experiential zones', namely, *Entertainment, Education, Escapist and Aesthetic* (see Fig. 2). The term 'involvement' refers to the level of interactivity between the supplier and the customer. Increased levels of involvement fundamentally change the way in which services are experienced, that is, suppliers no longer create an experience and pass it to the customer; instead, the supplier and customer are

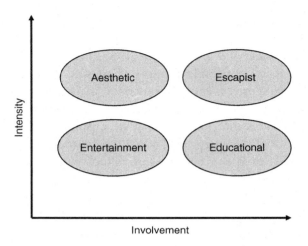

**Fig. 2** Experiential zones. (Adapted from Pine and Gilmore 1998)

interactively co-creating the experience. The term 'intensity' refers to the perception of the strength of feeling towards the interaction. The four experiential zones are not intended to be mutually exclusive; the richness of an experience is, however, a function of the degree to which all four zones are incorporated.

Those experiences we think of as *Entertainment*, such as fashion shows at designer boutiques and upmarket department stores, usually involve a low degree of customer involvement and intensiveness. For instance, flagship Gucci and Chanel stores in Tokyo have added restaurants and bistros with marquee chefs. Indeed, postmodern literature has consistently identified the cultural significance of shopping malls as entertainment, 'appropriated for forms of social interaction whose logic and experiential consequences are by no means a mere effort of retailing institutions' (Miller 1997). The suggestion that in this experiential zone, experiences are simply taken in may seem like an obvious application of much of the luxury experience. For luxury goods marketers, the key is, however, to apply a more holistic approach, that is, to incorporate entertainment into areas outside the immediate experience. Fendi's spectacular show staged on the Great Wall of China is, here, a compelling example.

Activities in the *Educational* zone involve those where participants are more actively involved, but the level of intensiveness is still low. In this zone, participants acquire new skills or increase those they already have. Many luxury goods offerings include educational dimensions. For example, cruise ships often employ well-known authorities to provide semi-formal lectures about their itineraries – a concept commonly referred to as 'edutainment'. Likewise, Ferrari Driving Experience (North America) is a two-day programme that is designed to narrow the gap between driving ability and a Ferrari's performance capability.

Despite the success of many such initiatives, the potential clearly exists for further increasing the 'educational' element of many luxury goods offers.

*Escapist* activities are those that involve a high degree of both involvement and intensiveness, and are clearly a central feature of much of luxury consumption. This is clearly evident within the luxury tourism and hospitality sector, characterised by the growth of specialised holiday offerings. The launch of the Royal Tented Taj Spa (Taj Hotels Resorts and Palaces) at the Rambagh Palace in Jaipur (India) recreates the mobile palaces used by the Mughal emperors of the sixteenth and seventeenth centuries, with chandeliers, royal pennants and Indian love swings. Within a broader context, exclusive membership of organisations, associations and clubs such as the P1 Prestige and Performance Car Club can also act as a form of escapist experience, allowing members to create new identities and realities for themselves. Likewise, celebrity endorsements for luxury products and services can help to foster escapism via association. This phenomenon is, however, not limited to celebrity endorsement advertising campaigns. The Tiger Woods Dubai is a private residential community and resort that will include the world's first golf course designed by Tiger Woods.

When the element of activity is reduced to a more passive involvement in nature, the event becomes *Aesthetic*. A high degree of intensiveness is clearly evident within this activity, but has little effect on its environment such as admiring the architectural or interior design of designer boutiques. The six-storey glass crystal design of the Prada store in Tokyo conceptualised by the architects Herzog and de Meuron has become a showcase for unconventional contemporary architecture. Likewise, Peter Marino's redesign of Ermenegildo Zegna's flagship store in New York inspired by its Italian textile-weaving heritage seeks to engage visitors via all the senses. Again, it is easy to conclude that much luxury goods activity is of an aesthetic nature, with consumers immersing themselves in the experience, but with little active participation.

## Strategies for Experiential Luxury Marketing

Academics and practitioners alike have developed frameworks to help formulate strategies for developing experiential branding strategies. Smith (2003) has put forward a six-step process. The first step is to conduct a customer experience audit in order to assess and evaluate the current experience of the brand. The second step is to create a brand platform that involves defining a clear brand-positioning statement. The third step is to design the brand experience. This involves the alignment of the brand's people, processes and products against the brand proposition. The next steps are to communicate the brand internally and externally. The final step is to monitor performance in order to ensure that the brand is delivering against defined objectives.

Likewise, the design and brand strategy consultancy Lippincott Mercer (Hogan et al. 2004) presented the following four principles of experience design. Identifying key customer segments is the first step. The trend towards the so-called democratisation of luxury has significantly changed luxury consumption patterns (Atwal and Williams 2007). The evaluation of customer data can help to identify the most profitable customer segments. This will ensure that the brand is connecting with the right target segment. The second step is to develop a touchpoint chain and gauge those with the greatest impact. Davis (2005) categorises touchpoints or interactions between the brand and the target according to the phases of pre-purchase, purchase and post-purchase. The third step is to turn findings into project priorities. Some luxury brand touchpoints will be more relevant than others. For example, Atwal and Khan (2008) found browsing as being critical to the purchase decision-making process among female fashion shoppers in India. These so-called moments of truth need to be aligned against what Pine and Gilmore (1998) refer to as the 'takeaways' of the experience. The final step is to implement and monitor. It is here essential that interactions are consistent with the desired brand experience.

It is apparent that the clearest implications of experiential marketing for luxury goods are in the design of marketing strategies. A compelling example of introducing experiential marketing in this way is BMW. This involves establishing a cohesive set of images and meanings for the experience. The recently opened BMW Welt (BMW World) in Munich, a cathedral-like showroom modelled on the Acropolis in Athens, evokes a marketing experience that includes a cohesive theme, an education project, engagement of the senses and the soliciting of feedback. According to the BMW website (BMW 2007), 'The BMW Welt embodies BMW in all dimensions. It unites tradition and innovation, emotion and precision, dynamism and aesthetics, exclusivity and openness. Here the company enters into dialogue with its customers, friends, neighbours and visitors – a site of encounter and change where BMW can be experienced with every sense'. A key question is, why have so few luxury brands sought to replicate such a winning marketing strategy?

The use of new technologies has also aided the potential for experiential marketing. This is of particular relevance given the increasing significance of the Internet as a communication and distribution channel within the luxury sector. The Luxury Institute (Pedraza 2007) found that 88 percent of wealthy consumers cite a preference for using the Internet to research a luxury services firm, and 38 percent prefer to purchase luxury goods online, versus 33 percent who favour face-to-face transactions.

This raises important implications for the luxury industry, as observed by Okonkwo (2007) who notes 'the need for luxury fashion brands to create a compelling, memorable, enjoyable and positive total customer experience for online shoppers'. Web experience models have been developed in order to guide the design of virtual experiences. The management consultancy, A.T. Kearney (2002) developed a 7Cs model to create a high-impact digital customer experience – content, customisation, customer care, communication, community, connectivity and convenience.

Likewise, Constantinides (2004) identified functional factors (usability, interactivity), psychological factors (trust) and content factors (aesthetics and marketing mix) as the main building blocks of web experience. A pioneer in developing virtual experiences was BMW's short Internet-based film series The Hire. Other experiential initiatives have since been an integral component of BMW's new media communications. For example, BMW TV can be viewed on the German BMW website, which reports on BMW-related features from Formula 1 to technological innovations. This website is updated every 2 weeks in order to 'lock in' the viewer. Only those firms that develop customer-valued web-based experiences will be successful in this domain.

## Conclusions and Implications

Experiential marketing is a relatively new orientation that is gaining ground not only in western but also emerging economies and provides a contrast to traditional marketing. Whereas traditional marketing frameworks view consumers as rational decision-makers focussed on the functional features and benefits of products, experiential marketing views consumers as emotional beings, focussed on achieving pleasurable experiences. As Firat and Schultz (1997) argue, 'The postmodern individual has involved into Homo consumericus, a creature defined by consumption and the experiences derived there from'. The difference between traditional and experiential marketing can be highlighted in a number of ways (Williams 2006). First, the focus is on customer experiences and lifestyles, which provide sensory, emotional, cognitive and relational values to the consumer. Second, there is a focus on creating synergies among meaning, perception, consumption and brand loyalty. Third, it is argued that customers are not rational decision-makers but are rather driven by rationality and emotion. Finally, it is argued that experiential marketing requires a more diverse range of research methods in order to understand consumers.

Although as we have seen there are examples of luxury brands using experiential marketing, there is significant scope for improvement. Many organisations suggest that they are using experiential marketing, when the reality is that they are simply repeating the mantra of traditional marketing strategies. Underpinning experiential marketing is the notion that experiences are central to luxury consumption activity. As Tsai (2005) argues, 'Marketers are faced with the challenge of finding ways in which consumer commitment is commensurate with the enhancement of unique and enjoyable experiences'. Referring back to the question with which we opened this chapter, we would argue that experiential marketing offers us the opportunity to consider a new approach to marketing, one with which to capitalise on the unique nature of luxury consumption. Innovative experience design will become an increasingly important component of luxury marketing.

# References

Atwal, G., & Khan, S. (2008, February). Luxury marketing in India: 'Because I'm worth it'. *Admap*, 36–38.

Atwal, G., & Williams, A. (2007, March). Experiencing luxury. *Admap*, 30–32.

Atwal, G., & Williams, A. (2008). Marketing in postmodern India: Bulgari meets Bollywood. *Indian Journal of Marketing*, *38*(1), 3–7.

Bauman, Z. (1992). *Intimations of postmodernity*. London: Routledge.

Berthon, P., & Katsikeas, C. (1998). Essai: Weaving postmodernism. *Internet Research: Electronic Networking Applications and Policy*, *8*(2), 149–155.

BMW. (2007). Mission and vision. The BMW experience for every sense. Retrieved 2 September 2007 from, www.bmw-welt.com/en/html/indexhtml

Constantinides, E. (2004). Influencing the online consumer's behaviour: The Web experience. *Internet Research*, *14*(2), 111–126.

Cova, B. (1996, November/December). The postmodern explained to managers: Implications for marketing. *Business Horizons*, 15–23.

Davis, S. (2005). Building a brand-driven organ-ization. In A. M. Tybout & T. Calkins (Eds.), *Kellogg on Branding*. Hoboken, NJ: John Wiley & Sons Inc.

Dubois, B., & Duquesne, P. (1993). The market for luxury goods: Income versus culture. *European Journal of Marketing*, *27*(1), 35–45.

Dumoulin, D. (2007, March). What is today's definition of luxury? *Admap*, 27–30.

Firat, A. F., & Schultz, C. J. (1997). From segmentation to fragmentation: Markets and marketing strategy in the postmodern era. *European Journal of Marketing*, *31*(3/4), 183–207.

Hogan, S., Almquist, E., & Simon, E. G. (2004). Building a brand on the touchpoints that count. *Mercer Management Journal*, *17*, 46–53. http://www.oliverwyman.com/content/dam/oliverwyman/global/en/files/archive/2004/MMJ17_Building_Brand_Touchpoints.pdf

Holbrook, M. B., & Hirschman, E. C. (1982). The experiential aspects of consumption: Consumer fantasies, feelings and fun. *Journal of Consumer Research*, *9*, 132–140.

Holt, D. B. (2002). Why do brands cause trouble? A dialectical theory of consumer culture and branding. *Journal of Consumer Research*, *29*, 70–90.

Kearney, A. T. (2002). Creating a high-impact digital customer experience: An A.T. Kearney white paper. Retrieved 8 June 2002 from, http://www.atkearney.com/pdf/eng/WP_Digital_Customer.pdf

Miller, D. (1997). Could shopping ever really matter? In P. Falk & C. Campbell (Eds.), *The Shopping Experience*. London: Sage.

Miller, G., & Real, N. (1998). Postmodernity and popular culture. In A. A. Berger (Ed.), *The Post-Modern Presence*. London: Sage.

Okonkwo, U. (2007). *Luxury fashion branding*. Basingstoke: Palgrave Macmillan.

Pedraza, M. (2007, March). Internet habits of the wealthy. *Admap*, 24–26.

Petkus, E. (2002). Enhancing the application of experiential marketing in the arts. *International Journal of Non-profit and Voluntary Sector Marketing*, *9*(1), 49–56.

Phau, I., & Prendergast, G. (2001). Consuming luxury brands: The relevance of the 'rarity principle'. *Journal of Brand Management*, *8*(2), 122–137.

Pine, B. J., & Gilmore, J. H. (1998, July/August). Welcome to the experience economy. *Harvard Business Review*, 97–105.

Pine, B. J., & Gilmore, J. H. (1999). *The experience economy*. Boston, MA: Harvard Business School Press.

Reeves, S. (2007, August). Grown to love. *Jaguar Enthusiast*, 50.

Schmitt, B. H. (1999). Experiential marketing. *Journal of Marketing Management*, *15*, 53–67

Silverstein, M., & Fiske, N. (2003). *Trading up: The new American luxury*. New York: Penguin Group.

Smith, S. (2003). Brand experience. In The Economist (Eds.), *Brands and branding*. London: Profile.

Tsai, S. (2005). Impact of personal orientation on luxury-brand purchase value. *International Journal of Market Research*, *47*(4), 427–452.

Unity Marketing. (2006). Unity marketing's luxury report 2006. Retrieved 5 August 2007 from, http://www.unitymarketingonline.com/reports2/luxury/pdf/LuxRep2006Intro.pdf

Vickers, S. J., & Renand, F. (2003). The marketing of luxury goods: An exploratory study – three conceptual dimensions. *The Marketing Review*, *3*(4), 459–478.

Vigneron, F., & Johnson, L. W. (2004). Measuring perceptions of brand luxury. *Brand Management*, *11*(6), 484–506.

Williams, A. (2006). Tourism and hospitality marketing; fantasy, feeling and fun. *International Journal of Contemporary Hospitality Management*, *18*(6), 482–495.

Yeoman, I., & McMahon-Beattie, U. (2006). Luxury markets and premium pricing. *Journal of Revenue & Pricing Management*, *4*, 319–328.

**Glyn Atwal** worked for Saatchi & Saatchi, Young & Rubicam and Publicis, and is Assistant Professor of Marketing at Rennes School of Business, France.

**Alistair Williams** is Professor of Marketing at Johnson & Wales University, USA, and has published widely in the field of leisure and hospitality.

# The Luxury Brand Strategy Challenge

## Uché Okonkwo-Pézard

In the last two decades, luxury brand management has generated much interest and discussions in both academic and business circles. Among business leaders, the debates have been related to the associated challenges and paradoxes that have emerged as a result of the evolution of luxury since it became a consolidated economic sector in the late 1990s, led by the vision of conglomerates such as LVMH, Gucci Group and Richemont.

The unprecedented growth of the luxury sector from a value of US$20 billion in 1985 to its current US$180 billion worth has been brought about by globalisation, wealth-creation opportunities, new

---

This chapter was Reprinted from Okonkwo, U. (2009) 'The Luxury Brand Strategy Challenge', *Journal of Brand Management*, 16, pp. 287-9. With kind permission from the *Journal of Brand Management*. All rights reserved.

U. Okonkwo-Pézard (✉)
Manchester, UK
e-mail: author@luxuryfashionbranding.com

© The Author(s) 2017
J.-N. Kapferer et al. (eds.), *Advances in Luxury Brand Management*,
Journal of Brand Management: Advanced Collections,
DOI 10.1007/978-3-319-51127-6_4

market segments, digital communications, international travel and culture convergence, and has led to a series of business challenges that luxury practitioners have never known. In addition to these, the expansion of the luxury client base and the subsequent lowering of the entry barriers to the industry have resulted to a rise in both offerings and competition across all luxury categories. Whether it is fashion and accessories, leather goods, fragrance, skincare, cosmetics, wines, spirits, timepieces, jewellery, automobiles, private jets, hotels, home decoration or concierge services, the supply of luxury is currently incessant. Brands such as Louis Vuitton, with 360 boutiques in 54 countries worldwide, are stretching the boundaries of access to luxury, whereas others such as Rolex and Cartier are leading the penetration of luxury in new regions and markets such as China and Russia. Additionally, issues such as counterfeiting, production outsourcing, country-of-origin effects and the extension of product ranges have all led to a mixed and expanded offering of luxury goods to a wider market, with accompanying complexities and expectations (Fig. 3).

In consequence, the expanded base of wealthy clients the world over are undergoing a parallel evolution in attitudes, interests, brand perceptions and overall psychology. They are driving the shift in the 'top-down' relationship that has existed for centuries with luxury brands to a bottom-up affiliation where the client has become as important as the product. An additional shift in power is taking place through the emergence of new luxury markets such as China, Russia, India, the Middle East, Brazil and Mexico. These markets, whose joint revenues

**Fig. 3** The scope of the luxury goods and services industry

in the next decade will surpass those of more established markets in Europe, North America and Japan, will drive the continuous evolution of luxury as the occidental luxury culture imposition gives way to the oriental luxury consumption style. Brands such as Burberry currently have more Russian clients in several UK locations than residents, and these new clients will continue to perceive luxury through different sets of references and parameters. These market dynamics are changing the luxury landscape, and therefore luxury management practices require revisiting and refining to accommodate these paradoxes.

Luxury as a concept is defined within the scope of socio-psychology as a result of its connection to a culture, state of being and lifestyle, whether it is personal or collective. When linked to brands, it is characterised by a recognisable style, strong identity, high awareness and enhanced emotional and symbolic associations. It evokes uniqueness and exclusivity, and is interpreted in products through high quality, controlled distribution and premium pricing. These core factors have led to the development of a US$180 billion global industry with an uninterrupted growth for over two decades. These elements have also led to the summarisation of luxury as a 'dream', leading to justifiable curiosity and interest.

The increased interest in luxury brand management among research and academic scholars in the last few years has been as a result of the aforementioned evolutionary factors. As a segment that was formerly linked purely to design and creativity, production and retail, luxury previously garnered minimal interest among researchers because of the general consensus that its impact on the academic and business worlds lacked adequate significance to merit consideration as a business domain or discipline. As the luxury segment evolved into an economic sector with the creation of LVMH and Richemont in the late 1990s and the subsequent consolidation of the Gucci Group in the early 2000s, several management issues linked to product design and strategic management, production, marketing, retail and above all branding emerged. Other organisational issues linked to resource management including people, material and finance also surfaced. This period also gave rise to the inclusion of client relationship management, which has led to the experiential marketing that is today a core aspect of luxury management. In parallel, branding as a business discipline also evolved in the 1990s, particularly with investigations into the measurement methods of brand equity as an intangible asset generator, and brand valuation as a core branding concept. Companies that invested substantially in brand building were shown to have a stronger competitive positioning than those whose core values were linked more to products and services than to branding. This evolution of branding influenced the introduction of assessments of several aspects of luxury products and services management.

As a consequence, several scholars from a wide range of business areas have published research papers in branding and marketing mainly linked to consumer behavioural science and corporate and consumer-based brand equity. Other research works have been in the areas of the intricate specificities of luxury management linked to branding, marketing and client relationship management. For a long time, however, research in luxury as a managerial science remained sparse in all exploratory, empirical, conceptual and strategic marketing aspects. This apparent gap prompted the publication of my book *Luxury Fashion Branding: Trends, Tactics, Techniques* (Okonkwo 2007, Palgrave Macmillan), which today serves as a reference for both academics and business practitioners in the luxury field. The need to make a further contribution of knowledge in luxury management has also led to other recent publications in the field by notable scholars and business leaders including the *Luxury Online* (2010, Palgrave Macmillan), which focuses on the challenges of adopting advanced Internet and digital strategies in luxury management, *Luxury Brand Management* (2012, Wiley) and *Luxury Strategy* (2012, Kogan Page).

In addition to these publications, several higher educational institutions, particularly business schools in France, Italy and beyond, have introduced research initiatives and academic programmes at both undergraduate and postgraduate levels, specialised in luxury management. The expansion of luxury management as a domain also led to the creation of the first research centre dedicated to the luxury domain, *The Luxury Centre* at ESC Rennes School of Business, France. Additionally, other scholars have recently enriched the luxury management research arena through their contributions, which have not only inspired and provoked our thinking but have also led to further interest in the field. This is evidenced by the level of attention this Special Issue on luxury brand management has attracted, and the wide range of topics which submitted papers have covered on the central theme of luxury. Initially designed as a single issue, the high number of submitted papers has led to the double issue that has been produced. This has ensured that the objective of this Special Issue, which is to present the latest management thinking and approaches to luxury brand management as a contribution to the widening of knowledge in the business of luxury.

The chapters in this edition of the *Journal of Brand Management* have been authored by both academics and luxury business practitioners, whose diverse backgrounds have led them to identify and examine the extensive range of challenging areas that the luxury sector is currently facing as a result of its current significant evolution. The subjects range from presentations of luxury management dynamics, the luxury fashion segment's branding dimensions, marketing specificities of luxury, evaluations of luxury brand perception models, online luxury challenges, luxury marketing environmental scanning, luxury client relationship management, experiential marketing in the luxury context, counterfeit goods effects on luxury brand equity and county-specific management aspects such as the impact of country-of-origin production on brand perceptions and the effects of country perception as the provenance of counterfeit luxury goods. Other areas are related to new dimensions of modern luxury marketing such as the place of the Internet and digital technology in the luxury sector, as well as an examination of the new mass luxury movement, and much more.

It has been a highly stimulating exercise to edit this first Special Issue on luxury brand management. The extensive subject ranges in the content and the diverse geographical representations of both the academics and practitioners who contributed to this issue have ensured a truly rich edition. I would like to thank all who submitted papers, and will add that as an active and passionate luxury advocate, I would have been only too glad to recommend the publication of all entries but due to feedback from reviewers and space limitations, we were only able to produce so much.

Special thanks also to Brenda Rouse, the managing editor of this Journal, whose diligence ensured that the quality of this Special Issue on luxury brand management matches luxury perceptions.

We hope that you will find this Special Issue dedicated to luxury, both enriching and thought-provoking and that the insights provided in the collection of research materials will inspire further interest and attention to luxury brand management.

## References

Okonkwo, U. (2007). *Luxury Fashion Branding. Trends, Tactics, Techniques Macmillan*. UK: Palgrave Macmillan. doi: 10.1007/978-0-230-59088-5.

Okonkwo, U. (2010). *Luxury Online. Styles, Systems, Strategies* Macmillan. UK: Palgrave Macmillan. doi: 10.1057/9780230248335.

Chevaller, M. Mazzalovo, G. (Eds.) (2012). *Luxury Brand Management: A World of Privilege, Second Edition*, John Wiley & Sons Singapore Pte. Ltd doi: 10.1002/9781119199168.

Kapferer, J.-N. Bastien, V. (2012). *The Luxury Strategy, Break the Rules of Marketing to Build Luxury Brands*.

**Uché Okonkwo-Pézard** is recognized worldwide as one of the pioneer business strategists and opinion leaders in the luxury industry. Uché Okonkwo-Pézard is one of the pioneer business strategy consultants in the luxury industry. Based in Paris, she is the executive director and founder of Luxe Corp. (www.luxe-corp.com), the leading strategy and management consultancy company specialized in the luxury industry and its affiliated sectors. Based at Paris' famed Place Vendôme, Luxe Corp currently advises and collaborates with major international luxury brands, including Louis Vuitton, Gucci, Richemont, Christian Dior, Coty, Piaget, and Fabergé, as well as emerging luxury brands including Daniele de Winter, André Ross, and Gottèsman. Uché is also the editor of the luxury business magazine, Luxe-Mag.Com (www.luxe-mag.com). A luxury veteran with extensive cross-sector experience in luxury management and strategy consultancy, Uché is a fellow of the American Luxury Marketing Council and sits on the Advisory Board of the Global Luxury Forum Moscow. She has MBA from Brunel University Business School London. She can be contacted through the book's website, www.luxuryfashionbranding.com.

# The Specificity of Luxury Management: Turning Marketing Upside Down

Jean-Noël Kapferer and Vincent Bastien

## Introduction

On 26 March 2008, the news was confirmed: the prestigious luxury brand Jaguar, along with the mythical brand Land Rover, were sold to the Indian conglomerate Tata, which had just announced some months earlier its own launch of the cheapest car in the world. The price paid by Tata for both brands (2.3 billion US$) was half of the price paid by Ford in November 1989 (5.2 billion US$), and several billion dollars have been invested by Ford during those 9 years. This demise of Ford Corporation in rebuilding a profitable Jaguar is intriguing: all modern techniques of industrial

---

This chapter was Reprinted from Kapferer, J. and Bastien, V. (2009) "The Specificity of Luxury Management: Turning Marketing Upside Down", *Journal of Brand Management*, 16, pp. 311–22. With kind permission from the *Journal of Brand Management*. All rights reserved.

J.-N. Kapferer (✉) · V. Bastien
Inseec Business School, Paris, France
e-mail: jnkapferer@inseec.com; bastien@hec.fr

© The Author(s) 2017
J.-N. Kapferer et al. (eds.), *Advances in Luxury Brand Management*, Journal of Brand Management: Advanced Collections,
DOI 10.1007/978-3-319-51127-6_5

management had been applied to Jaguar (re-engineering, re-focus on quality, and so on). Modern marketing had also been introduced in the management of this brand to make it more competitive and attract more consumers. In the automobile industry, critical size is a determinant factor of profitability, and Jaguar brand extensions were launched to reach this critical size in volume. Despite the introduction of marketing, or maybe because of it, Jaguar sales dropped from 130,000 to 60,000 in 5 years.

In fact, all over the world, in most Luxury Groups, marketing is introduced fiercely: experienced brand managers, typically MBAs, well trained in classic marketing at Procter and Gamble (P&G) or Johnson & Johnson, are hired to promote their methodologies within the management of luxury brands. This is the beginning of the problem soon faced by these brands. Certainly, most luxury brands do market products that themselves are not luxury products: these trading-down extensions aim at leveraging the prestige of the name they carry in order to harvest the royalties of, say, masstige fragrances, eyewear, accessories, and so on. In these segments, classical marketing does apply, by bringing efficiency through methodologies and techniques inherited from mass products (segmentation, positioning, pre-testing, surveys of consumers' desires and expectations, benchmarking, and so on). They have an allure of luxury but are not luxury (Thomas 2007).

The current problem is the growing extension of these classical marketing techniques to the core business of luxury brands. Extant approaches are simply not working: Jaguar, Calvin Klein or Cardin are some of the examples of this. Jaguar has never been profitable, although its perceived quality had been remarkably upgraded by Ford, as indicated by all J.D. Power consumer surveys in the United States. Calvin Klein has slowly moved out of the luxury market, as Cardin did before: these two brands are no longer luxury brands. There is nothing wrong in not being a luxury brand: Zara and Mango are very profitable, while being in the accessible fashion market. Our point is that in order to enter the luxury market, to build a successful luxury brand and to make it remain a luxury brand, one has to forget the classical marketing rules. The successful luxury goods marketers *turn traditional marketing practices upside down* to achieve profitable success. This has obvious consequences on the human resources policy of these brands.

## Luxury Marketing: A Difference of Level or of Nature?

Looking at the literature on luxury, one is amazed by the recent profusion of concepts: trading up, new luxury, mass luxury, masstige, opuluxe, hyper-luxury, luxury fashion, and so on. Each one tries to identify a new segment, nuance or form of luxury, opposing it to former forms of luxury called 'traditional luxury' (Danziger 2005; Okongwo 2007; Silverstein and Fiske 2003; Tungate 2004). In fact, it is commonly assumed that an underlying continuum goes from mass consumer goods to luxury. Doyle's (2002) classic marketing textbook presents a graph with cost as horizontal axis and quality as vertical axis: economy products, mass-market products, premium products and luxury are all plotted on the same line, meaning that there is a linear progression from one to the other (p. 84). This graph implies that marketing luxury goods would have no strong specificities: it would only exhibit differences in level, not in nature, with the marketing used by all fast-moving consumer goods companies. For instance, the luxury brand would be the most selective in its distribution; the most image-driven; the most extreme in its product quality and in the services that go with the products, and so on; and the most expensive (Sicard 2003).

The proper look at the way truly profitable luxury brands are managed reveals that sticking to a luxury strategy implies a very strict set of rules (called 'The luxury strategy', *stricto sensu*) in all facets of their management, including financial and human resources (Kapferer and Bastien 2009). In fact, one does not launch a luxury brand; one builds it progressively by managing the allocation of resources in a very specific way. Growth that brings more sales and profits while keeping the brand luxury status also needs the strict obedience to this set of rules. At an operational level, the luxury strategy means abandoning some of the classic principles of marketing, as fruitfully practiced by P&G or L' Oreal in the food and drug traditional markets or in masstige markets (mass fragrances). To become what it is now, transforming small family companies such as Ferrari, Chanel, Cartier, Louis Vuitton, Gucci, Prada, and so on into worldwide successes, luxury has had to invent its own marketing rules, which are too often unknown or forgotten, today, by many so-called luxury brands, and the word 'luxury' itself seems to have lost its meaning and the clear perception of its implications.

Going back to fundamentals, this chapter highlights the specificities of marketing luxury brands: it cannot be just a set of rules, but must explain why these rules are a consequence of what luxury is, and its role in modern societies (Kapferer and Bastien 2009). Luxury is a culture, which means that you have to understand it to be able to practice it with flair and spontaneity. The reason why marketing does not seem to work with luxury goods the same way it does with everyday consumer goods, even top-of-the-range or premium consumer goods, is that the two are fundamentally different.

If we want to be able to market luxury, we need first to understand what luxury is all about. Any set of new rules must be firmly grounded in scholarship. In this chapter, we shall make a brief historical, sociological and anthropological detour to grasp the functions of luxury and hence, how to implement them.

## The Essence of Luxury: Recreating the Social Distance

Let us start with history.

- Originally, luxury was the visible result – deliberately conspicuous and ostentatious – of hereditary social stratification (kings, priests and the nobility, versus the gentry and commoners). Aristocrats had to show their inherited rank to the crowds: ostentatious spending was a social obligation for the aristocrats, even the least well off. On the other hand, social distance was preserved: the rich Bourgeois were not allowed to dress like aristocrats. This was forbidden by royal rules (sumptuary laws) (Berry 1994; Castar è de 2008).
- Eighteenth-century rational thought and Enlightenment philosophy resulted in the gradual disappearance of the founding myths that

gave legitimacy to this social structure, and led to our present-day western society. Globalisation is inexorably conquering the world, that is to say, a materialistic and fluid society in which any kind of transcendent social stratification has disappeared. Meritocracy has been substituted with aristocracy. Each person in a democratic world has even chances of succeeding: one makes one's own destiny through work. This is a much more fluid and open world. Some people even speak of 'classless societies'.
– What has not disappeared, on the other hand, is man's need for some form of social stratification, which is vital to him; he needs to know his place in society (Frank 1999; Frank 2007; Veblen 1899).
– Luxury, then, has this fundamental function of recreating this social stratification. Moreover, it does it in a democratic manner, meaning that everyone can recreate (up to a certain point) his strata according to his dreams – whence a new kind of anxiety, that of freedom: before, the strata were known and respected; now hierarchical codes need to be recreated, and this produces a demand for advice on how to recreate them, placing the 'luxury brand' *in a position of superiority with respect to its client*, a notion that will have major consequences in luxury brand management. This is a necessary condition for the richest and most powerful people to crave for luxury brands.

'Trading Up' (see the book by Silverstein and Fiske 2003) – or persuading a client to choose an item from further up the range, to go 'up-market' – essentially plays on the many excuses people can always find for treating themselves well by indulging in buying something better and more expensive. Trading up is very different from luxury, for it does not have the latter's sociological dimension – its function is not so much social stratification as personal indulgence, improving brand performance thanks to emotional and experiential rewards. Typical examples developed in 'Trading Up' are Victoria's Secret, Belvedere vodka, and Callaway golf clubs: none qualify as luxury brands.

## Luxury as a Badge: Luxury for Others

Clearly, luxury is a social marker, which is why there is such a need for brands.

With luxury recreating some degree of social stratification, people in a democracy are therefore free – within the limit of their financial means – to use any of its components to define themselves socially as they wish. What we have here is *'democratic luxury': a luxury item that extraordinary people would consider ordinary is at the same time an extraordinary item to ordinary people*. The DNA of luxury, therefore, is the symbolic desire (albeit often repressed) to belong to a superior class, which everyone will have *chosen* according to their dreams, because *anything that can be a social signifier can become a luxury*. By the same token, anything that ceases to be a social signifier loses its luxury status. Once, a swimming pool was a luxury, but it is no longer so. A private elevator still is one, for it harks back to the multistorey private hotel.

The codes of luxury are cultural, in as much as the luxury brand lies at the confluence between culture and social success. Money (high price of products) is not enough to define luxury goods: it only measures the wealth of the buyer. But money is not a measure of taste. This is why the luxury brand must first encode social distinction (Bourdieu 1985). *Luxury converts the raw material that is money into a culturally sophisticated product that is social stratification.*

## Luxury for Oneself

In addition to this key social function, *luxury should have a very strong personal and hedonistic component, otherwise it is no longer luxury but simple snobbery* (it would in effect be allowing others to impose a paradigm for us to follow, instead of us making our own choice according to our personal tastes), and we would quickly fall into the trap of *provocation* ('I have the biggest automobile in the whole neighborhood') or of *'Potlatch'* – a highly complex ritual ceremony practiced in Melanesia and among certain indigenous peoples on the

Pacific north-west coast of the United States and Canada, especially the Kwakiutl tribe, in which the object of the exercise is to overawe the other person and outdo him by offering him the most luxurious gifts possible, which he cannot reciprocate, placing him in a position of weakness in a society in which every gift must be followed by a return gift of equal or greater munificence (Mauss 1990).

Undoubtedly, there does exist a consumer market for symbols (ostentatious logos on leather bags and accessories). But no luxury brand can hope to survive if it relies purely on clients who are only interested in reputed signs of recognition, the symbol rather than the substance; these people – those who are only interested in symbols – will drift from one symbol to another, from one logo to another: tycoons will today be drinking Dom Perignon by the case and tomorrow something else.

As a result, *luxury is qualitative and not quantitative*: the number of diamonds in a necklace is an indication of the opulence of the wearer, but says nothing about his taste. Also, when it comes to luxury, *hedonism takes precedence over functionality*: this is a major distinction with premium brands. Luxury is closer to art than to mere function. It has to be *multisensory and experiential*: it is not only the appearance of a Porsche that matters but also the sound of it; not only the odour of a perfume but also the beauty of the bottle it comes in (Chevalier and Mazzalovo 2008). It is a multisensory compression.

Luxury being a social phenomenon, and society being composed of human beings, *luxury, whether object or service, must have a strong human content* and must be of human origin. This has two major consequences:

(a) *To qualify as luxury, the object or part of it must be handmade*, the service rendered by a human to another human. Even the widely sold Lacoste shirt is handmade in the final part of its product process.
(b) *Exclusive services are a* sine qua non *part of luxury management*. Merits that call for personal honours, making each one of us a prince for a short while, are the key differences between the customer relationship management (CRM) of luxury brands and that of mass brands or premium brands (Cailleux et al. 2009).

## Luxury and Fashion

Both luxury and fashion play a key role in our social life:

– Luxury, by recreating a social stratification that was done away with by democracy
– Fashion, by recreating the rhythm of the seasons that was done away with by urbanisation, and a social differentiation while avoiding being engulfed by the anonymous crowd

Fashion is intimately tied to the ebb and flow of time (Okongwo 2007; Tungate 2004). Luxury aims at timelessness: the great classics represent a high share of the sales of a luxury brand, whereas last years' fashion has little value and can be bought on sale on the Internet.

Luxury and fashion, then, represent two worlds – both economically important but still very different (the 'luxury streets' are not to be found in the 'fashion quarters') – and they overlap only marginally (limited to haute couture); in these cases, success relies on a tandem arrangement, where you have a brand (which covers the luxury side) and a creator (who covers the fashion side), and the best examples of this are Chanel and Karl Lagerfeld.

## Turning Marketing Upside Down

Having looked at, through history, anthropology, and sociology, the role of luxury in democratic societies, we are now able to infer its consequences for marketing practice and offer prescriptive advice.

What are some imperatives that should reign in managing luxury brands?

### Forget About 'Brand Positioning', Worship Brand Identity

In consumer marketing, at the heart of every brand strategy you will find the concept of positioning, of the 'Unique Selling Proposition', and

'Unique and Convincing Competitive Advantage'. Every classic brand has to specify its positioning *vis-à-vis* a set of competitors it has chosen. Positioning is *the difference with these other brands that creates the preference* (Kapferer 2008).

Nothing is more foreign to this approach than luxury. When it comes to luxury, *being unique is what counts, not any comparison with a competitor.* Luxury is the expression of a taste, of a creative identity, of the intrinsic passion of a creator; luxury makes the bald statement, 'this is what I am', not 'that depends' – which is what positioning implies. What made the Christian Lacroix brand is its image of bright sunshine, full of this designer's bright, vivid colours, suffused with the culture of the Mediterranean; it certainly is not concerned with its positioning with respect to this or that other established designer, held as competitor. This image is born of itself – not of surveys showing where there might be a niche or a business opportunity, but in the very spontaneous identity of this man, his background and his idiosyncrasies. One should use all that helps to forge authenticity, psychological and social depth, and that creates close bonds with the psyche of clients who will be seduced by this identity.

As a result, the luxury brand should tell a story, its own story, be it real (History) as for Coco Chanel and René Lacoste (Kapferer and Gaston-Breton 2000) or completely invented from scratch as for Ralph Lauren or Tod's. Stories create emotional involvement, build an appealing identity and travel fast like rumours (Kapferer 1990).

## Be Superlative, Never Comparative

In luxury, the word 'competitors' is irrelevant: can you imagine someone comparing the merits of Andy Warhol and Roy Lichtenstein? These are two different identities, stories, and so on, each one being the best of its own kind.

In traditional marketing, there is this obsession with poaching clients from other brands. Lexus, the top-of-the-range Toyota brand, took as its primary goal taking customers away from Mercedes in the United States – its target as a potential source of business. The Lexus brand introductory model was purposely designed taking the Mercedes E Class as the model to overtake; externally it resembled it very closely, though in fact it was superior to the E Class technically, and was substantially cheaper to buy. Hence, the launch advertising for its first automobile in the United States in 1999: 'This is perhaps the first time it has happened, that by choosing a 36,000 US$ car over a 72,000 US$ car the customer has been able to go up-range'.

Although in statistical terms Lexus claims to reign as the Number 1 imported luxury brand in the US car market, its behaviour betrays a strong lack of identity and an obsession with by-passing competition. This is typical of a premium brand, not a luxury brand. In fact, in Japan, Lexus is not perceived at all as a luxury brand: Japanese consumers feel it is a remarkable output of Toyota's engineers but associated with no vision or heritage of its own; what's the story beyond the product performance and the hybrid engine? There is none.

## Should You Aim at the Pursuit of Perfection? No Flaws, No Charm

The most overused word in luxury is 'perfection': advertising campaigns on the latest models speak repeatedly of their 'perfection'. It is true that in surveys on the perception of luxury, consumers from all over the world were interviewed, and the consensus was that 'product excellence' is the primary prerequisite of luxury. In the United States, Robb Report regularly publishes a 'best of' guide: for example, which is the best golf club, the best MP3 player, the best automobile. Lexus has almost no defaults, functionally speaking: it is a premium brand. The Lacoste shirt is held as the 'best polo in the world', its quality being far above that of Ralph Lauren's own shirt.

The aim of a premium product is to be a perfect product. It would take a touch of madness for it to be counted a luxury. Functionally, a Seiko watch is superior to many luxury watches – it is more accurate (because it is a quartz watch) and shows the time directly and in a perfectly legible manner (because it is displayed on a digital face). If you were to buy a luxury watch, such as Patek Philippe, you would be warned that it loses

2 min every year. The flaw is not only known, it is assumed – one could say that that is both its charm and its guarantee of authenticity. It is the specific and singular nature of their movement that is responsible for this. Luxury watches like adding complications, and indeed seek it out in their endless quest of art for art's sake. This is the 'madness' touch that goes beyond perfection and makes people collect them.

Of course, if a luxury product is not a flawless product, the reverse is not true: adding flaws does not turn a regular product into a luxury product.

## Resist Clients' Demands

In traditional marketing, client is king. P&G's success relies on a methodology that puts the customer at the heart of the business: P&G does this by listening to its customers – listening to what they have to say or are trying to say – then transforming these wishes into global, or at least regional, products that are then sold through mass distribution channels. The same holds true for fragrances: consumers' dreams and stars are clustered, and each fragrance of a brand aims at one dream cluster. The luxury brand, on the other hand, comes from the mind of its creator, driven by a long-term vision.

Yves Saint Laurent himself invented from scratch Opium, as Thierry Mugler invented Angel, two long-lasting worldwide blockbusters, not to mention of the iconic Chanel N°5, invented in 1921 at a time marketing did not exist.

There are two ways to go bankrupt: not listening to the client, and also listening to him too much. One of the most respected brands in the world is BMW. This ever-growing brand has been successful in creating a cult, a body of owners who are extremely faithful, devoted and committed to their brand. According to *BusinessWeek* (6 August 2007), it is the thirteenth brand in the world in terms of brand equity: 21.6 billion US$, third in the automobile sector, behind Toyota (world's top auto builder) with 32 billion and Mercedes Benz with 23.5 billion US$. It is in fact, according to the Luxury Institute, 'the most admired car company in the world'.

What is less well known, however, is that despite its success, the brand has remained true to itself thanks to its *willingness to resist client demands* when these did not correspond to the company's very precise vision as to what made for a true BMW (Kiley 2004).

An example that says a great deal about this brand is that consumers regularly curse each time a new Series 5 car is released, because this model does not give rear passengers enough legroom. According to them, such stubbornness defies reason and good sense. But the makers object that meeting client demands would spoil the purity of design of this car, its proportions having been meticulously calculated, as indeed were its aerodynamics. Some may remember the loss of performance and aesthetics that the Jaguar E-type suffered following the addition of two full-size rear seats.

## Don't Look for Equality with Your Clients

Luxury is a consequence of meritocracy. Once the exclusive privilege of the aristocracy, luxury today is what restratifies our so-called classless societies, but on the basis of merit, no longer simply on birth. So everyone is looking for ways to haul themselves up – luxury brands are at the same time a reward and a token of gradual elevation. To preserve this status, the brand must always dominate its client. This is not the same as saying do not respect him: parents dominate their children, but that does not mean that they do not respect them; on the other hand, if they treat them as 'best buddies', making themselves out to be equals with them, they lose their aura, and profoundly disturb their offspring. This relationship between parents and their children is very close to that between brand and client.

As a result, a certain distance is preserved that is not supercilious or aloof, but nevertheless maintains an aura of mystery. If you eat in a high-class restaurant, you do not visit the kitchen – that is the place where they craft the magic creation. This is the whole problem with so-called relational programmes, CRM, those that seek in traditional marketing to involve customers in the shaping of a brand, in co-creation, in consumer empowerment and in creating a relational intimacy (Cailleux et al. 2009). Nothing could be more alien to a luxury brand. It is true, of course, that Louis Vuitton does occasionally organise vintage sports car rallies, bringing together knowledgeable oglers at the wheel of their prestige coupés, legacies of the past. But that is not the same as getting involved in client relations – it is keeping the myth alive.

In contrast to the premium market or trading up, luxury is the domain of culture and taste. Even if many well-off buyers do not actually have the codes themselves, they deduce from the limitless consumption of a luxury brand the fact that it must be coded as a luxury. In all fast-growing countries where there is an emerging wealth class, the so-called BRIC (Brazil, Russia, India, China), the luxury brands should be ready to play this role of advisor, educator, and sociological guide even to the richest people of this world (Chaddah and Husband 2006; Dubois et al. 2001).

## Make It Difficult for Clients to Buy

The luxury brand is something that has to be earned. The greater the inaccessibility – whether actual or most often virtual – the greater the desire. As everyone knows, with luxury there is a built-in time factor – the time spent searching, waiting, longing – so far removed from traditional marketing logic, which does everything to facilitate quick access to the product through mass distribution, with its self-service stores, self-checkout systems, the Internet, call centres, and introductory offers. Luxury has to know how to set up the necessary obstacles to the straining of desire, and keep them in place. People do eventually get to enjoy the luxury after passing through a series of obstacles – financial obstacles, needless to say, but more particularly cultural (they have to know how to appreciate the product, wear it, and consume it), logistical (find the shops), and time obstacles (wait 2 years for a Ferrari or a Mikimoto pearl necklace).

Luxury needs to excel in the practice of distributing rarity, especially when there are no real shortages. It is quite natural: just as actual shortages stand in the way of growth, the absence of rarity leads to the immediate dissipation of desire, and so does the disappearance of the waiting time that sustains luxury. To create this obstacle to immediate consumption, it should always be necessary to wait for a luxury product – time is a key dimension of luxury, as with all desire for anything even remotely sophisticated.

## The Role of Advertising Is Not to Sell

How does one evaluate an advertising campaign at P&G? By means of comparison of sales, before and after the campaign.

Interviewed about his role, the head of BMW in the United States replied that with its customers trading up, and the collective aspiration of the younger drivers, BMW's sales target for the following year had already been 90 percent met virtually automatically. Did that mean that he would have nothing to do then? His reply was simple, direct and highly illuminating: 'My job is to make sure that the 18-year-olds in this country decide that, as soon as they have the money, they will be buying a BMW. I have to see to it that when they go to bed at night they are dreaming of BMW' (Kiley 2004).

In luxury, advertising aims exclusively at recreating the dream. In fact, this dream is permanently eroded by sales growth and media over-visibility: for the desire engine to work, the tank must be refilled with dream. Do not measure dream by the immediate effect on sales: there will not be much.

## Advertise to Those Whom You Are Not Targeting

In traditional marketing, the keyword is effectiveness, but over and above effectiveness there has to be a return on investment: this is efficiency. In advertising, for example, the media plan must focus on the target consumers and nothing but the target consumers – every person reached beyond the target is a waste of investment money.

In luxury, if somebody is looking at somebody else and fails to recognise the brand of his watch, and to *have an idea of* (know) the price that goes with it, part of its value is lost. It is essential to spread brand and worth awareness far beyond the target group. This is the only way to build the distinctive facet of the brand (creating desire in the eyes of others).

The functional analysis of luxury (see above) reminded us that luxury has two value facets – luxury for oneself and luxury for others. To sustain the latter facet it is essential that there should be many more people that are familiar with the brand than those who could possibly afford to buy it for themselves.

## Raise Your Prices Continuously in Order to Increase Demand

Marketing is a discipline that tries – and sometimes succeeds – to bend the rigid laws of economics. In the standard market model, when the price falls, demand rises. This is why to increase sales, most brands do capitalise on economies of scale, experience curves to lower their prices and earn a dominant market share: this is typical of Dell.

To live in luxury you have to be above others, not be 'reasonable', in both senses of the word. A reasonable price is a price that appeals to reason, and therefore to *comparison*. Now, recalling our second imperative, presented above, luxury is 'superlative', not 'comparative'. To be reasonable is also to reduce the object to its tangible dimension and to deny the intangible.

By increasing prices, you lose the bad customers, but now you suddenly become dazzlingly attractive to people who would previously not have given you a second glance.

It would be wrong, ridiculous, to believe that all luxury means is being the most expensive in the market. First, it attracts the segment of luxury buyers for whom luxury means showing one's richness: this does not create much loyalty, for pricing high can always be imitated. Richard Mille created the hyper-luxury segment of tourbillon watches (beyond 500,000 US$): it was soon imitated in the United States by Jacob Arabo in New York. This would also fall into the volume trap. It is true that luxury follows a strategy that is the very opposite of that used by traditional marketing – which often talks a lot about its value strategy, but is secretly pushing volume – but it should not be put in a niche.

For a status brand, it is important for the range of products, which are mostly out of reach of the average man in the street – like a made-to-measure trunk at around $150,000 from Louis Vuitton – also to include more affordable products (like a Louis Vuitton key holder at $150), provided that such items live up to the brand and are significantly more expensive than equivalent products from other sources. This is why Louis Vuitton pens are dearer than a Montblanc or an Omas.

Now, this does not prevent the brand from creating some more accessible product lines (to let new clients enter the brand universe), as long as the average price of the whole range goes up.

The final point of this policy of systematically raising prices is that it gives the whole company a sense of responsibility. Price is a decisive factor in bringing about a change in mentality; indeed, we see quite profound internal changes in mentality, as every person in the company in his own way is constantly trying to find new ways of creating more value for the customer. It is all a matter of living up to the price.

## Unveiling the Specific Marketing of Luxury Brands

For readers of extant classic marketing literature, the above prescriptions probably look counter-intuitive, if not provocative. The problem of marketing extant literature is that it bases its analyses and models on brands that do not qualify as luxury, although for advertising purposes they claim being so. As a result, this literature has so far little relevance for luxury brands. It has not explored the inside of the luxury companies or tried to understand the working models of the managers of companies such as Louis Vuitton, the most valuable luxury brand in the world according to Interbrand (20,321 billion US$ in 2007, ranking seventeenth among all global brands). This would have been most enlightening. It is time to rediscover the true fundamentals of luxury marketing, those used by these small family companies that have become worldwide successes while keeping the luxury status of their brands.

## The Luxury Sector Hit by the Economic Crisis

Today luxury brands face a rare and violent economic crisis. Not only are the middle class buyers gone, but many wealthy consumers have also been hit; traders for instance. Even those wealthy people who have not been personally affected by the crisis are changing their purchasing behaviour. These people are reducing their conspicuous consumption, although they still have the means to buy expensive goods and brands. This is their way of symbolically participating in the national effort and exhibiting solidarity.

In fact, it can be argued that the luxury sector is more affected than other sectors by consumers' generalised trading down. Compared to January 2008, hotel occupancy rates fell 12.9 percent in the United States. The figure for luxury hotels is worse, it fell by 24.4 percent (International Herald Tribune 2009). New corporate guidelines encourage managers to downgrade their standards; for instance, by staying at a three star rather than a four star hotel. Another direct effect of the crisis is the postponement of major purchases by the wealthiest themselves: furniture, antiques, art shops are relatively empty. Consumers are rethinking their spending priorities and values.

Which luxury brands will survive? A former Cartier chief operating officer (COO) once said that the main luxury brands have already endured two world wars, one global economic depression, many local revolutions, two oil crisis, and are still standing. The weakest brands are those that capitalised on an inherited prestige to sell non-luxury products. Today many of these so-called luxury brands have seen their sales slashed. They thrived on the allure of luxury and seducing a target group that has been called the 'excursionist', that is, consumers who were not within the core luxury target market but who bought these accessible items. The fact is that many luxury brands have become unable to remain profitable in their core business. These luxury brands have increasingly targeted the middle class and have marketed products that are not luxury products. Their trading down was aimed at leveraging the prestige of the name and seducing irregular buyers who were, in turn, seduced by the ostentatious logo. These excursionists have stopped buying and frivolous consumption has all but gone.

The regular buyers consider luxury as *an art de vivre*. They do appreciate the many exclusive features of the luxury product. Interestingly they might for now postpone their purchase, but delaying one's purchase means that one dreams about it, and as a result, there is an increased desire to purchase the product. It is crucial for these brands to sustain the dream, for instance, by advertising superb innovations. As Ernst Lieb, COO of Mercedes USA puts it: 'If I can get a customer interested today in our new product, that is a good thing, because in three years, when he is ready to buy again, he'll buy our product' (Elliott 2009).

## The Future of Luxury Brands: From Retreat to Rebound

Luxury brands will lose sales and consumers, like most other sectors. However there is a clear difference between those brands whose profitability is made in their core business (e.g., leather goods for Louis Vuitton) and those brands whose profitability is achieved only through brand extensions outside of their core activity. The brand extension activity is often a trading down. The latter will now face a double difficulty because their luxury status was already fragile. Slashing prices will dilute their status. The questions one must ask are these: Will it make some irregular buyers purchase on impulse? Isn't it a sign of lack of value to discount products?

Luxury purchases have two facets: indulging in one's pleasure (luxury for self) and demonstration of success (luxury for others). The latter will cease to be a major driver in Europe and in the United States. The brands which can prove the exclusive qualities of their products, their undeniable heritage, and their unique experience will bounce back first. In emerging countries however, the driver will still be to demonstrate that one is not poor anymore: luxury for others will remain dominant.

Luxury brand owners will seize the opportunity given by this crisis to regain the balance, beauty, and attractiveness of their brand and to regenerate them. They will take the brand back to its roots, by cutting their brand extensions or unprofitable store locations. Another strategy to preserve profitability will be to cut unnecessary overheads and non-essential public relations programmes. These brand owners will also take the opportunity to review their outsourcing operations, which might have been formulated only for cost reduction purposes, and not to create value per se. Finally they will look to the future and consider the desires of the luxury consumer, for whom luxury is more than a logo. For them luxury is an appreciation of fine works, fine craftsmanship, creativity, and the making of a legend. The luxury consumer needs to be seduced once again.

# References

Berry, C. J. (1994). *The idea of luxury: A conceptual and historical investigation.* Cambridge: Cambridge University Press.
Bourdieu, P. (1985). *Distinction.* Cambridge, MA: Harvard University Press.
Cailleux, H., Mignot, C., & Kapferer, J. N. (2009). Is CRM for luxury? *Journal of Brand Management Special issue on luxury, 16*(5–6), 406–412.
Castar è de, J. (2008). *Luxe et Civilisation.* Paris: Eyrolles.
Chaddah, R., & Husband, P. (2006). *The cult of the luxury brand.* Boston, MA: Nicholas Brealey.
Chevalier, M., & Mazzalovo, G. (2008). *Luxury brand management.* Singapore: John Wiley & Sons.
Danziger, P. M. (2005). *Let them eat the cake.* Chicago, IL: Dearborn.
Doyle, P. (2002). *Marketing management and strategy* (3rd edn.). London: Prentice-Hall.
Dubois, B., Laurent, G., & Czellar, S. (2001, 1 October). Consumer relationship to Luxury: Analyzing complex and ambivalent attitudes. *HEC Paris Research Paper.*
Elliott, H. (2009, 14 January). Luxury cars aren't selling either. *Forbes.com.*
Frank, R. H. (1999). *Luxury fever.* New York: Free Press.
Frank, R. H. (2007). *Richistan.* London: Piatkus Books.
International Herald Tribune. (2009, 28 January). *International Herald Tribune*, 17.
Kapferer, J. N. (1990). *Rumours: Nature, functions and uses.* New Brunswick, NJ: Transaction Books.
Kapferer, J. N. (2008). *The new strategic brand management.* London: Kogan Page.
Kapferer, J. N., & Bastien, V. (2009). *The luxury strategy.* London: Kogan Page.
Kapferer, P., & Gaston-Breton, T. (2000). *Lacoste: The Legend.* Paris: Cherche Midi.
Kiley, D. (2004). *Driven: Inside BMW.* New York: Wiley.

Mauss, M. (1990). *The Gift: Form and reason for exchange in archaic societies.* London: Routledge.
Okongwo, U. (2007). *Luxury fashion branding.* London: Palgrave Macmillan.
Sicard, M. C. (2003). *Luxe, Mensonge et Marketing.* Paris: Village Mondial.
Silverstein, M., & Fiske, N. (2003). *Trading up.* New York: Portfolio.
Thomas, D. (2007). *Deluxe: How luxury lost its luster.* London: Penguin Books.
Tungate, M. (2004). *Fashion brands: Branding style from Armani to Zara.* London: Kogan Page.
Veblen, T. (1899). *The theory of the leisure class: An Economic Study in the Evolution of Institutions.* USA: Macmillan.

**Jean-Noël Kapferer** is a worldly renowned authority on luxury. HEC Paris Graduate and Emeritus Professor, PhD Kellogg Business School (USA), he conducts his research at INSEEC Luxury on the mutations of luxury and luxury brand management. Honorary editor of the *Luxury Research Journal*, he has widely published his articles in international journals. Co-author of the reference book *The Luxury Strategy: Break the Rules of Marketing to Build Luxury Brands*, author of *How Luxury Brands Can Grow Yet Remain Rare*, he leads executive seminars on luxury all around the world (USA, China, Korea, and Europe) and is advisor to the president of INSEEC business school. JN Kapferer enjoys travelling, skiing, and windsurfing.

**Vincent Bastien** is one of the most experienced senior managers in the luxury business. For over 25 years, he has been CEO or MD of international companies including Louis Vuitton Malletier and the beauty division of Sanofi group (including Yves Saint Laurent, Nina Ricci, and Parfums Oscar de la Renta, Van Cleef & Arpels, and Fendi). He is now Affiliate Professor at HEC Paris. He has just published *The Luxury Strategy* (Kogan Page ed.).

# Luxury Consumption in the Trade-Off Between Genuine and Counterfeit Goods: What Are the Consumers' Underlying Motives and Value-Based Drivers?

Klaus-Peter Wiedmann, Nadine Hennigs and Christiane Klarmann

## Introduction

The significant growth of luxury consumption in recent decades has been accompanied by a prevalence of pirated and counterfeited goods. The market for counterfeit goods is estimated to account for as much as 10 percent of world trade and has spread to almost all product categories. Counterfeiting is

---

This chapter was Reprinted from Wiedmann, K., Hennigs, N. and Klarmann, C. (2012) 'Luxury Consumption in the Trade-off between Genuine and Counterfeit Goods: What are the Consumers' Underlying Motives and Value-based Drivers?', *Journal of Brand Management*, 19, pp. 544–66. With kind permission from the *Journal of Brand Management*. All rights reserved.

K.-P. Wiedmann · N. Hennigs (✉) · C. Klarmann
Institute of Marketing and Management, Leibniz University of Hannover, Hannover, Germany
e-mail: wiedmann@m2.uni-hannover.de; hennigs@m2.uni-hannover.de
klarmann@m2.uni-hannover.de

© The Author(s) 2017
J.-N. Kapferer et al. (eds.), *Advances in Luxury Brand Management*,
Journal of Brand Management: Advanced Collections,
DOI 10.1007/978-3-319-51127-6_6

often related to organized crime and international terrorism and harms the legitimate producers who have invested in research, product development and marketing (Green and Smith 2002; Furnham and Valgeirsson 2007). The availability of substandard imitations may lead to a reduction of the perceived quality of the genuine product and might potentially erode consumer confidence in the brand (Green and Smith 2002). Consequently, genuine brands face a loss of both revenues and intangible values, such as brand reputation and consumer goodwill (Bush et al. 1989). In a luxury product context, the prevalence of low-cost counterfeits may reduce the perceived exclusiveness of luxury goods (Wilke and Zaichkowsky 1999). Nevertheless, most consumers disregard the negative effects of counterfeiting (Phau et al. 2009a), while in turn, many suppliers of counterfeits argue that their actions are satisfying the demand of people who strive to own status-laden brands without being able or willing to pay for the original (Wilke and Zaichkowsky 1999). Researchers claim that the investigation of the demand side of counterfeiting is still deficient (Wee et al. 1995; De Matos et al. 2007; Swami et al. 2009). Regardless of whether a multitude of studies on consumer attitudes and purchase intentions of counterfeits exists, a clear concept of consumer counterfeit purchase behavior and of the perceived value as a motivational driver of this kind of consumer misbehavior is still missing. However, all governmental actions to curtail counterfeit activities will be insufficient so long as counterfeiters face such an immense demand for their products and as the importance of focusing on the demand side becomes evident (Ang et al. 2001).

Given that the market for counterfeit luxury brands relies on consumers' desire for real luxury brands (Hoe et al. 2003; Penz and Stöttinger 2005), it is critical for researchers and marketers to understand the reasons why consumers buy genuine luxury brands, what they believe real luxury is, and how their perception of luxury value affects their buying behavior in the trade-off between authentic or counterfeit products. The focus of our study is to explore the underlying motives of counterfeit luxury buyers and to develop implications for the management of genuine luxury brands. Based on a comparison of studies that provides a holistic view of the phenomenon of counterfeit consumption and a comprehensive model, the key drivers of perceived value will be defined, helping to reduce the complexity of counterfeit consumption and enabling the development of customized countermeasures. An overview of recent anti-counterfeiting strategies by governments, industry associations and companies will be provided to examine the most effective arguments in designing anti-counterfeiting measures and in discouraging consumers from buying counterfeits.

# Theoretical Background and Construct Definition

## The Luxury Concept and Motives for Luxury Consumption

Although routinely used in our everyday lives to refer to products, services or a certain lifestyle, the term "luxury" elicits no clear understanding. Viewed as goods for which the simple use or display of a particular branded product brings esteem for its owner, luxury goods enable consumers to satisfy psychological and functional needs. The psychological benefits are considered the main factor distinguishing luxury from non-luxury products (Nia and Zaichkowsky 2000). In the literature, the concept of exclusivity or rarity is well documented (Pantzalis 1995). Luxury brands are those whose price and quality ratios are the highest in the market (McKinsey 1990), and even though the ratio of functionality to price might be low with regard to certain luxury goods, the ratio of intangible and situational utility to price is comparatively high (Nueno and Quelch 1998). Therefore, luxury brands compete based on the ability to evoke exclusivity, brand identity, brand awareness and perceived quality from the consumer's perspective (Phau and Prendergast 2000). Because luxury is a subjective and multidimensional construct, a definition of the concept should follow an integrative understanding. This chapter uses the luxury brand definition of Vigneron and Johnson (1999) as the highest level of prestigious brands encompassing several physical and psychological values. To explain consumer behavior in relation to luxury brands, apart from interpersonal aspects, such as snobbery and conspicuousness (Leibenstein 1950; Mason 1992); personal aspects, such as hedonism and perfectionism (Dubois and Laurent 1994); and situational conditions, such as economic, societal and political factors, are relevant (Vigneron and Johnson 1999, 2004). While the consumption of prestige or status brands involves purchasing a higher-priced product to boost one's ego (Eastman et al. 1999), the consumption of luxury goods involves buying a product that represents value to both the individual and significant others.

## Definition of Counterfeiting

In general, four common forms of intellectual property rights (IPRs) infringements exist: counterfeiting, piracy, imitation and gray market (Lai and Zaichkowsky 1999; Kwong et al. 2003). The focus of this study is on counterfeiting, which can be defined as " any manufacturing of a product which so closely imitates the appearance of the product of another to mislead a consumer that it is the product of another or deliberately offer a fake substitute to seek potential purchase from non-deceptive consumers" (OECD 1998). However, even though counterfeits attempt to look like the original product, it is generally accepted from a consumer's perspective that counterfeiting can be either deceptive or non-deceptive (Wilcox et al. 2008).

While previous literature has focused on a two-sided concept of deceptiveness (Grossman and Shapiro 1988), the great variance in counterfeits implies that deception can vary from "super-deceptive" (branded and counterfeited goods appear identical and indistinguishable from the original) to completely non-deceptive (all buyers are able to discern the difference between the counterfeit and genuine articles) depending on the customer's awareness, knowledge and experience (Eisend and Schuchert-Güler 2006). This chapter focuses on non-deceptive counterfeiting, which prevails in the luxury market, as the basis for identifying the motives of counterfeit luxury consumers compared to those buying the genuine luxury brand.

# Conceptual Model: Determinants of Consumers' Luxury Value Perceptions

Several researchers have attempted to identify determinants that influence the formation of attitudes toward counterfeiting and thus the intention to buy faked goods. Assuming that the market for counterfeit brands relies on consumers' desire for real luxury brands (Hoe et al. 2003; Penz and Stöttinger 2005), it is necessary to understand the motives and value-based drivers for luxury consumption that affect their buying behavior in the trade-off between authentic and counterfeit products. With regard to consumption values that directly explain why consumers choose to either buy or avoid particular products (Sheth et al. 1991), different types of values influence consumers' purchase choices. Inspired by the work of Dubois and Laurent (1994), Leibenstein (1950), Mason (1992), Kapferer (1998), Eastman et al. (1999), Phau and Prendergast (2000), and Dubois et al. (2001) on the evaluation of luxury brands, Vigneron and Johnson (2004) proposed that the consumer's decision-making process can be explained by five main factors: personal perceptions in terms of perceived extended self, perceived hedonism and non-personal perceptions referring to perceived conspicuousness, perceived uniqueness and perceived quality. To enhance the understanding of consumer motives and value perceptions in genuine or counterfeit luxury consumption, the model presented here draws on and extends Bourdieu's capital theory (1986) as well as existing luxury research literature (Vigneron and Johnson 2004; Wiedmann et al. 2007, 2009).

Beginning from an integral perceived value concept (Fig. 4) shows the proposed conceptual model encompassing several influencing variables and value drivers that may be related to the four key dimensions of luxury value perception. The *financial dimension* addresses direct monetary aspects, such as price, resale cost, discount and investment, and refers to the value of the product – expressed, for example, in dollars, euro or yen – as well as to what is given up or sacrificed to obtain it (e.g., Ahtola 1984; Monroe and Krishnan 1985; Chapman 1986; Mazumdar 1986). The *functional dimension* refers to such core product benefits and basic utilities as quality, uniqueness, usability, reliability and durability (Sheth et al. 1991). The *individual dimension* focuses on a customer's personal orientation toward luxury consumption and addresses personal matters such as materialism (e.g., Richins and Dawson 1992), hedonism, and self-identity (e.g., Hirschman and Holbrook 1982; Vigneron and Johnson 2004). Finally, the *social dimension* refers to the perceived utility individuals perceived with products or services recognized within their own social group(s), such as conspicuousness and prestige value, that may significantly affect the

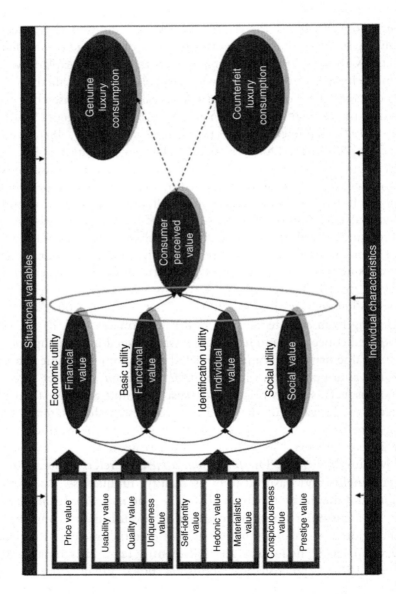

**Fig. 4** The conceptual model

evaluation and propensity to purchase or consume luxury brands (Bearden and Etzel 1982; Brinberg and Plimpton 1986; Kim 1998; Vigneron and Johnson 1999). Although these value dimensions operate independently, they interact with each other and have various influences on individual value perceptions and behaviors that can be used to further identify and differentiate different types of luxury or counterfeit consumers.

## Financial Value

Prestige pricing – setting a rather high price to suggest high quality or status (McCarthy and Perreault 1987) – may even make certain products or services more desirable (Groth and McDaniel 1993), which is often mentioned when explaining luxury consumption. In this context, value consciousness as "a concern for price paid relative to quality received" (Lichtenstein et al. 1993, p. 235) is supposed to impact consumer behavior. Luxury counterfeit consumption is driven by low price (in combination with status-laden brands) due to a perception of financial value. Given the increasing quality of counterfeit products and the fact that searching for bargains is an aspect of human nature, consumers are tempted to engage in illicit purchase behavior, especially in the case of price pressures (Ang et al. 2001). Individuals longing for prestige, brand, and image benefits probably consider counterfeits as being a good value for the money spent, despite some possible quality defects (Bloch et al. 1993). Consequently, we propose

> **Proposition 1:** The financial value as perceived by consumers is supposed to influence the evaluation of genuine versus counterfeit luxury goods.

## Functional Value

In general, a product or service is designed to perform a particular function; therefore, the core benefit can be observed in its ability to satisfy consumer needs. Consumers associate luxury products with a superior brand quality and reassurance; in this way, they perceive more value from them (Aaker 1991). On the basis of product characteristics, one can distinguish between search goods, whose quality can be rated before purchase (e.g., a polo shirt), and experience goods, where the determination of quality is difficult even after purchase (e.g., electrical appliances) (Eisend and Schuchert-Güler 2006). Owing to perceived performance and functional risks associated with faulty or unreliable products (Wee et al. 1995), consumers might be more willing to buy a counterfeit when the quality of the product can be determined before purchase. Furthermore, the perceived exclusivity and uniqueness of a luxury product enhances a consumer's desire or preference for it (Verhallen 1982; Lynn 1991; Pantzalis 1995), which is also supposed to convey the perception of the fake and influence consumers' willingness to buy the counterfeit (Eisend and Schuchert-Güler 2006).

**Proposition 2:** The functional value as perceived by consumers is supposed to influence the evaluation of genuine versus counterfeit luxury goods.

## Individual Value

Referring to individuals' need to enjoy the "finer things in life" and the fact that luxury brands arouse affective states received from personal rewards (Sheth et al. 1991; Westbrook and Oliver 1991), the emotional desire for sensory gratification is an important driver of luxury consumption (Ang et al. 2001). Furthermore, highly materialistic consumers may use luxury products to integrate symbolic meaning into their own identity (Holt 1995; Vigneron and Johnson 2004), or they may use the brands to portray impressions of who they perceive themselves to be and what their status or position is (Douglas and Isherwood 1979; Belk 1985). Assuming that a counterfeit product does not provide the same pleasure or satisfy the individual need for sensory gratification, consumers who place importance on hedonistic and materialistic aspects might have a negative attitude toward a counterfeit purchase because they are aware of the self-deceiving aspect of this behavior. However, low-cost or fake luxuries allow consumers to conform to fashion without spending an exorbitant amount of money on goods that are only "in-vogue" for a short period of time (Gentry et al. 2006).

> **Proposition 3:** The individual value as perceived by consumers is supposed to influence the evaluation of genuine versus counterfeit luxury goods.

## Social Value

Luxury brands often encompass prestige values, social referencing and the construction of self-identity; buying to impress others and conspicuous consumption play a significant role in shaping preferences for many luxury products (Braun and Wicklund 1989; Hong and Zinkhan 1995; Bagwell and Bernheim 1996; Corneo and Jeanne 1997; Vigneron and Johnson 2004). Regarding the evaluation of genuine versus counterfeit luxury goods, individuals' desire to possess luxury brands as well as luxury counterfeits is supposedly influenced by the reference group they are embedded within: consumers who are aware that their peers or reference groups have expert knowledge in determining the difference between genuine and counterfeit goods will fear the negative consequences of being unmasked as a counterfeit consumer and may abstain from purchasing fake merchandise (Phau and Teah 2009).

> **Proposition 4:** The social value as perceived by consumers is supposed to influence the evaluation of genuine versus counterfeit luxury goods.

# Counterfeiting Research: Selection Method and State of the Art

To provide a review of the past and current research on counterfeiting in the luxury sector, as a selection method, we focused on leading and influential academic journals. Using keywords such as "counter-feiting," "counterfeit," "knock-offs," "fake," and "product piracy," in the databases of "Emerald," "Jstor," "Highbeam," and "EBSCO-host" and related references, we selected studies addressing the consumer perception of counterfeit luxury goods. The resulting chronological review as presented in the Appendix (Table A1) comprises studies referring to luxury counterfeits and the importance of determinants that influence the attitude toward counterfeiting, the purchase intention and post-purchase feelings. After having reviewed the existing literature on consumer evaluations and purchasing intentions of luxury counterfeits, the complexity of underlying motives and their interrelations has become apparent. The selected studies reveal the multifaceted reasons explaining counterfeit consumption referring to the economic, functional, individual, and social evaluation of the product.

## Price and Price–Quality Relationship

In comparison with the price of the genuine luxury product, the low price of the counterfeit alternative was the most cited reason for purchasing counterfeits in all studies (e.g., Harvey and Walls 2003; Staake and Fleisch 2008). The individual price sensitivity and the amount a person is normally willing to spend on such a product influence the intention to buy the counterfeit product. (Kim et al. 2009). With regard to quality perception, both consumers and non-consumers of counterfeits state "originals are cheaper in the long run" (Staake and Fleisch 2008, p. 54). However, the price–quality relationship of counterfeit products is regarded as offering good value for the money (Ang et al. 2001; Wang et al. 2005; Furnham and Valgeirsson 2007).

## Product Characteristics and Related Involvement

The product category and the individual involvement with this product-class is expected to have a negative impact on counterfeit purchase intention because highly involved consumers think more about the consequences of their purchases (d'Astous and Gargouri 2001). However, consumers who hold favorable attitudes toward counterfeit goods will more likely rely on this pre-disposition in case of high product involvement (Huang et al. 2002). With reference to counterfeit luxury goods in the domain of fashion, Penz and Stöttinger (2005) found that fashion involvement indirectly negatively influences the willingness to purchase counterfeits because it diminishes the idea that counterfeit consumption is a savvy shopper behavior and simultaneously enhances the perceived embarrassment potential. Consequently, it can be assumed that the more knowledgeable consumers are about the product, the less likely they are to choose a counterfeit alternative.

## Individual Characteristics

Profiling consumers of counterfeit luxury goods based on demographic information is difficult because gender, age, income, and educational level provide no clear picture of counterfeit consumers. Some studies state that females are more prone to buy counterfeit clothes and accessories than males (Cheung and Prendergast 2006); others reveal that the intention to buy counterfeit leather wallets and purses is negatively related to household income and education (Wee et al. 1995), whereas another study shows that counterfeit luxury products are bought regardless of the income level (Yoo and Lee 2005). Moreover, it is suggested that a high level of integrity, measured by items such as honesty, politeness, responsibility, and self-control (Ang et al. 2001), leads to unfavorable attitudes toward counterfeit consumption. However, even when integrity was found to be a significant predictor of attitudes, it did not necessarily reflect a person's buying decision (Phau et al. 2009a) – particularly, if the consumer's interest in the product is higher than the person's moral values (Sivacek and Crano 1982). In this context, Phau et al. (2009b) argue that external factors such as normative or informative susceptibility undermine ethical decision making. With regard to the cultural background of consumers, some studies show a positive influence of collectivism on attitudes toward counterfeits (Wang et al. 2005) and a slightly higher intention to purchase counterfeits reported by Asian respondents than by American respondents (Harvey and Walls 2003). Furthermore, there is a strong influence of perceived risk in counterfeit perception: the fear that the product is not worth the money (financial risk), the fear that the product's functionality might be limited or unreliable (performance risk), the fear of shame or loss of face in the reference group or rejection by peers (social risk), and the fear of legal consequences (legal risk) are reported to influence the intention to buy counterfeit luxuries (e.g., Leisen and Nill 2001; Vida 2007; Bian and Veloutsou 2008). Concerning the importance of materialistic traits, studies found out that highly materialistic consumers desire to own genuine, authentic goods; consequently, they choose genuine over counterfeit products (Furnham and Valgeirsson 2007).

## Status-Oriented Consumption

Empirical evidence found that individuals who base their purchase decisions on the expert opinions of others (information susceptibility) are less inclined to buy counterfeit luxury goods, while those who decide on the basis of what would impress significant others (normative susceptibility) are more inclined to purchase counterfeit luxuries (Phau and Teah 2009). Consumers who are more susceptible to external influences attempt to gain peer's approval by using the signaling effect of branded goods and thus are more tempted to purchase counterfeit goods (Penz and Stöttinger 2005). In contrast to this, individuals with high self-esteem are more inclined to choose genuine brands that convey status, wealth, and affluence and reflect a high self-identity (Wee et al. 1995; Yoo and Lee 2009). In an attempt to differentiate between counterfeit consumption driven by a social-adjustive function and a value-adjustive function, Wilcox et al. (2008) discovered that image-conscious consumers showed a higher tendency to purchase counterfeits with a logo exposed in contrast to those consumers who try to communicate their central beliefs and values through their purchase decision and product usage. This finding leads to the assumption that consumers motivated by social reasons are more likely to choose the counterfeit over the original because, in their perception, both products fulfill the salient goals of self-presentation, but the counterfeit dominates in price. Furthermore, the associated status of luxury goods is supposed to influence counterfeit purchase intention, even if empirical results did not provide clear evidence in support of this assumption (Wee et al. 1995; Phau et al. 2009a, b; Kim and Karpova 2010).

# Implications for Countermeasures Against Counterfeit Consumption

Encompassing the multifaceted reasons explaining counterfeit consumption as described above, previous shopping experiences have been shown to have the strongest predictive power. Especially those consumers who previously bought counterfeits are more likely to exhibit this behavior again: they evaluate counterfeiting as less risky (Ha and Lennon 2006), have more favorable attitudes toward counterfeiting, and have higher purchase intentions for such goods (Tom et al. 1998). Given that circumstances remain stable, behavior becomes habit-forming, such that future behavior will be based on past behavior rather than on cognitive considerations (Bamberg et al. 2003). Once established as a form of accepted behavior, it will be difficult to discourage counterfeit consumption. Consequently, it is crucial to develop strategies to inhibit counterfeit purchases from the beginning, before it becomes internalized behavior. Ethical, legal, and economic countermeasures may restrain consumers from buying counterfeits and therefore increase the desire for genuine luxury brands, as shown in (Fig. 5)

## Legal Countermeasures

The legal environment is a key factor combating counterfeit consumerism, whereby law enforcement and severe penalties constitute prerequisites for successful prosecution of and legal action against counterfeiters (Chaudhry and Walsh 1996). To limit counterfeit trade, the World Trade Organization (WTO) introduced the agreement on Trade-Related Aspects of Intellectual Property Rights (TRIPs), which sets a minimum standard of protection and to which

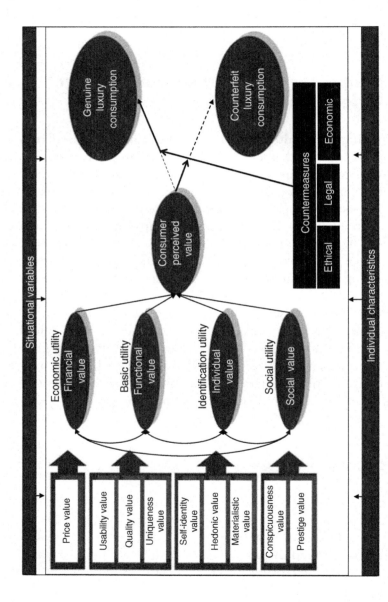

Fig. 5 The effect of anti-counterfeiting countermeasures

all member states must adhere (WTO, 2010). However, taking legal action against counterfeiters may induce long-term and costly litigation processes with uncertain outcomes, especially in emerging countries where TRIPs have not yet been ratified, and IPR infringement is not considered a criminal activity (Nill and Shultz 1996). Both the French and the Italian governments have begun to prosecute the purchasers of counterfeits as well. According to the National Anti-Counterfeit Commission (CNAC), French customs agents are not only allowed to confiscate fake products but also to impose a fine in the amount that corresponds to one or two times the value of the original product. The Italian government's tourist board informs that the new legislation, implemented in 2005, imposes fines of up to 10 000 euros for purchasing counterfeits.

## Ethical Countermeasures

The fact that in most countries the purchase of counterfeits does not incur a penalty might send a wrong signal to the populace, implying that purchase of counterfeits is not a serious offense. Apart from governmental authorities, there are many non-governmental organizations and business associations involved in the fight against counterfeiting and piracy. Most of these associations place a great emphasis on consumer education as a means to reduce the demand for counterfeits. The messages point either to ethical considerations – by highlighting the close connection between counterfeiting and organized crime and by referring to the equivocal production practices – or messages emphasize the negative effects for the individual – by referring to health and safety risks as well as quality defectives that counterfeit (luxury) products can carry, by illustrating potential job losses, or by warning of the loss of self-esteem or group acceptance when purchasing counterfeits. For instance, a campaign by the International Anti-Counterfeiting Coalition (IACC), called *Blood Money: The Steep Human Cost of the Counterfeit Culture*, appeals to the ethical conscience of consumers by displaying the terrible working Motives of counterfeit consumption conditions (including child labor) under which counterfeits are produced.

## Economic Countermeasures

Owing to the flourishing business of faked products, companies have combined their strengths in global mutual cooperation and various industry associations, such as the International Trademark Association (INT), the International Anti-Counterfeiting Coalition (IACC), the Business Action to Stop Counterfeiting and Piracy (BASCAP), and the Haute Horlogerie (dedicated to luxury watches). To curtail the counterfeit business, they use diplomatic and legislative remedies or use technological possibilities, such as high-tech product labels that are difficult and costly to copy (Nill and Shultz 1996). As one of the most copied luxury brands, Louis Vuitton employs 40 in-house lawyers and additionally collaborates with 250 external investigators; the extent of these actions becomes apparent (Chevalier and Xiao 2009). In general, experts suggest that a corporate anti-counterfeit strategy should address both the supply and demand sides of counterfeit business and comprise four "D's": defend, detect, doubt, and discourage (Nunes and Donnelly 2010). To *defend* the company's intellectual property, the control of the supply chain and a selective distribution are important. Tracking technologies and human expertise guarantee a complete surveillance of a product's manufacturing process, beginning with the raw materials and components, to the production and distribution, and finally to the final point of sale. Measures directed at the demand side should focus on educating wholesalers, retailers, and consumers on how to *detect* counterfeits and to inform them of what characteristics carry the authentic articles (e.g., typical design and price level). By raising the risks and cost of counterfeit production by the means of legal remedies, it is important to make the counterfeiters' life as hard as possible and to *discourage* them. Furthermore, companies should let the public know that counterfeiting is not a victimless crime to make consumers *doubt* whether it is worth engaging in this kind of business.

# Conclusions and Further Research Steps

The global impact of counterfeiting is increasing at an alarming rate; its effects are perceptible on a both macro – and microeconomic levels. Governments, supranational organizations, and industry associations have undertaken considerable efforts to curtail the illegitimate business through IPR protection and law enforcement. Nevertheless, an attempt where countermeasures focus on the supply side only falls short; any remedy will be insufficient so long as there is a maintained demand for counterfeit products. A better understanding of consumer motivation for purchasing these goods builds the basis for the development of strategies that aim to reduce the global appetite for counterfeits. Based on the perceived value dimensions as key motives for luxury consumption and a literature review on drivers of counterfeit consumption, our findings reveal that counterfeit luxury products are primarily purchased due to their low price and the widespread opinion that they offer a good value for the money. In this context, there is empirical evidence that counterfeit and authentic consumers sometimes overlap (Staake et al. 2009); the report *Counterfeiting Luxury: Exposing the Myths* (Davenport Lyons, 2007) revealed that 20 percent of counterfeit consumers in the United Kingdom have annual household earnings of £50 000 and above. Further evidence is provided by Gosline (2009), who found in a long-term study with 100 consumers that approximately 40 percent adopted the legitimate product over time. Therefore, the key challenge is to inform consumers about the risks associated with counterfeit consumption, raise ethical considerations, display the negative consequences for society, and convince them that – compared to the value of genuine luxury – in the long run, counterfeit products are not worth the money. Possible arguments in an awareness campaign are as following: While a genuine luxury good is made of high-quality materials with filigree craftsmanship and technical know-how, counterfeit products often break down, fade, or even bear health risks (e.g., allergic reactions). In addition, luxury brands demonstrate social responsibility in their raw material sourcing, production processes, employment politics, and cultural projects, whereas counterfeiters are only interested in short-term profits. With regard to its owner, only for a genuine luxury product might a strong message such as *You are unique, you deserve to own something genuine* or *If you don't value yourself you are not valued by others* be useful to make individuals think about their self-image and the impression that they are making on others. In sum, the consumer's value perception determines the individual trade-off between authentic and counterfeit products and should be the object of development for effective legal, ethical, and economic countermeasures.

With regard to possible directions for future research, it must be stated that even if governments, international organizations, industry associations, and companies have recognized the importance of addressing the problem of counterfeiting from the demand side as well, valid measures of the success of these efforts are still lacking. Based on qualitative experiments and quantitative analyses, future research should examine the reasons why consumers choose the counterfeit over the authentic product and how consumers respond to anti-counterfeit campaigns and activities in different countries and product categories. Furthermore, an interesting approach would be to analyze the booming online business with replicas and high-class counterfeits that are often sold for hundreds of dollars because they represent a growing concern for luxury brand managers.

# Appendix

**Table A1** Literature review – consumer value perception of luxury counterfeits

| Study | Study design (method, participants) | Counterfeit product | Determinants | Dependent variable | Main results |
|---|---|---|---|---|---|
| Wee et al. (1995) | Survey, 949 students and working adults in South-East Asia (potential buyers of counterfeits) | Literature, software, leather wallet/purses, watches | Psychographic variables (attitude toward piracy, brand status, materialism, novelty-seeking, risk taking), product attribute variables (purpose, quality, perceived fashion content, physical appearance, image, durability), demographic variables (education, age, household income) | Intention to purchase pirated products | The link between attitude toward piracy and purchase intention confirmed for all product categories. Brand status, materialism, novelty-seeking, and risk-taking seemed to be insignificant. For adults, educational attainment negatively influences purchase intention for fashion-related products (counterfeit watches) but positively impacts functional products (pirated literature and counterfeit software), whereas students' educational background only impacts their willingness to purchase counterfeit fashion products. Quality perception has a strong influence on purchase intention for all product types. Only for counterfeit watches, the perceived fashion content seems to be of interest. For leather wallets/purses and watches, the physical appearance enhances purchase intention, while image and durability have no influence. Results show a negative relationship of income and purchase intention of counterfeit leather goods. |

*(continued)*

Table A1 (continued)

| Study | Study design (method, participants) | Counterfeit product | Determinants | Dependent variable | Main results |
|---|---|---|---|---|---|
| Ang et al. (2001) | Survey, 3251 Singaporean consumers (previous buyers and non-buyers of counterfeits) | Counterfeit CDs | Social influences (informative and normative susceptibility) Personality characteristics (value consciousness, integrity, personal gratification) and demographics | Attitude toward piracy (mediator), purchase intention | There is a positive correlation between attitude and purchase intention. There is a negative influence of normative susceptibility, integrity and personal income on attitudes toward piracy. A positive relation between value-consciousness and attitude toward piracy was found. Males tend to accept piracy with a more positive attitude than females. |
| d'Astous and Gargouri (2001) | Survey, 160 randomly selected residents from a mid-size Canadian city | Two convenience goods: bread and shampoo; two luxury goods: Ralph Lauren polo shirt, Ray Ban sunglasses | Value of brand imitation, store image (in the absence/presence of the original brand), level of involvement, product familiarity, brand sensitivity, brand loyalty, price sensitivity | Evaluations of the brand imitator | Consumers evaluate imitations of luxury goods better when they are distributed in stores with a good image. For both luxury products, neither the goodness of imitation nor the presence of the original brand has a significant effect on consumer evaluations. Except for the polo shirt product category, involvement is negatively related with consumer evaluations of brand imitations. Product familiarity is only significant for convenience goods. Brand sensitivity + loyalty are negatively correlated with evaluations; and price sensitivity has a positive effect. |

| | | | | |
|---|---|---|---|---|
| Leisen and Nill (2001) | Survey, 144 US students (potential buyers of counterfeits) | Pain reliever, sunglasses, watch | Perceived shopping environment and product attributes, perceived financial performance, social and legal risk, awareness of social consequences | Purchase intention to buy counterfeit products | The purchase intention for watches and sunglasses depends on the perceived shopping environment. Perceived financial and performance risks are negatively related with the willingness to purchase pain relievers. The consumer's perceived social and legal risks were not found to have any effect on purchase intentions for any of the examined counterfeit products. |
| Huang et al. (2002) | Survey, 107 undergraduate students in Taiwan | Gray-market goods (beverages, watches and mobile phones) | Price-consciousness, price-quality inference, risk averseness, level of involvement | Consumer attitude toward and purchase intention of gray-market goods | Price consciousness was shown to be insignificant across the three product categories. A consumer who places great importance on the price-quality inference tends to have a negative attitude toward gray-market goods. Risk averseness has a negative impact on consumer attitudes toward gray-market goods. There is a positive correlation between involvement and purchase intention. |

*(continued)*

**Table A1** (continued)

| Study | Study design (method, participants) | Counterfeit product | Determinants | Dependent variable | Main results |
|---|---|---|---|---|---|
| Harvey and Walls (2003) | Experiment, 120 students, 60 from Hong Kong and 60 from Las Vegas | Laboratory market of various counterfeits | Real monetary price of the authentic goods, expected penalty associated with purchase of counterfeit, culture, interaction | Choice/purchase of pirated goods (proportion of students) | If the monetary price of the authentic good increases, consumers choose the counterfeit item. The expected penalty of buying counterfeits shifts consumer preferences in the direction of the genuine goods. This effect is even stronger than the price effect. Students from Hong Kong are more prone to purchase counterfeits than students from Las Vegas. |
| Penz and Stöttinger (2005) | Survey, 1040 Austrian consumers (previous buyers and non-buyers of counterfeits | Counterfeit goods in general | Attitude toward counterfeiting and subjective norm influenced by personality traits (readiness to take risk, fashion involvement, ethical predisposition); perceived behavioral control, self-identity, price consciousness, access to counterfeits; price level | Attitudes toward counterfeiting (mediator), purchase intention, (past) purchases of counterfeits | Consumer attitudes toward counterfeiting and self-identity positively influence the purchase intentions, particularly at low price levels. Social pressure and perceived behavioral control have a positive effect on buying intentions at both price levels. Personality traits influence a consumer's attitude toward counterfeiting and subjective norms, whereas price consciousness has no significant effect. The availability and accessibility of counterfeits has a positive impact on buying intention. Results show that purchase intention predicts buying behavior. |

| | | | | |
|---|---|---|---|---|
| Wang et al. (2005) | Survey, 314 Chinese students (previous buyers and non-buyers of counterfeits) | Counterfeit software | Attitude toward piracy, social influences (informative + normative susceptibility), personality (value consciousness, integrity, personal gratification) | Attitude toward piracy (mediator), purchase intention | Attitude toward (software) piracy is a significant predictor of purchase intention. Value consciousness, novelty seeking, and collectivism have a positive impact on attitudes toward piracy. Consumers who previously bought pirated software have more positive attitudes than those consumers with no buying experience. |
| Yoo and Lee (2005) | Study 1: Survey, 500 students from Korea; Study 2: Experiment, 420 students from Korea | Study 1: handbags, designer shoes, apparel, sunglasses, jewelry Study 2: handbags | Experience with counterfeits, experience with genuine items; additionally in Study 2: brand and price information for genuine and counterfeit items | Purchase intention of counterfeits vs. originals | Respondents demonstrated a preference for genuine products regardless of their previous shopping experience. Price information reduces the demand for original products. Consumers who previously purchased counterfeits are more likely to do so again. The intention to buy counterfeits does differ among buyers and non-buyers of genuine products. |
| Cheung and Prendergast (2006) | Survey, 1152 adult consumers from Hong Kong, Shanghai, Wuhan (previous light and heavy buyers of counterfeits) | Video CDs (VCDs), clothing or accessories | Demographics, income gender occupation, education, age, marital status | Light vs. heavy buyers of counterfeit goods | Middle- and high-income families were the main buyers of pirated VCDs, but for clothing and accessories, family income is insignificant. Pirated VCDs are mostly purchased by young male consumers, who are mostly white-collar workers with a tertiary education. Females are more likely buyers of counterfeit clothing and accessories; for this category, no other variable was significant. |

(continued)

**Table A1** (continued)

| Study | Study design (method, participants) | Counterfeit product | Determinants | Dependent variable | Main results |
|---|---|---|---|---|---|
| Ha and Lennon (2006) | Qualitative study, interviews conducted among undergraduate students at a large US University with a sample-size of 115 in the first and 326 in the second study | Fashion products | Ethical ideologies, idealism, relativism, perceived risk | Ethical judgments, intention to purchase counterfeit fashion products | Ethical ideology showed to be insignificant in predicting counterfeit purchase intention. Perceived risk has a negative influence on the intention to buy counterfeit fashion products. Non-buyers ranked higher on idealism and perceive counterfeit purchases as more risky. Those who have already bought counterfeits are more prone to purchase counterfeits again. Uncertainty about consequences influences purchase intention, while uncertainty about physical performance and perceived risk associated with post-purchase service seem to be insignificant. Idealism affects ethical judgments, which in turn influences the purchase intention of fashion counterfeits. Relativism has no effect on ethical judgments. |
| Furnham and Valgeirsson (2007) | Survey, 103 participants from all ages, interviewed in the British museum district in central London | Various | Good value, law and danger, experience, background information, personal values and materialism | Willingness to buy counterfeit goods | Consumers who rate a counterfeit product as a good value for money are more willing to purchase it. Background information (being the first child, having children, being married, having religious beliefs, and political orientation) proved to be the strongest predictor of willingness to buy counterfeits. |

| | | | | |
|---|---|---|---|---|
| Vida (2007) | Survey, 223 consumers from Slovenia | t-shirts, software, watches | Socio-demographic variables: age, gender, education, income, marital status, religiosity; mediators: attitude toward piracy, innovativeness, social consequences | Willingness to purchase counterfeit goods | Out of 10 tested values, only tradition has a (negative) effect on willingness to buy counterfeits; materialism: the factor "centrality" negatively influences the willingness to buy counterfeit goods.<br>Religious observation is negatively related to attitudes toward piracy for all product types.<br>In case of software and watches, men hold more positive attitudes toward counterfeit activities.<br>Better-educated respondents are more concerned with social consequences when buying or using counterfeit watches than lower-educated people.<br>Innovativeness and respondents' perceptions of social risk are strongly negatively correlated. Innovative people have a higher ability to justify counterfeit activities.<br>For fashion counterfeits (t-shirts and watches), results showed a direct interaction between attitudes, perceived social risk, and willingness to purchase. |

*(continued)*

Table A1 (continued)

| Study | Study design (method, participants) | Counterfeit product | Determinants | Dependent variable | Main results |
|---|---|---|---|---|---|
| Bian and Veloutsou (2008) | Survey, 525 consumers: 230 from the UK and 295 from China | Sunglasses | Social risk, time risk, physical risk, performance risk, financial risk, psychological risk, cultural background | Overall risk and its explanatory power when purchasing counterfeits | Both British and Chinese consumers perceive the same overall risk of counterfeits, but with differences in the sub-dimensions of risk; there are correlations between the various risk dimensions. Only psychological risk is a significant predictor of overall risk for both British and Chinese consumers. British respondents ranked psychological risk the highest, followed by financial risk and performance risk, while Chinese emphasize the physical risk over psychological risk and time risk. |
| Han et al. (2008) | Survey, 127 students at two large universities in South-Korea (potential buyers of counterfeits) | Logo-exposed luxury fashion goods, especially Louis Vuitton handbags | Aesthetic appeal, conformity, conspicuousness, durability | Attitude and intention to buy logo-exposed counterfeit luxury goods | Logo exposure has a greater impact than the consumer's pursued values. Only 2.7 percent of participants were willing to purchase non-logo-bearing products. Those consumers who scored high on aesthetic appeal are less prone to buy logo-exposed products. Conformity and conspicuousness are positively related to attitude and purchase intention of logo-exposed luxury goods. |
| Tom et al. (1998) (Study 1) | Survey, 128 US consumers | Not specified | Experience with counterfeit purchase | Attitude toward counterfeiting | Previous counterfeit shopping experiences positively influence attitudes toward counterfeiting. |

| | | | | |
|---|---|---|---|---|
| Tom et al. (1998) (Study 2) | Survey, 435 US consumers (potential buyers of counterfeits) | CD, software, t-shirts, purses | Perceived importance of brand, function, durability/quality, price; demographics | Preference for legitimate or counterfeit product, attitude | For t-shirts, perceived importance of brand, function, and durability is negatively correlated with purchasing a counterfeit, while price is positively related. Those consumers who emphasize durability will choose the genuine purse over the counterfeit version age, income, and education is negatively related to choosing the counterfeit. |
| Tom et al. (1998) (Study 3) | Survey, 126 US consumers (previous buyers and non-buyers of counterfeits) | Watches, clothing, purses, perfume, CDs, software, video | Satisfaction with counterfeits products, demographics | Propensity to purchase counterfeits in the future | Perceived satisfaction with counterfeits bought at a flea market is a significant predictor for future purchases across all product categories. Younger, less well-off consumers are more likely to admit counterfeit purchases. |
| Wilcox et al. (2008) Study 1 | Survey, 79 undergraduate students from a North Eastern university | Luxury fashion counterfeits | Value-expressive function and social-adjustive function of attitudes, brand conspicuousness, consumer's moral belief | Likelihood of purchasing counterfeit luxury brands; preferences for the real brand | Individuals whose consumption is driven by the social-adjustive function are more inclined to purchase counterfeits, whereas the value-expressive function has no effect on purchase intent. Moral beliefs predict purchase intent, but only when value-expressive function is strong. |

*(continued)*

**Table A1** (continued)

| Study | Study design (method, participants) | Counterfeit product | Determinants | Dependent variable | Main results |
|---|---|---|---|---|---|
| Wilcox et al. (2008) Study 2 | Experiment, 138 female students from a North Eastern university | Louis Vuitton handbag (with and without logo) | Value-expressive function and social-adjustive function of attitudes, brand conspicuousness, consumer's moral belief | Purchase intent and preference change | Participants were clustered by their dominative attitudes. Social-adjustive respondents are more prone to purchase the counterfeits LV bag than value-expressive participants; purchase intention for value-expressive group varied significantly with their moral beliefs. Attitudes in interaction with brand conspicuousness are the strongest predictors of purchase intention. When the social-adjustive function is dominating exposure to counterfeits leads to a negative preference change (because authentic and counterfeit fulfill the same needs, but the counterfeit is much cheaper). |
| Wilcox et al. (2008) Study 3 | Survey, 176 students from a large North Eastern university | Tissot watches | Value-expressive vs. social-adjustive advertising, positive | Purchase intent (change in attitude) | Purchase intention is higher among consumers who viewed the social-adjustive ad compared with those who were exposed to the value-expressive campaign; the impact of moral beliefs on purchase intention is higher for consumers who viewed the value-expressive advertising. The shift in preferences toward the counterfeit watch is stronger after watching the social-adjustive advertising compared to the value-expressive advertising. |

| | | | | |
|---|---|---|---|---|
| Kim et al. (2009) | Survey, 313 women on a Midwestern or Southeastern university in the United States | Handbags | Moral judgment, moral intensity and moral affect, specifically shame and guilt | Purchase intention and moral judgment | Moral intensity had a significant positive effect on moral judgments, which in turn are negatively related to the purchase intent for counterfeit and imitation products.<br>Proneness to guilt had a significant negative effect on purchase intent concerning a gray-market product, but no impact on counterfeits or imitations.<br>The higher the amount of money a consumer typically spent on a handbag, the less likely than he was to purchase a counterfeit, gray-market or imitation product. |
| Phau et al. (2009b) | Survey, 202 students from a large Australian university | Ralph Lauren polo shirt | Attitude toward lawfulness and legality of counterfeits, status consumption, materialism, integrity, buyers and non-buyers of counterfeits | Consumers' willingness to knowingly purchase counterfeit luxury brands | Attitudes toward lawfulness or legality of counterfeits have no impact on willingness to purchase counterfeits.<br>Only integrity showed to be a significant predictor of consumers' willingness to knowingly purchase a faked Ralph Lauren shirt. Neither status consumption nor materialism has significant effects on purchase intention of low-involvement luxury goods. |

(*continued*)

Table A1 (continued)

| Study | Study design (method, participants) | Counterfeit product | Determinants | Dependent variable | Main results |
|---|---|---|---|---|---|
| Phau and Teah (2009) | Survey, 202 shoppers in a mall in downtown Shanghai | Luxury brand counterfeits | Informational/normative susceptibility, and collectivism, value consciousness, integrity, personal gratification, novelty seeking, and status consumption | Attitudes toward counterfeits of luxury brands and buying intention | While status consumption and integrity have a strong effect on purchase intention, normative as well as informational susceptibility, personal gratification, value consciousness, and novelty seeking are only weak influencers on purchase intention. There is a significant relationship between attitude and willingness to purchase counterfeit luxury brands. Collectivism does not predict attitudes nor purchase intention of luxury counterfeits. |
| Yoo and Lee (2009) | Survey, 324 female college students from South Korea | Luxury fashion: handbags, designer shoes, apparel, sunglasses, and jewelry | Past purchase behavior, economic benefits, hedonic benefits, materialism, perception of future social class, self-image | Purchase intention of counterfeits vs. originals | Past purchase experiences positively predict purchase intention of luxury counterfeits. Both economic and hedonic benefits showed to have a positive impact on willingness to buy counterfeits. The purchase intention for originals was higher for consumers who previously bought original luxury fashion and who scored high on materialism, self-identity, and perceived future social class status, but lower for those who hold positive attitudes toward counterfeits; purchase intention of counterfeits has a positive influence on purchase intention of genuine goods, but vice versa, the relation is negative. |

| | | | | |
|---|---|---|---|---|
| Kim and Karpova (2010) | Survey, random sample of 336 female college students from a large Midwestern University (previous buyers and non-buyers of counterfeits) | Fashion counterfeits | Informational and normative susceptibility, value consciousness, integrity, status consumption, materialism, product appearance, past purchase behavior, perceived behavioral control, subjective norm | Attitude toward fashion counterfeit goods and purchase intention | Product appearance, past purchase behavior, and value consciousness have a positive influence on attitude toward purchasing fashion counterfeit goods, whereas normative susceptibility has a negative influence on attitude; integrity, materialism, and status consumption showed to be insignificant Product appearance seems to be the major reason for buying fashion counterfeits. Past purchase behavior has a positive effect on attitude and purchase intentions, implying that consumers who previously bought counterfeits will more likely purchase counterfeits again. Perceived behavioral control has a minimal influence on purchase intent. |

# References

Aaker, D. A. (1991). *Managing Brand Equity: Capitalizing on the Value of a Brand Name.* New York: Free Press.

Ahtola, O. T. (1984). Price as a "give" component in an exchange theoretic multicomponent model. *Advances in Consumer Research, 11*(1), 623–636.

Ang, S. H., Cheng, P. S., Lim, E. A. C., & Tambyah, S. K. (2001). Spot the difference: Consumer responses towards counterfeits. *Journal of Consumer Marketing, 18*(3), 219–235.

Bagwell, L. S., & Bernheim, B. D. (1996) Veblen effects in a theory of conspicuous consumption. *American Economic Review, 86*(3), 349–373.

Bamberg, S., Rölle, D., & Weber, C. (2003). Does habitual car use not lead to more resistance to chance of travel mode? *Transportation, 30*(1), 97–108.

Bearden, W. O., & Etzel, M. J. (1982). Reference group influence on product and brand purchase decisions. *Journal of Consumer Research, 9*(2): 183–194.

Belk, R. W. (1985). Materialism: Traits aspects of living in the material world. *Journal of Consumer Research, 12*(3): 265–280.

Bian, X., & Veloutsou, C. (2008). A cross-national examination of consumer perceived risk in the context of non-deceptive counterfeit brands. *Journal of Consumer Behaviour, 7*(1), 3–20.

Bloch, P. H., Bush, R. F., & Campbell, L. (1993). Consumer "accomplices" in product counterfeiting: A demand side investigation. *Journal of Consumer Marketing, 10*(4), 27–36.

Bourdieu, P. (1986). The forms of capital. In J. Richardson (Ed.), *Handbook of Theory and Research for the Sociology of Education* (pp. 241–258). New York: Greenwood.

Braun, O. L., & Wicklund, R. A. (1989). Psychological antecedents of conspicuous consumption. *Journal of Economic Psychology, 10*(2), 161–186.

Brinberg, D., & Plimpton, L. (1986). Self-monitoring and product conspicuousness on reference group influence. *Advances in Consumer Research, 13*(1), 297–300.

Bush, R. F., Bloch, P. H., & Dawson, S. (1989, January–February). Remedies for product counterfeiting. *Business Horizons*, 59–65.

Chapman, J. (1986). The Impact of Discounts on Subjective Product Evaluations. Working paper, Virginia Polytechnic Institute and State University.

Chaudhry, P. E., & Walsh, M. G. (1996). An assessment of the impact of counterfeiting in international markets: The Piracy Paradox Persists. *The Columbia Journal of World Business, 31*(3), 34–48.

Cheung, W.-L., & Prendergast, G. (2006). Buyers' perceptions of pirated products in China. *Marketing Intelligence and Planning, 24*(5), 446–462.
Chevalier, M., & Xiao, P. (2009). *Luxury China – Market Opportunities and Potential.* Singapore: John Wiley & Sons.
Corneo, G., & Jeanne, O. (1997). Conspicuous consumption, snobbism and conformism. *Journal of Public Economics, 66*(1), 55–71.
d'Astous, A., & Gargouri, E. (2001). Consumer evaluations of brand imitations. *European Journal of Marketing, 35*(1/2), 153–167.
Davenport, L. (2007). *Counterfeiting Luxury: Exposing the Myths* (2nd Edn.). London: Ledbury Research.
De Matos, C., Augusto, C., Ituassu, T., & Rossi, C. A. V. (2007). Consumer attitudes toward counterfeits: A review and extension. *Journal of Consumer Marketing, 24*(1), 36–47.
Douglas, M., & Isherwood, B. (1979). *The World of Goods.* New York: Basic Books.
Dubois, B., & Laurent, G. (1994). Attitudes toward the concept of luxury: An exploratory analysis. *Asia Pacific Advances in Consumer Research, 1*(2), 273–278.
Dubois, B., Laurent, G., & Czellar, S. (2001). Consumer Rapport to Luxury: Analyzing Complex and Ambivalent Attitudes. Consumer Research Working Paper No. 736, HEC, Jouy-en-Josas, France.
Eastman, J., Goldsmith, R. I., & Flynn, L. R. (1999). Status consumption in consumer behavior: Scale development and validation. *Journal of Marketing Theory and Practice, 7*(3), 41–51.
Eisend, M., & Schuchert-Güler, P. (2006). Explaining counterfeit purchases: A review and preview. *Academy of Marketing Science Review, 10*(12), 214–229.
Furnham, A., & Valgeirsson, H. (2007). The effect of life values and materialism on buying counterfeit products. *The Journal of Socio-Economics, 36*(5), 677–685.
Gentry, J. W., Putrevu, S., & Shultz, C. J. (2006). The effects of counterfeiting on consumer search. *Journal of Consumer Behaviour, 5*(3), 1–12.
Gosline, R. R. (2009). *The Real Value of Fakes: Dynamic Symbolic Boundaries in Socially Embedded Consumption.* Boston, MA: Harvard Business School. http://proquest.umi.com/pqdlink?did=1872995361&Fmt=6&VType=PQD&VInst=PROD&RQT=309&VName=PQD&TS=1280130728&clientId=79356. Accessed 26 July 2010.
Green, R. T., & Smith, T. (2002). Countering brand counterfeiters. *Journal of International Marketing, 10*(4), 89–106.
Grossman, G. M., & Shapiro, C. (1988). Foreign counterfeiting of status goods. *The Quarterly Journal of Economics, 103*(1), 79–100.

Groth, J., & McDaniel, S. W. (1993). The exclusive value principle: The basis for prestige pricing. *Journal of Consumer Marketing, 10*(1), 10–16.

Ha, S., & Lennon, S. (2006). Purchase intent for fashion counterfeit products: Ethical ideologies, ethical judgments, and perceived risks. *Clothing and Textiles Research Journal, 4*(4), 297–315.

Han, J.-M., Suk, H.-J., & Chung, K.-W. (2008). The influence of logo exposure in purchasing counterfeit luxury goods: Focusing on consumer values. International DMI Education Conference Design Thinking: New Challenges for Designers, Managers and Organizations, Design Management Institute (DMI).

Harvey, P. J., & Walls, D. (2003). Laboratory markets in counterfeit goods: Hong Kong. *Applied Economic Letters, 10*(14), 883–887.

Hirschman, E. C., & Holbrook, M. B. (1982). Hedonic consumption: Emerging concepts, methods and propositions. *Journal of Marketing, 46*(3), 92–101.

Hoe, L., Hogg, G., & Hart, S. (2003). Fakin' it: Counterfeiting and consumer contradictions. *European Advances in Consumer Research, 6*(1), 60–67.

Holt, D. B. (1995). How consumers consume: A typology of consumption practices. *Journal of Consumer Research, 22*(1), 1–16.

Hong, J. W., & Zinkhan, G. M. (1995). Self-concept and advertising effectiveness: The influence of congruency, conspicuousness, and response mode. *Psychology & Marketing, 12*(1), 53–77.

Huang, J.-H., Lee, B. C. Y., & Hoe, S. H. (2002). Consumer attitude toward gray market goods. *International Marketing Review, 21*(6), 598–614.

Kapferer, J.-N. (1998). Why are we seduced by luxury brands? *Journal of Brand Management, 6*(1), 44–49.

Kim, H., & Karpova, E. (2010). Consumer attitudes toward fashion counterfeits: Application of the theory of planned behavior. *Clothing and Textiles Research Journal, 28*(2), 79–94.

Kim, J.-E., Cho, H. J., & Johnson, K. P. (2009). Influence of moral affect, judgment, and intensity on decision making concerning counterfeit, gray-market, and imitation products. *Clothing and Textiles Research Journal, 27*(3), 211–226.

Kim, J. S. (1998). Assessing the causal relationships among materialism, reference group, and conspicuous consumption of Korean adolescents. *Consumer Interests Annual, 44*(1), 155–156.

Kwong, K. K., Yau, O. H. M., Lee, J. S. Y., Sin, L. Y. M., & Tse, A. C. B. (2003). The effects of attitudinal and demographic factors on intention to buy pirated CDs: The case of Chinese consumers. *Journal of Business Ethics, 47*(3), 223–235.

Lai, K. K.-Y., & Zaichkowsky, J. L. (1999). Brand imitation: Do the Chinese have different views? *Asia Pacific Journal of Management, 16*(2), 179–192.

Leibenstein, H. (1950). Bandwagon, snob, and Veblen effects in the theory of consumers demand. *Quarterly Journal of Economics, 64*(2), 183–207.

Leisen, B., & Nill, A. (2001). Combating product counterfeiting: An investigation into the likely effectiveness of a demand-oriented approach. *American Marketing Association Conference Proceedings, 12*(1), 271–277.

Lichtenstein, D. R., Ridgway, N. M., & Netemeyer, R. G. (1993). Price perceptions and consumer shopping behavior: A field study. *Journal of Marketing Research, 30*(2), 234–245.

Lynn, M. (1991). Scarcity effects on value: A quantitative review of the commodity theory literature. *Psychology & Marketing, 8*(1), 45–57.

Mason, R. S. (1992). Modeling the Demand for Status Goods. Working paper, Department of Business and Management Studies, University of Salford, U.K., New York, St Martin's.

Mazumdar, T. (1986) Experimental Investigation of the Psychological Determinants of Buyers' Price Awareness and a Comparative Assessment of Methodologies for Retrieving Price Information from Memory. Working paper, Virginia Polytechnic Institute and State University.

McCarthy, E. J., & Perreault Jr, W. D. (1987). *Basic Marketing: A Managerial Approach* (9th edn.). Home-wood, IL: Irwin.

McKinsey. (1990). *The Luxury Industry: An Asset for France*. Paris: McKinsey.

Monroe, K. B., & Krishnan, R. (1985). The effect of price on subjective product evaluations. In J. Jacoby & J. Olsen (Eds.), *Perceived Quality* (pp. 209–232). Lexington, MA: Lexington Books.

Nia, A., & Zaichkowsky, J. L. (2000). Do counterfeits devalue the ownership of luxury brands? *Journal of Product & Brand Management, 9*(7), 485–497.

Nill, A., & Shultz, C. J. (1996). The scourge of global counterfeiting. *Business Horizons, 39*(6), 37–42.

Nueno, J. L., & Quelch, J. A. (1998). The mass marketing of luxury. *Business Horizons, 41*(6), 61–68.

Nunes, P. F., & Donnelly, C. (2010). Is it the real thing? – Counterfeiting is a bigger problem than you probably think. *The Conference Board Review*, Winter. http://www.tcbreview.com/pdfs/is-it-the-real-thing-w10.pdf. Accessed 25 July 2010.

OECD. (1998). The economic impact of counterfeiting. http://www.oecd.org/dataoecd/11/11/2090589.pdf. Accessed 23 July 2010.

Pantzalis, I. (1995). Exclusivity strategies in pricing and brand extension. Unpublished doctoral dissertation, University of Arizona, Tucson, AZ.

Penz, E., & Stöttinger, B. (2005). Forget the real thing-take the copy! An explanatory model for the volitional purchase of counterfeit products. *Advances in Consumer Research, 32*(1), 568–575.

Phau, I., Sequeira, M., & Dix, S. (2009a). Consumers' willingness to knowingly purchase counterfeit products. *Direct Marketing: An International Journal, 3*(4), 262–281.

Phau, I., Sequeira, M., & Dix, S. (2009b). To buy or not to buy a 'counterfeit' Ralph Lauren polo shirt: The role of lawfulness and legality toward purchasing counterfeits. *Asia-Pacific Journal of Business Administration, 1*(1), 68–80.

Phau, I., & Prendergast, G. (2000). Consuming luxury brands: The relevance of the "rarity principle". *Journal of Brand Management, 8*(2), 122–138.

Phau, I., & Teah, M. (2009). Devil wears (counterfeit) Prada: A study of antecedents and outcomes of attitudes towards counterfeits of luxury brands. *Journal of Consumer Marketing, 26*(1), 15–27.

Richins, M., & Dawson, S. (1992). A consumer values orientation for materialism and its measurement: Scale development and validation. *Journal of Consumer Research, 19*(3), 303–316.

Sheth, J. N., Newman, B. I., & Gross, B. L. (1991). Why we buy what we buy: A theory of consumption values. *Journal of Business Research, 22*(2), 159–170.

Sivacek, J., & Crano, W. D. (1982). Vested interest as a moderator of attitude-behavior consistency. *Journal of Personality and Social Psychology, 43*(1), 210–221.

Staake, T., Thiesse, F., & Fleisch, E. (2009). The emergence of counterfeit trade: A literature review. *European Journal of Marketing, 43*(3/4), 320–349.

Staake, T., & Fleisch, E. (2008). *Countering Counterfeit Trade – Illicit Market Insights, Best-Practice Strategies, and Management Toolbox*. Berlin, Germany: Springer.

Swami, V., Chamorro-Premuzic, T., & Furnham, A. (2009). Faking it: Personality and individual difference predictors of willingness to buy counterfeit goods. *The Journal of Socio-Economics, 38*(5), 820–825.

Tom, G., Garibaldi, B., Zeng, Y., & Pilcher, J. (1998). Consumer demand for counterfeit goods. *Psychology & Marketing, 15*(5), 405–421.

Verhallen, T. M. (1982). Scarcity and consumer choice behavior. *Journal of Economic Psychology, 2*(4), 299–321.

Vida, I. (2007). Determinants of consumer willingness to purchase non-deceptive counterfeit products. *Managing Global Transitions, 5*(3), 253–270.

Vigneron, F., & Johnson, L. W. (1999). A review and a conceptual framework of prestige-seeking consumer behaviour. *Academy of Marketing Science Review, 1*(1), 1–15.

Vigneron, F., & Johnson, L. W. (2004). Measuring perceptions of brand luxury. *Journal of Brand Management, 11*(6), 484–506.

Wang, F., Zhang, H., Zang, H., & Ouyang, M. (2005). Purchasing pirated software: An initial examination of Chinese consumers. *Journal of Consumer Marketing, 22*(6), 340–351.

Wee, C.-H., Ta, S.-J., & Cheok, K.-H. (1995). Non-price determinants of intention to purchase counterfeit goods: An exploratory study. *International Marketing Review, 12*(6), 19–46.

Westbrook, R. A., & Oliver, R. L. (1991). The dimensionality of consumption emotion patterns and consumer satisfaction. *Journal of Consumer Research, 18*(1), 84–91.

Wiedmann, K.-P., Hennigs, N., & Siebels, A. (2007). Measuring consumers' luxury value perception: A cross-cultural framework. *Academy of Marketing Science Review, 7*(1), 1–21.

Wiedmann, K.-P., Hennigs, N., & Siebels, A. (2009). Value-based segmentation of luxury consumption behavior. *Psychology & Marketing, 26*(7), 625–651.

Wilcox, K., Kim, H. M., & Sen, S. (2008). Why do consumers buy counterfeit luxury brands? *Journal of Marketing Research, 46*(2), 247–259.

Wilke, R., & Zaichkowsky, J. L. (1999). Brand imitation and its effects on innovation, competition, and brand equity. *Business Horizons, 42*(6), 9–18.

WTO, World Trade Organization. (2010). Intellectual property: Protection and enforcemen.http://www.wto.org/english/thewto_e/whatis_e/tif_e/agrm7_e.htm. Accessed 23 July 2010.

Yoo, B., & Lee, S.-H. (2005). Do counterfeits promote genuine products? Hofstra University, http://www.hofstra.edu/pdf/BIZ_mlc_workingpaper7.pdf. Accessed 22 July 2010.

Yoo, B., & Lee, S.-H. (2009). Buy genuine luxury fashion products or counterfeits? *Advances in Consumer Research, 36*(1), 280–228.

**Klaus-Peter Wiedmann** is a Full Chaired Professor of Marketing and Management and the Director of the Institute of Marketing and Management at the Leibniz University of Hannover, Germany. His main subjects of research and teaching as well as consulting are Strategic Management, Brand & Reputation Management, Corporate Identity, International Marketing, Luxury Marketing, Innovation & Technology

Marketing, Corporate Culture & Change Management, Consumer Behavior, Marketing Research & Controlling, Online & Mobile Marketing.

**Nadine Hennigs** is Assistant Professor at the Leibniz University of Hannover, Germany, Institute of Marketing and Management. Her main subjects of research and teaching as well as consulting are: Luxury Marketing, Strategic Management, Brand & Reputation Management, Marketing Research, Consumer Behavior.

**Christiane Klarmann** is Scientific Research Assistant at the Leibniz University of Hannover, Germany, Institute of Marketing and Management. Her main focus in research and teaching as well as consulting are: Luxury Marketing, Strategic Management, Brand & Reputation Management, Marketing Research, Consumer Behavior.

# Is Luxury Compatible with Sustainability? Luxury Consumers' Viewpoint

Jean-Noël Kapferer and Anne Michaut-Denizeau

## Introduction

Despite the recent global financial crisis and economic turmoil, luxury brands are doing well with a growth of over 10 percent per year since 2009 (Bain and Co 2012). As a result of their unique performance, luxury brands become a focus of attention through multiple articles in the press. The downside of this growth and high visibility has also increased exposure to criticism. In particular, as luxury brands become more visible and promote themselves to wider audiences, the most recognised luxury brands also turn into more attractive targets for

---

This chapter was Reprinted from Kapferer, J. and Michaut-Denizeau, A. (2014) 'Is Luxury Compatible with Sustainability? Luxury Consumers' Viewpoint', *Journal of Brand Management*, 21, pp. 1-22. With kind permission from the *Journal of Brand Management*. All rights reserved.

J.-N. Kapferer (✉) · A. Michaut-Denizeau
Inseec Business School, Paris, France
e-mail: jnkapferer@inseec.com; michaut@hec.fr

© The Author(s) 2017
J.-N. Kapferer et al. (eds.), *Advances in Luxury Brand Management*,
Journal of Brand Management: Advanced Collections,
DOI 10.1007/978-3-319-51127-6_7

sustainable development activists and watchgroups such as Greenpeace (www.thefashionduel.com).

As they are well aware of the challenges of sustainability in today's business context, some luxury companies have emphasised the way sustainability issues feature in their business practices, and today, most luxury companies produce extensive reports of their efforts.

Faced by this increasingly relevant challenge for luxury brands, it seems to us relevant to detach ourselves from the companies' reports on sustainability to focus more extensively on the perceptions that consumers have of the sustainable orientation of luxury companies.

The present chapter, therefore, intends to explore issues related to luxury brands and sustainability, with two main objectives: (i) to explore the extent of the perceived contradiction between their luxury consumption and sustainability in the eye of the luxury consumer and (ii) to understand the drivers of this perceived contradiction. A study enabling to uncover the drivers of the perceived contradiction between luxury and sustainability is an effective management tool for luxury brands to better develop their sustainability strategies and associated communication.

In order to achieve these objectives, this chapter is organised as follows. In its first part, the chapter focuses on explaining why sustainability has not been central to luxury brands concerns, at least in an explicit manner, until recently. In a second step, it emphasises how recent evolutions in the context have dramatically changed the situation and increased the importance of sustainability for luxury brands. The research investigates the level of sensitivity of actual luxury buyers to the cause of sustainability, insofar as it concerns the luxury sector, luxury brands and their purchases. The dependent variable, their perception of a contradiction between luxury and sustainability, allows identifying the variables that increase consumers' scepticism about the coexistence of luxury and sustainability ideals.

## Luxury and Sustainability

The meaning of luxury is manifold, and its definition is elusive, with nuances suggesting an absolute concept tied to an idealised life, extras beyond necessity, needlessly expensive items or intimate exceptions of self-indulgence. A vast number of studies have intended to define luxury products and brands, inspired by prior economic or psychological theories, and often based on consumers' perceptions (De Barnier et al. 2006). A major issue related to the definition and measurement of luxury thus arises from its subjective character (De Barnier et al. 2012). In an effort to develop a new scale, with a spectrum of dimensions relating to the most complete possible perception of luxury, De Barnier et al. (2012) have combined three most quoted existing scales: Kapferer (1998), Dubois et al. (2001) and Vigneron and Johnson (2004). They have proposed a hybrid scale formed of a combination of eight of the dimensions belonging to the original scales: elitism, distinction and status, rarity, reputation, creativity, power of the brand, hedonism and refinement. Each criterion is necessary to differentiate luxury from fashion goods, premium offerings or even ultra-premium products (Kapferer and Bastien 2012).

Following the most widely used definition developed by the World Commission on Environment and Development, we view sustainability as 'meeting the needs of the present without compromising the ability of future generations to meet their own needs' (Brundtland Report 1987, p. 8). This definition emphasises the importance of the conservation of nature's assets while consuming (Strong 1997). It challenges the practices of companies and brands, from their supply chain down to consumers' retail experience. All industries, including luxury, need to preserve rare materials, guarantee safe manufacturing of their products, avoid pollution and exhibit respect for workers upstream; they also need to consider downstream practices, such as packaging and wrapping practices in retail locations, and recycling waste at the end of life of products. We see sustainability as a triple bottom line of economic profitability, respect for the environment and social responsibility (Johnson 2009).

## The Relative Silence of Luxury Houses on Sustainability Issues

Luxury companies, though slow to engage in communication on sustainability, have started to publish their activities (DeBeers 2009), such that most luxury brand websites contain special sections dedicated to social and environmental responsibility. Yet, few luxury companies take proactive sustainable development stances. This sector, though clearly aware of the stakes, thus remain discreet, which some critics interpret as uninvolved.

In truth, since 2000, most of the major luxury groups have created dedicated positions or task forces. Luxury groups do not operate like other groups though, in that they are not integrated, nor do they have a top-down decision-making culture. Instead, the independence of the craftspeople or maisons is a key element of their sustained aura, and there are few synergies across brands (Ijaouane and Kapferer 2012). Each brand therefore conducts its own audits and sets up its own controls, ideally in line with the group's ambitions.

Furthermore, luxury brands tend to communicate little. They might stage shows, provide luxury experiences or host events, but they rarely talk about themselves and their functions. For example, the family companies (Armani, Hermès, Chanel) are not required to publish financial data or strategic information; they actively seek to maintain the dream image they are selling by avoiding to diffuse much of any other type of information. Finally, these brands seemingly perceive that sustainability suffers from so much greenwashing that remaining silent is the best way to avoid boomerang effects.

Most luxury brands start small and stay small, often as family businesses. The products may be made by hand, and they move slowly and with reluctance towards higher volumes. As a result, these brands control the whole supply chain, from the raw materials to the merchandising and consumer experiences in stores. With their focus on high-quality and family-like working conditions, such firms are unlikely to thrive by relying on poor practices, unfair labour conditions, poor animal treatments or spoiling the environment. A basic tenet of a luxury strategy is to produce local objects, with the assistance of talented craftspeople who need years to develop their talent. French luxury is produced in France; Italian luxury comes from Italy (though this trend also is evolving, as we describe subsequently).

## Luxury Beyond the Radar of SD Sentinels

Although no industry can avoid sustainability concerns, activist groups seemingly have found few axes to grind in the luxury sector. Bendell and Kleanthous (2007), in a pioneering 'Deeper Luxury Report' for the World Wildlife Fund, highlighted sustainability issues. Yet, this report itself includes brands such as Garnier, which is not a luxury brand. It appears that commodities represent the main site for activists' concerns, not luxury. Activist groups' own interests focus on important issues with strong ecological impact, such as mass killings of whales by the Japanese fishing industry, sweatshops, unacceptable working conditions for makers of mass premium brands (e.g., Nike's famous sweat-shops with child labour, Apple's Chinese Foxconn factories), the oil industry (e.g., risks tied to offshore drilling, unreliable mass tanker transportation), the automobile industry, mining and energy industries, and chemical waste.

In luxury, criticisms tend to refer to hidden parts of the supply chain, such as raw material sourcing (e.g., checking the source of all animal skins, gold, gemstones), animal treatments (e.g., the anti-foie gras lobby, exploitation of crocodile farms, killing baby seals for fur), human work conditions (e.g., gold), manufacturing methods polluting the local environment (e.g., mercury for tanning skins) or destruction of the environment (e.g., endangered tree species used in the luxury furniture business, exploitation of rare water resources by luxury golf clubs and hotels situated in poor countries). Another major facet of sustainability relates to economic and social equilibrium, or its lack thereof. The luxury sector must realise the reputational risks, especially considering modern communication techniques, which allow activist groups and regular consumers to spread rumours rapidly and widely (Kapferer 1990). The Internet is a worldwide social solidarity and resistance network: nothing can stay hidden anymore (Okonkwo 2009).

The general public has mirrored this selective focus of activists and acted in the ways that seemed most efficient in terms of the impacts of their efforts, which apparently entail low-cost commodity products (Davies et al. 2012). Jones (1991) has proposed what he calls the six 'moral intensity factors' that drive consumers to act immediately: the magnitude of the consequences, social consensus about the negativity of the activity, the probability of harm, temporal immediacy, proximity and the concentration of the harmful effect on a small group or its dispersion over a large number of people. These factors help explain why, for example, consumers buy fair trade coffee: As a commodity, coffee is regularly bought by millions of people at a low price. They see the immediate effect of millions of extra pennies spent on fair trade brands and products when this money gets sent to poor growers in Colombia or elsewhere in the world. The same reasoning holds for the fashion industry, which is mostly a low-cost industry with global, mass fashion brands such as Zara, Mango, C&A, H&M, Uniqlo or even Polo Ralph Lauren. They have delocalised their high volume production in low labour cost countries, such as China or Thailand. In contrast, some consumers prefer to spend a few more dollars to create a personal link with small, eco-friendly cotton growers who supply small fashion brands positioned on their eco-concerns or the eco-lines of the big fashion retailers (Chan and Wong 2012). Although these consumers still represent a small segment (Weller and Walter 2008), they believe their choices can have a positive impact; these repeated purchases allow them to insert their ethical criteria in the consumers' decision process (Davies et al. 2012).

The same reasoning explains why luxury purchasers have been far less concerned by sustainability preoccupations and decision criteria. Luxury purchases are rare, irregular and expensive, which differentiates them from Jones's (1991) morality factors. In an industry in which everything makes consumers feel special and unique, there is no reason for consumers to anticipate a volume impact. Not only do most consumers see no evil in buying a Dior leather bag, but they also can seek sustainable alternatives in the luxury market, such as Stella McCartney, who refuses to use animal skins and works only with substitutes.

In summary, activists' lack of emphasis on luxury thus far likely has resulted from the presence of bigger issues as greater sources of concern in other industries. Consumers make such irregular purchases of luxury items that the impact of sustainability information campaigns might have lacked resonance. Furthermore, luxury has a notable role in modern societies, namely, to elevate people from their day-to-day routines and hardships. Once limited to the very rich, growth in this sector has come about by expanding the offerings to the middle classes. Buying a luxury product once in a while is an exceptional experience; luxury boutiques thus seek to help people forget the difficulties of their lives and the world. In turn, questions about manufacturing and supply chains are remote from buyers' decision criteria. Consumers see no contradiction in these Janus-faced desires for repetitive day-to-day purchases, for which they show sustainability consciousness, and exceptional purchases, for which they escape from reality and its corollaries.

## Recent Evolutions: Why Luxury Has Come Under Scrutiny

Recently more attention has centred on the relationships between luxury brands and sustainability. According to sustainability literature, businesses can justify their sustainability actions with several main rationales (Porter and Kramer 2006), including the license to operate (i.e., businesses identify social issues that matter to their stakeholders) and reputation (i.e., businesses seek to satisfy external audiences). Financial investment funds also increasingly take sustainability facets into consideration when they make recommendations to investors, out of fear of the risks associated with a brand that uses unethical practices. Reputation also offers pricing power, and any breach decimates this power. Clearly, luxury brands have more to lose; in the meantime, questions raised in published reports (e.g., Bendell and Kleanthous 2007) have forced luxury companies to communicate more about their actions (e.g., DeBeers 2009).

In all these realms, the growth of the luxury sector, close to 10 percent annually for the past decade (Bain and Co 2012) despite the global economic crisis, has created challenges. What was once a tiny sector is now very visible; as Chadha and Husband (2007) suggest, half of all Tokyo secretaries have a Louis Vuitton bag that costs the equivalent of a month's salary. Such visible luxury reinitiates the moral condemnation that has always accompanied this industry.

Despite claims of craftsmanship, hand-made items or the perpetuation of tradition, many luxury brands also are growing by expanding their operations to low-cost factories, while licensed operators pursue volume and sell fashionable, high margin accessories. A few brands may stick to the stringent principles of a luxury strategy (Kapferer and Bastien 2009, 2012), but many others have abandoned them: Burberry closed its historical UK factory in 2007 and moved its production to China. In 2010, Prada announced it would delocalise from Italy to China. Coach is manufactured in China, as is Polo Ralph Lauren. These brands try to make more money at both ends: by minimising the cost of manufacturing and maximising the retail price. As such, they are far from their public image (experienced craftspeople making unique products by hand), and their production more accurately reflects a fashion industry. A true luxury strategy instead seeks to maximise brand uniqueness and control the entire value chain (Kapferer and Bastien 2012). As part of the luxury industry is now acting like any fashionable mass retailer, it is logical that sustainability advocates would pay more attention to its practices. The pursuit of higher volume puts more strain on sustainability concerns, such as rare species preservation, origin of raw ingredients and working conditions in factories.

The era of mass luxury also evokes the idea that happiness is a by-product of owning things, which creates a clear ethical issue in sustainable development terms. If the luxury sector targets more consumers, it seemingly might go too far and entice people to invest considerable amounts of their disposable income in objects or experiences they do not need (Kapferer 2012a). In the hotel business, the expansion of five star hotels and resorts in sunny tourist destinations, which are often in impoverished countries, or in previously well-preserved natural zones raises also sustainability issues related to social harmony. Should the happy few enjoy these resorts while the wider population is starving a few yards from their dining rooms? The dis-equilibrium in the allocation of rare resources in these places (e.g., water, energy, food) creates further questions. Although the luxury sector certainly cannot be blamed for growing inequalities witnessed in many nations, the visibility of the disequilibrium raises concerns.

In summary, whereas luxury historically aligned with sustainability ideals (Kapferer 2010; De Barnier et al. 2012), by producing rare products of ultra high quality, made by hand and with respect for tradition, it has come to look more like consumer or fashion goods, made to fill trash bins after they achieve structural and rapid obsolescence. Therefore, the real issue entails the sustainability of this new form of mass luxury. Such issues have been predicted by opinion leaders, such as Hollywood stars, cautious about their personal branding, who prefer to be seen driving a Tesla electric roadster rather than traditional sport cars.

## Hypotheses and Method

Beyond opinion leaders though, it becomes necessary to measure public opinion, especially considering the few wide-scale studies available on sustainability and luxury. The dependent variable, luxury consumers' perception of a contradiction between luxury and sustainability, will enable us to identify which variables increase consumers' scepticism about the coexistence of luxury and sustainable development ideals.

We measure the respondents' present degree of concern about the issue and their consideration of sustainability as a purchase criterion when buying luxury goods or services. We did not expect their degree of concern to be high (because luxury promotes the ideal of helping people forget about the harsh realities of life), so we decided to test the sensitivity of the public to actual potential issues of concern, which we elaborated and presented to the luxury buying interviewees.

Finally, we asked about their predictions for the future of luxury in a world concerned with sustainability. To determine which factors might cause people to perceive a contradiction between luxury and sustainability, we considered nine main variables.

## Hypotheses

### Socio-Demographics

One robust and well-replicated finding has been that women report greater concern for social and environmental issues. At the behavioural level, they also report more socially and environmentally friendly purchase behaviours

(Luchs and Mooradian 2012). Yet, there is no evidence that this should lead to a difference in the perceived contradiction between luxury and sustainability. More generally, as emphasised by Shrum et al. (1995) a relative large number of studies have found little or no relationship between demographic characteristics and environmental attitudes and behaviours. In turn, we offer no specific hypotheses with regard to gender and age.

With respect to income, luxury buyers with lower income could be more likely to purchase lower-end luxury goods that are less representative of the hand-made traditional luxury approach and thus more likely to find a contradiction between sustainability and luxury.

> **Hypothesis 1**: Luxury consumers with lower incomes are more likely to perceive a higher contradiction between luxury and sustainability.

*Consumers' sensitivity to sustainability issues:* Clients likely vary in their sensitivity to sustainability. To measure this sensitivity, we used an existing scale developed by BVA (a survey organisation) for the French National Energy Saving Agency. This scale supports a comparison of sustainability sensitivity between our sample of luxury buyers and national populations. It also enables us to investigate whether attitudes towards sustainability, emerging from other sectors of public or economic life, exert an influence on our sample's perception of luxury itself, or if luxury is a world completely apart.

Consumers most sensitive to sustainability are disenchanted with mindless consumption and its impact on society (Kozinets and Handleman 2004). As a result, they look for more sustainable alternatives in their consumption or even substantially decrease their consumption, cutting down all non-necessary purchases. Presenting luxury brands as fulfilling an ecological need is likely to appear rather controversial to these consumers in particular considering the premise that luxury is accessible primarily to the fortunate (Joy et al. 2012). Hence, we anticipate that sensitive consumers consider luxury and sustainability more contradictory than insensitive consumers.

> **Hypothesis 2**: Luxury consumers' perception of the contradiction between luxury and sustainability increases with consumers' sensitivity to sustainable development issues.

*Consumers' sustainable behaviours:* Social psychology has demonstrated that not all attitudes transform into behaviour. In particular, despite concern towards the environment (attitude) consumers fail to purchase sustainable products (behaviour) (Gupta and Ogden 2009). Therefore, we used a specific scale to measure consumers' actual implementation of sustainable acts (e.g., using a bike or public transportation to commute to the office, saving energy at home, recycling batteries). In terms of behaviour, past research has shown that green consumers have increased interest in new products, are information seekers and consider themselves opinion leaders (Shrum et al. 1995). Such consumers are more likely to uncover all non-sustainable issues in luxury and therefore more likely to perceive a contradiction. Besides, acting according to the principles of sustainable development signals an ability to master consumption and exert control, in contrast with the essence of luxury, for which excess is key (e.g., excess creativity, materials, detail, comfort, performance). We hypothesise that active consumers should declare sustainability and luxury more contradictory.

**Hypothesis 3:** Luxury consumers' perceived contradiction between luxury and sustainability increases with consumers' actual behaviours related to sustainable development.

*Consumers' degree of liking of luxury:* According to Osgood's balance theory (Osgood and Tannenbaum 1955) or Heider's (1958) congruence theory, people who love luxury should forgive any ethical issues or at least minimise them, to maintain a cognitive balance. Therefore, we hypothesise a negative relationship between love of luxury and perceptions of a contradiction with sustainability.

**Hypothesis 4:** Luxury consumers' perceptions of a contradiction between luxury and sustainability decreases with consumers' degree of liking of luxury.

*Consumers' perception of luxury as promoting 'true' versus 'superficial' values:* On the one hand, the stringent principles of luxury based on very high product quality, rarity, crafts-manship and tradition are in line with sustainability objectives (Kapferer 2010). Very high quality and rarity account for durability and resilience; craftsmanship and respected artisans take care of the equity dimension. Through their prominent concern for quality and craft, luxury brand could effectively turn into opinion leaders on sustainability issues. For consumers perceiving such elements of luxury, which we labelled luxury's true values, there should be less contradiction between luxury and sustainability. On the other hand, greater conspicuous consumption and prominent logos are closely linked to luxury (Han et al. 2010), which conveys a superficial dimension, the antipode of sustainability principles. Accordingly:

> **Hypothesis 5**: Luxury consumers' perception of the contradiction between luxury and sustainability (a) decreases with consumers' perceptions of luxury as promoting true values but (b) increases with consumers' perception of luxury as promoting superficial values.

*Consumers' perception that luxury creates social unrest:* By encouraging people to buy products they cannot really afford, luxury as symbol of inequality is likely to be accused of fostering social unrest. In 2011, billboards promoting a luxurious lifestyle were banned in Beijing, because of concerns that the end-less advertisements would simply remind people of the wealth gap. In their provocative 'Deeper Luxury' report, Bendell and Kleanthous (2007) argue that the pursuit of luxury is linked to the brand's stance on important social issues, such as saving the planet. Yet, the social question appears much more challenging in an endemic definition of luxury making it accessible to only the fortunate. Consumers who believe that luxury creates social unrest should declare that sustainability and luxury are contradictory.

> **Hypothesis 6**: Luxury consumers' perception of the contradiction between luxury and sustainability increases with consumers' perception that luxury creates social unrest.

## Methodology

For this exploratory research, we focus on 966 luxury buyers exclusively and depend on descriptive statistics to assess the level of concern among this population.

We used multiple regression analysis to test the explanatory power of our various hypotheses. To collect the data, we conducted a survey among luxury buyers, recruited from the BVA Internet regular national panel in France. This major survey and polling company recruited people who indicated they had purchased at least five products above a certain price (Champagne above €45, shoes above €250, sunglasses beyond €250 and so on). All 966 respondents even declared having bought expensive Champagne in the previous 12 months (in France, the average retail price of a bottle of real Champagne is €13.75).

## Measures

We first measured a number of items related to the perception of luxury, the perception of the contradiction between luxury and sustainability, and potential drivers. These variables were measured by 5-point Likert type scales and later used in factor analyses to develop the dependent and explanatory variables of our regression analysis.

First, the perceived contradiction between luxury and suitability was measured by two items, the literal contradiction as well as the perception that 'luxury has no future in a sustainably driven world'.

With respect to sustainability sensitivities, we used BVA's existing 10-item scale (e.g., 'one should stop using cars in midtowns', 'I am worried about the degradation of the planet'). Similarly, regarding the sustainable behaviours of respondents, we measured consumers' actual engagement in sustainable development, in the form of small, everyday acts based on a BVA existing scale as well. Using these existing scales allows comparing the sample of luxury consumers to a national sample. These scales are adapted from the ones developed by the International Institute for Sustainable Development (Michalos et al. 2012).

Consumers' degree of liking of luxury consisted of three items as well as the perception of luxury as being superficial and the perception of luxury as creating social unrest. Finally, we also developed an item based on the perception of what we labelled luxury 'true values', that is, the quality and longevity typical of luxury products as well as the preservation of know-how.

All these scales are presented in Appendix A (Table A2).

Finally, two factors are expected to be strong determinants of the relationship: the superficial value factor and the social unrest factor. The first factor consists of three items related to personal guilt, superficiality and an unwillingness to display big logos. The second factor also contains three items, involving luxury as a symbol of human wealth inequality, people overspending despite their lower resources and encouragement of a lack of self-control.

Finally, we also measured a number of variables related to 'shocking' elements about luxury brands potential misbehaviour, if sustainability is considered. These variables included for instance, 'Killing animals for their fur' or 'Exploiting cheap workforce in China'. These variables are listed in (Table 2) in the results section and were measured on a 10-point Likert type scale.

## Sample Description

Our sample included luxury consumers from 18 to 75 years old with a balance between men and women (54 percent men) and a monthly income ranging from less than €5000 to more than €15,000. (Table 3) presents the socio-demographic breakdown of the sample.

Table 4 compares the sustainable development sensitivity of our luxury sample with that of a national sample. We used the typology built by BVA Institute for the National Energy Saving Agency, which defines five types according to two major factors: sustainable development sensitivity (low to strong) and sustainable development behaviour (low to strong).

From (Table 4), we note that relative to the national sample, luxury buyers more prominently appear in the Type 1 category (sustainable development sensitive and active) or the Type 4 category (very indifferent and willing to do the least). In contrast, they are less of Type 3 than the nation, which includes pragmatists who are less sensitive but perform sustainable development – oriented acts.

**Table 2** Shocking news about luxury brands' misbehaviour

| | N | Minimum | Maximum | Mean | σ |
|---|---|---|---|---|---|
| Some luxury brand exploit cheap workforce in China | 941 | 1 | 10 | 7.73 | 2.749 |
| Killing animals for their fur | 931 | 1 | 10 | 7.72 | 2.849 |
| Having to kill crocodiles to make a luxury handbag | 942 | 1 | 10 | 7.68 | 2.860 |
| Destroying unsold products rather than selling them at a discount | 939 | 1 | 10 | 7.62 | 2.807 |
| Hearing that French or Italian luxury brands produce in China, Romania, Morocco and so on | 938 | 1 | 10 | 7.57 | 2.742 |
| Private yachts that require 150,000 litres of fuel | 932 | 1 | 10 | 7.49 | 2.839 |
| Creating golf courses and luxury hotels in countries where people are Starving | 944 | 1 | 10 | 7.43 | 2.857 |
| Luxury cars with high carbon emissions | 941 | 1 | 10 | 7.29 | 2.854 |
| Spending holidays in five star hotels in underdeveloped countries where inhabitants lack for everything | 937 | 1 | 10 | 7.02 | 2.888 |
| The tradition of wrapping luxury products in multiple wrappings that all end in a trash bin | 944 | 1 | 10 | 7.02 | 2.680 |
| Piles of exotic fruit out of season transported by airplane | 944 | 1 | 10 | 6.80 | 2.787 |
| Stuffing geese and ducks for the pleasure of eating foie gras | 945 | 1 | 10 | 6.33 | 3.051 |
| Young consumers buying luxury goods at hefty prices | 944 | 1 | 10 | 6.23 | 2.824 |
| Transporting heavy Champagne bottles across the globe | 944 | 1 | 10 | 6.16 | 2.931 |
| Luxury billboards in the street when there is an economic crisis and precariousness in our country | 943 | 1 | 10 | 6.14 | 2.946 |

**Table 3** Sample description: Demographics

| Frequencies | | N | In percentage | Valid percentage |
|---|---|---|---|---|
| Age | 18–25 | 186 | 19.3 | 19.3 |
| | 26–35 | 217 | 22.5 | 22.5 |
| | 36–45 | 209 | 21.6 | 21.6 |
| | 46–55 | 147 | 15.2 | 15.2 |
| | 56–65 | 156 | 16.1 | 16.1 |
| | 66–75 | 51 | 5.3 | 5.3 |
| | Total | 966 | 100.0 | 100.0 |
| Gender | Men | 520 | 53.8 | 53.8 |
| | Women | 446 | 46.2 | 46.2 |
| | Total | 966 | 100.0 | – |
| Income (monthly) | Less than €5,000 | 427 | 44.2 | 50.0 |
| | Between €5,000 and €10,000 | 214 | 22.2 | 25.1 |
| | Between €10,000 and €15,000 | 80 | 8.3 | 9.4 |
| | €15,000 and more | 133 | 13.8 | 15.6 |
| | Missing | 112 | 11.6 | – |
| | Total | 966 | 100.0 | – |

*Notes*: Age was measured as a continuous variable: minimum = 18, maximum = 75, mean = 41.04, standard deviation = 14.76.

**Table 4** Sample description: Sustainable development sensitivity and behaviour

| Sample | Luxury buyers (in percentage) | National (in percentage) |
|---|---|---|
| Type 1: Sustainable development sensitive and active | 22 | 11 |
| Type 2: Sustainable development sensitive, not active | 14 | 15 |
| Type 3: Sustainable development insensitive, yet active | 27 | 40 |
| Type 4: Sustainable development indifferent, doing the least | 30 | 19 |
| Type 5: Sustainable development hostiles, inactive | 7 | 5 |

# Results

## Descriptive Statistics

As a preliminary analysis, we analysed consumers' sensitivity to sustainable development, using 5-point Likert scales (from fully agree to fully disagree).

From (Table 5), we derive a few insights. It should come as no surprise that a sample selected on the basis of their declared purchases of selected expensive items loves luxury brands (70 percent agree or fully agree, all sample M = 3.83). Nevertheless, one-third of luxury buyers hold mixed feelings towards luxury as a concept. It thus appears that luxury brands create an ideal image, but luxury as a concept or industry provokes a different perception. Whereas these consumers expect luxury to serve as a pioneer, 54.1 percent of the sample also think luxury has been a late mover in terms of sustainable orientation (all sample M = 3.53). The meaning of sustainability was explicitly provided at the beginning of the survey interview, including mentions of its three facets (biodiversity, preservation of resources, human social harmony). Furthermore, 61.8 percent of the sample indicated that the modern luxury industry pursues wider markets and exerts pressure on them to buy items that they cannot really afford without sacrifices (all sample M = 3.67).

Only one-third of respondents (34.9 percent) declared that they cared about sustainability when they made purchase decisions about luxury products (all sample M = 2.91). For a majority of consumers, sustainability thus is not a part of their decision-making agenda (when we combine those who disagree and those who do not know). Images of hardship and exploited workforces have little association with luxury in their minds, nor do consumers imagine whom they might be hurting by buying such products (cf. mass market goods) or recognise any alternatives. The percentage indicating this perspective, 34.9 percent, is higher than that reported in recent research (Davies et al. 2012), which was based on 199 UK respondents approached on a main street and selected according to socio-economic quotas, not luxury purchases. The previous study also focused on the relative weight of ethics considerations for commodity versus luxury purchases. Davies et al. (2012, p. 44) thus

**Table 5** Consumers' opinions on luxury and standard deviation (N = 966)

| | N | Minimum | Maximum | Mean | σ |
|---|---|---|---|---|---|
| I love luxury brands | 944 | 1 | 5 | 3.83 | 1.060 |
| I feel a bit guilty when I buy a luxury good | 947 | 1 | 5 | 2.81 | 1.304 |
| I prefer packs without the big logo of the store | 942 | 1 | 5 | 3.05 | 1.332 |
| I appreciate the extreme quality of luxury goods | 949 | 1 | 5 | 4.05 | 1.027 |
| Liking luxury is liking a superficial way of life | 942 | 1 | 5 | 2.98 | 1.300 |
| Luxury and sustainability are contradictory | 934 | 1 | 5 | 2.96 | 1.252 |
| Luxury should be exemplary in terms of sustainability | 941 | 1 | 5 | 4.00 | 1.024 |
| Given their price, it would be shocking to hear that luxury brands are not compliant | 942 | 1 | 5 | 3.92 | 1.108 |
| Long-lasting luxury products match sustainability ideals | 928 | 1 | 5 | 3.37 | 1.090 |
| Luxury makes people buy products far too expensive for their means | 945 | 1 | 5 | 3.67 | 1.123 |
| Symbol of human inequalities, luxury contradicts sustainability | 936 | 1 | 5 | 3.20 | 1.242 |
| Luxury brands are late in terms of sustainability | 913 | 1 | 5 | 3.53 | 1.055 |
| Sustainable Development must look after other priority sectors than luxury | 941 | 1 | 5 | 3.45 | 1.222 |
| Luxury encourages excess spoilage; sustainability encourages self-control, Austerity | 934 | 1 | 5 | 3.29 | 1.212 |
| Luxury is not ethical | 931 | 1 | 5 | 3.24 | 1.151 |
| When I buy luxury products, I don't care about sustainability | 938 | 1 | 5 | 2.91 | 1.261 |
| Luxury has no future in a world driven by sustainability | 922 | 1 | 5 | 2.88 | 1.260 |
| Sustainability will kill the creativity and dream of luxury | 923 | 1 | 5 | 2.72 | 1.326 |

conclude that 'ethics in production is a low priority to consumers when buying luxury products'. Our 34.9 percent figure thus could have been inflated by a yea-saying effect or social desirability bias.

The global picture emerging from these answers is a three-part segmentation: luxury buyers who are quite critical and even guilty, those who say they have no idea and those for whom luxury carries no harm. Overall, the majority (52.8 percent) of these respondents believe that luxury should not be a priority for sustainable development activism (all sample M = 3.45), because they regard it as far cleaner than many other sectors, in which sustainability efforts could have a much higher and more immediate impact.

## Shocking Information for Luxury Consumers

We expected this result, as already evoked by Davies et al. (2012). Accordingly, we included several news items in the survey, to test their emotional resonance and the ability of information to shock this sample of luxury buyers. Table 2 presents the results, in descending magnitude of emotional sensitivity.

The most 'shocking' items were evocative of activists' classic struggles: Killing animals topped the list (45 percent of the sample rated 10, all sample M = 7.72). Following close behind were globalisation issues, such as production in countries with cheap labour (41.7 percent rated 10, all sample M = 7.73), a topic that also has received substantial media attention recently. Waste-related issues, such as destroying unsold goods (36.9 percent rated 10, all sample M = 7.62), luxury cars with high carbon emissions (32.1 percent rated 10, all sample M = 7.49) or yachts' fuel consumption (36.4 percent rated 10, all sample M = 7.29), were also issues for consumers. Finally, consumers were shocked by the presence of luxury hotels in less developed areas (36.3 percent rated 10, all sample M = 7.43).

To identify differences in perception of these variables between respondents, we use INDSCAL (Individual Differences Scaling), a procedure that allows for individual differences in multidimensional scaling developed by Carroll and Chang (1970). The 'shocking' items are evocative of activists' classic struggles and split along two major dimensions: human welfare and animal welfare as shown in Figure 6.

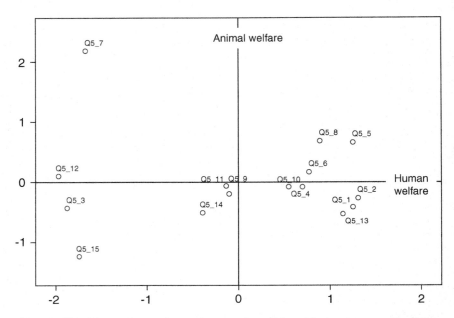

**Fig. 6** Shocking news about luxury brands' misbehaviour – Euclidian Distances. INDSCAL (stress = 0.10462, RSQ = 0.96)

5.1 Destroying unsold products rather than selling them at a discount
5.2 Some luxury brand exploit cheap workforce in China
5.3 Luxury billboards in the street when there is an economic crisis and precariousness
5.4 Luxury cars with high carbon emissions
5.5 Killing animals for their fur
5.6 Creating golf courses and luxury hotels in countries where people are starving
5.7 Stuffing geese and ducks for the pleasure of eating foie gras
5.8 Having to kill crocodiles to make a luxury handbag
5.9 Five star hotels in underdeveloped countries where inhabitants lack for everything
5.10 Private yachts that require 150,000 litres of fuel
5.11 The tradition of wrapping luxury products in multiple wrappings that all end in a trash bin
5.12 Transporting heavy Champagne bottles across the globe
5.13 Hearing that French or Italian luxury brands produce in China, Romania, Morocco and so on
5.14 Piles of exotic fruit out of season transported by airplane
5.15 Young consumers buying luxury goods at hefty prices

Perhaps even more important for luxury management, consumers expect brands to return to their basic luxury principles, such as craftsmanship and localisation of production. Keeping production local appears as an essential element to maintain the ideal image of luxury for consumers (Kapferer 2012b).

## Explaining the Luxury–Sustainability Contradiction

In Table 4, 33.8 percent of the luxury buyers declared luxury contradicted with sustainability (all sample, M = 2.96), once they received a reminder of the definition of sustainability. Yet, an approximately equal number (36.1 percent) considers them non-contradictory. To investigate what motivates these answers, we used a dependent variable measured with two items ('contradictory' and 'luxury has no future in a sustainably driven world'). All variables used in our subsequent analyses, except socio-demographics, were derived from factor analyses. Appendix A provides the details of the items represented by each factor.

Our nine key variables explain 51 percent of the variance (F = 94.73, P ≤ 0.001), as we reveal in Table 6.

Table 6 Explaining the perceived contradiction between luxury and sustainability

|  | Standard β | t | Significance |
|---|---|---|---|
| (Constant) | – | 0.746 | 0.456 |
| Gender | −0.032 | −1.182 | 0.238 |
| Age | −0.041 | −1.382 | 0.167 |
| Income | 0.061 | 2.178 | 0.030 |
| Consumers' sensitivity to sustainability issues | −0.059 | −2.078 | 0.038 |
| Consumers' actual sustainable behaviours | −0.106 | −3.412 | 0.001 |
| Consumers' degree of liking of luxury | 0.062 | 2.062 | 0.040 |
| Consumers' perception of luxury as promoting 'true values' | 0.050 | 1.706 | 0.088 |
| Consumers' perception of luxury as superficial | 0.182 | 6.064 | 0.000 |
| Consumers' perception that luxury creates social unrest | 0.590 | 19.345 | 0.000 |
| $R^2$ | 0.51 | – | – |

Gender and age are not significantly linked to the dependent variable, which supported our theoretical choice not to hypothesise about these variables. Income is marginally significant (t = 2.178, s = 0.030): Higher declared incomes lead to greater perceptions of a contradiction (Hypothesis 1 is not supported). This finding may arise because in our sample of luxury buyers, many of the consumers do not actually represent the high-net worth individuals who can afford the most exceptional luxury products; rather, they may be consumers of the kind of mass luxury that delocalises production and produces massively. Their higher income might only be the indication that they can afford more of this kind of luxury products, thus contradicting sustainability principles.

What about the impact of general sustainable development sensitivities? It had hardly any impact on perceptions of the contradiction (t = −2.078, s = 0.038; β weight = −0.059) and Hypothesis 2 is not supported. One explanation is that sustainable development scales focus heavily on items related to the planet, pollution, the environment, food and health. These facets are less often evoked in criticisms of luxury, which instead pertain to social or self-oriented facets.

We also measured consumers' actual engagement in sustainable development, in the form of small, everyday acts. We hypothesised a positive relationship (Hypothesis 3); instead, the relationship was negative and significant (t = −3.412, s = 0.001; β weight = −0.106). Why would more active people find less contradiction between luxury and sustainability? We offer two explanations. First, to avoid cognitive dissonance, they might seek to diminish any sense of self-contradiction because of their concomitant purchase of luxury items and their participation in sustainable development – related acts by simply saying that luxury is not harmful. Second, the acts mentioned by these respondents included recycling batteries, using bikes or public transportation instead of cars if possible, and buying more expensive bio-food, but these aspects of sustainability are less salient for luxury. Criticisms of mass luxury instead take ethical stands against targeting non-wealthy people for future growth.

Loving luxury is marginally related to perceptions of the contradiction (t = 2.062, s = 0.040; β weight = 0.062), which was an unexpected outcome (Hypothesis 4 not supported). In contrast with our hypothesis, consumers express doubts about the contradictory nature between luxury and sustainability, whatever their degree of liking of luxury. This results shows that respondents manage their Janus-faced desire in their luxury consumption. In the sample, descriptives (Table 5) show that consumers exhibit a high level of love for luxury goods (M = 3.83) and share a feeling that luxury corresponds to a superficial way of life (M = 2.98).

Because luxury is often portrayed as promoting true values in line with sustainable development ideals, we predicted a negative relationship of true values with contradiction perceptions. However, the data do not support this hypothesis (Hypothesis 5a not supported), and the factor is not significant (t = 1.706, s = 0.088; β weight = 0.050), though it suggests a positive relation with perceptions of the contradiction, with a very small β weight.

Two factors reveal extremely significant relationships with perceptions of the contradiction and high-β weights (Hypothesis 5b supported and Hypothesis 6 supported): the superficial value factor (t = 6.064, s = 0.000; β weight = 0.182) and the social unrest factor (t = 19.345, s = 0.000; β weight = 0.590). Thus, the perceptions of a contradiction appear to stem not from alleged misbehaviours in the supply chain but rather from the essence of what luxury signals (rich versus poor) and the modern marketing practices the luxury industry uses to expand its social pressure far beyond consumers with high-disposable incomes (Table 7).

## Discussions and Implications

This study aimed to test whether luxury consumers perceive a contradiction between their luxury consumption and sustainability. Beyond this descriptive result, we also sought to uncover the drivers of any perceived contradiction.

At the descriptive level, most luxury buyers believed luxury should not be a priority on sustainability groups' agenda. Nevertheless, we have identified issues that could harm luxury brands if luxury consumers were to learn of them, including not only classical topics such as animal

Table 7 Explanatory variables and relationships with perceived contradiction between luxury and sustainability

| Explanatory variable | Hypotheses | Findings |
| --- | --- | --- |
| Socio-demographics: Gender | na | |
| Socio-demographics: Age | na | |
| Socio-demographics: Income | Hypothesis 1 negative | ✓ marginally positive |
| Consumers' sensitivity to sustainability issues | Hypothesis 2 positive | ✓ marginally negative |
| Consumers' actual sustainable behaviours | Hypothesis 3 positive | ✓ but negative |
| Consumers' degree of liking of luxury | Hypothesis 4 negative | ✓ marginally positive |
| Consumers' perception of luxury as promoting 'true values' | Hypothesis 5a negative | ns |
| Consumers' perception of luxury as superficial | Hypothesis 5b positive | ✓ |
| Consumers' perception that luxury creates social unrest | Hypothesis 6 positive | ✓ |

Notes: na non-available; ns non-significant.

welfare but also concerns about the delocalisation of production. The descriptive findings also enable us to identify three, roughly equally represented types of luxury buyers, according to their perceptions of the contradiction between luxury and sustainability: those who perceive a contradiction, those who do not and those who have no opinion. We have identified a similar distribution with regard to the attention dedicated to sustainability issues when purchasing luxury items.

To explain these distinct groups, we note two main motives for perceiving a contradiction between luxury and sustainability. In a regression analysis, these two variables alone accounted for 50 percent of the variance explained in the dependent variables, which reinforces their standing as the only two strong drivers of the perceived contradiction between luxury and sustainability. First, consumers' perception of luxury as superficial positively affects perceptions of the contradiction. This finding, combined with the recognition that consumers still consider the 'true values' of luxury significant, suggests that luxury brands need to promote their true values credibly to consumers. If consumers cannot perceive how the true values of luxury are in line with sustainable development principles, they continue to perceive only superficiality in the industry. In this respect, credibility is critical; Britain's Advertising Standards Agency banned Louis Vuitton ads for misleading customers into thinking that the bags were made by hand with no machinery.

Second, consumers' perception that luxury created social unrest enhances the perceived contradiction with sustainability. This feature may create the greatest challenge for the years to come. In a rapidly changing environment, in which inequalities are becoming more apparent and consumption is both conspicuous and for status, luxury brands need to manage the risk of creating social turmoil. In China, the wealth gap is considered a serious threat, so the government has taken the lead and banned aspirational advertisements, arguing that they create a politically unhealthy climate. This issue is all the more sensitive when we consider that luxury brands must use social recognition to communicate about their products.

Although luxury brands tend to focus on the products themselves and materials used when approaching sustainability topics, they may benefit more from shifting their focus to other issues. That is, brand should communicate about luxury's true values to customers. Existing examples include special days ('journées particulières') when Louis Vuitton Moet Hennessy (LVMH) opens its workshops to the public to show how products are made, or Hermès' movie Les Mains d'Hermès, which emphasises the know-how possessed by each métier of the house. Such initiatives could have notable impacts in the long run.

A main ongoing challenge relates to equity, which is entirely unique to luxury when sustainability issues are the topic. This challenge is substantial, because the sustainable development priority directly opposes one of the functions of luxury, namely, social stratification (Kapferer and Bastien 2012). Our finding that the motives linked to sustainable development sensitivity and actual behaviours insignificant or negatively linked to perceptions of a contradiction is interesting too, because it provides more evidence that the domain of luxury is disconnected from daily purchases.

Finally, companies may have different motives for engaging into sustainable practices, such as the potential for upside benefits, managing downside costs or risks, and value creation (Esty and Winston 2007). Although our results suggest that luxury buyers' interest in sustainability when purchasing luxury goods is still relatively minimal, it is clear that avoiding the negative effects of non-compliance may offer a compelling avenue for further efforts by the luxury sector.

## Limitations and Future Research

This study refers to only one country, France. Although it is interesting to analyse a large, representative sample of real luxury buyers from a country very closely associated with luxury, many luxury cultures also exist throughout the world (Kapferer and Bastien 2012), defined by their structural factors, such as:

- The relationship to money, accumulation and acceptance of exhibits of wealth: These variables in turn often reflect the religious base of the country (Catholicism versus Protestantism) and its economic dynamism.
- The rate of growth of the national economies: For example, in the BRIC (Brazil, Russia, India and China) countries, there are vast opportunities for vertical mobility. Success is open to young entrepreneurs whose parents were very poor; they tend to like signs of success. New Chinese millionaires are young and express no guilt about their luxury spending.

Because of these limitations, an extension of this research should cover countries that exhibit vastly different cultural and economic parameters (China, Japan, the United States, the United Kingdom and Germany).

Another limitation is the self-selected nature of the sample. However, the related bias should not be overestimated. Respondents to this survey participate in a larger panel and regularly answer short questionnaires. In our sample, the respondents were selected on the basis of their declared luxury purchases, but they did not know the research topic or the focus of the survey.

In terms of concepts used, this research clearly is based on a general definition of both luxury and sustainability. As such, it does not consider luxury brands that are particularly oriented towards sustainability such as Loro Piana, participating in protection programmes for vicunas for instance, or Stella McCartney who refuses to use any leather or fur in her creations. Rather, this research gives a broader vision of luxury as a sector without differentiating between brands. Similarly, this research does not consider any specific sustainable orientation of luxury brand. For instance this chapter does not distinguish sustainability in production from sustainability in consumption. In the case of the equity dimension in sustainability, the distinction would be essential though as luxury brands might take care of this dimension with their employees or suppliers at the production level, yet have a consumption that reflects social stratification.

**Acknowledgements** The authors acknowledge funding and support from the Pernod Ricard Company.

# Appendix A

**Table A2** Construction of explanatory variables

| Explanatory variables | Items |
|---|---|
| Consumers' sensitivity to sustainability (Cronbach's $\alpha$ = 0.927; variance explained = 0.61) | Q32.1. One has to limit car usage in city centres. |
| | Q32.2. I am concerned about environment degradation. |
| | Q32.3. I am ready to boycott a company that does not comply with social and environmental regulations. |
| | Q32.4. It is through technical progress that we will find solutions to prevent environmental degradation. |
| | Q32.5. It is by significantly modifying our lifestyles that can prevent the degradation of the environment. |
| | Q32.6. I prefer healthy products, without risk to my health. |
| | Q32.7. I often talk about pollution and the environment with my family, children, friends. |
| | Q32.8. During elections, issues regarding the environment are instrumental in my choice of candidate. |
| | Q32.9. I am in favour of awarding a penalty for products negatively impacting the environment. |
| | Q32.10. I am interested in sustainable development. |

*(continued)*

Table A2 (continued)

| Explanatory variables | Items |
|---|---|
| Consumers' actual sustainability behaviours (Cronbach's $\alpha$ = 0.860; variance explained = 0.55) | Q33.4. I always choose products with less packaging.<br>Q33.5. I make sure to buy local and seasonal vegetables.<br>Q33.7. I always turn off electrical devices that are in standby.<br>Q33.8. I bring batteries to appropriate places for collection.<br>Q33.10. I regularly give items that I no longer use to associations.<br>Q33.11. I buy products from organic farms.<br>Q33.12. I always invest in the most efficient appliances/energy. |
| Consumers' degree of liking of luxury (Cronbach's $\alpha$ = 0.756; variance explained = 0.68) | Q1.1. I love luxury brands.<br>Q1.4. I am ready to completely deprive myself to be able to purchase a beautiful luxury item.<br>Q1.7. Luxury makes me dream. |
| Consumers' perception of luxury as promoting true values (Cronbach's $\alpha$ = 0.691; variance explained = 0.76) | Q7.5. Luxury is about high quality products, known for their longevity.<br>Q7.6. Luxury preserves know-how and enhances manual skills. |
| Consumers' perception of luxury as superficial (Cronbach's $\alpha$ = 0.654; variance explained = 0.60) | Q1.3. I feel a little guilty when I buy a luxury product.<br>Q1.5. When I buy a luxury item I prefer not to get out of the store with its big logo bag.<br>Q1.6. Loving luxury is like living in a superficial way. |
| Consumers' perception that luxury creates social unrest (Cronbach's $\alpha$ = 0.750; variance explained = 0.67) | Q7.7. Luxury is about symbols of wealth inequality in humans.<br>Q7.8. Luxury led many people to buy products that are too expensive relative to their means.<br>Q7.11. Luxury encourages overconsumption; sustainable development encourages restraint and austerity. |
| Perceived contradiction (Cronbach's $\alpha$ = 0.750; variance explained = 0.80) | Q7.4. Luxury and sustainable development are contradictory.<br>Q7.12. Luxury has no future in a sustainably driven world. |

# Appendix B

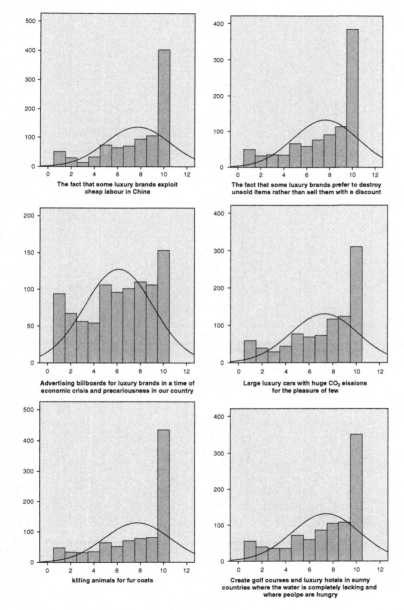

'Shocking' variable distribution

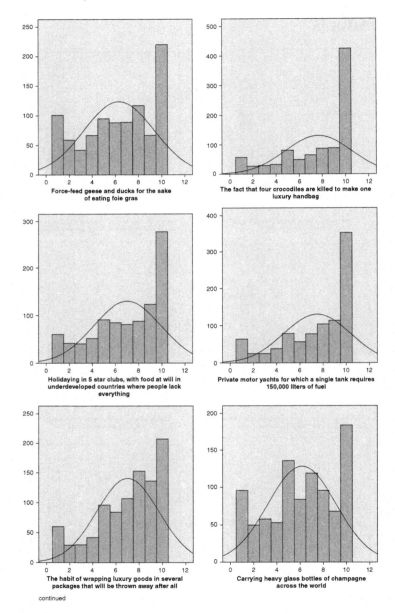

(Continued)

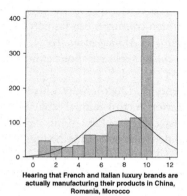
Hearing that French and Italian luxury brands are actually manufacturing their products in China, Romania, Morocco

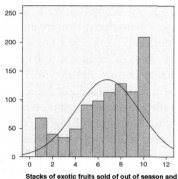
Stacks of exotic fruits sold of out of season and transported by airplane across the world

Young people who buy expensive accessories luxury brands, sunglasses, watches, bags

(Continued)

# References

Bain & Co. (2012). *Luxury goods worldwide market study 2012.* Milan: Altagamma.
Bendell, J., & Kleanthous, A. (2007). Deeper luxury: quality and style when the world matters (world wildlife federation-UK). www.wwf.org.uk/deeper luxury.
Brundtland Report. (1987). *Our common future.* New York: United Nations World Commission on Environment and Development.
Chadha, R., & Husband, P. (2007). *The cult of luxury: Asia's love affair with luxury.* London: Nicholas Brealey.

Chan, T.-Y., & Wong, C. W. Y. (2012). The consumption side of sustainable fashion supply chain: Understanding fashion consumer eco-fashion consumption decision. *Journal of Fashion Marketing & Management, 16*(2), 193–215.

Davies, I., Lee, Z., & Ine, A. (2012). Do consumers care about ethical luxury? *Journal of Business Ethics, 106*(1), 37–51.

De Barnier, V., Rodina, I., & Valette-Florence, P. (2006). Which luxury perceptions affect most consumer purchase behavior? A cross cultural exploratory study in France, the United Kingdom and Russia. *Congrés Paris-Venise des Tendences Marketing*, Paris. http://www.escp-eap.net/conferences/marketing/2006_cp/Materiali/Paper-/Fr/DeBarnier_Rodina_Valette Florence.pdf, pp. 1–27.

De Barnier, V., Falcy, S., & Valette-Florence, P. (2012). Do consumers perceive three levels of luxury? A comparison of accessible, intermediate and inaccessible luxury brands. *Journal of Brand Management, 19*(7), 623–636.

DeBeers. (2009). *Luxury: Considered*. London: Ledbury Research.

Douglas, C. J., & Chang, -J.-J. (1970). Analysis of individual differences in multidimensional scaling via an N-Way generalization of 'Echart-Young' decomposition. *Pshychometrika, 35*(September), 283–319.

Dubois, B., Laurent, G., & Czellar, S. (2001). Consumer rapport to luxury: Analyzing complex and ambivalent attitudes. Working Paper Series: CR 736/2001, HEC, Paris, France.

Esty, D. C., & Winston, A. S. (2007). *Green to Gold: How Smart Companies Use Environmental Strategy to Innovate, Create Value, and Build Competitive Advantage*. New York: John Wiley.

Gupta, S., & Ogden, D. T. (2009). To buy or not to buy? A social dilemma perspective on green buying. *Journal of Consumer Marketing, 26*(6), 376–391.

Han, J. J., Nunes, J., & Drèze, X. (2010). Signalling status with luxury goods: The role of brand prominence. *Journal of Marketing, 74*(4), 15–30.

Heider, F. (1958). *The Psychology of Interpersonal Relations*. New York: Wiley.

Ijaouane, V., & Kapferer, J. N. (2012). Developing luxury brands within luxury groups – Synergies without dilution. *Marketing Review St. Gallen, 1*(2012), 24–29.

Johnson, R. L. (2009). Organizational motivations for going green or profitability versus sustainability. *The Business Review, 13*(1), 22–28.

Jones, T. M. (1991), Ethical decision making by individuals in organizations: An issue contingent model. *Academy of Management Review, 16*(2), 366–395.

Joy, A., Sherry, J. F., Venkatesh, A., Wang, J., & Chan, R. (2012). Fast fashion, sustainability and the ethical appeal of luxury brands. *Fashion Theory, 16*(3), 273–296.

Kapferer, J. N. (1990). *Rumors*. New Brunswick, NJ: Transaction Books.
Kapferer, J. N. (1998). Why are we seduced by luxury brands? *Journal of Brand Management, 6*(1), 40–45.
Kapferer, J. N. (2010, November–December). All that glitters is not green: The challenge of sustainable luxury. *European Business Review*, 40–45.
Kapferer, J. N. (2012a). Abundant rarity: Key to luxury growth. *Business Horizons, 55*(5), 453–462.
Kapferer, J. N. (2012b, March–April). Why luxury should not delocalize: A critique of a growing tendency. *European Business Review*, 58–62.
Kapferer, J. N., & Bastien, V. (2009). The specificity of luxury management: Turning marketing upside down. *Journal of Brand Management, 16*(5/6), 311–322.
Kapferer, J. N., & Bastien, V. (2012). *The Luxury Strategy: Break the Rules of Marketing to Build Luxury Brands*. London: Kogan Page.
Kozinets, R., & Handleman, J. (2004). Adversaries of consumption: Consumer movements, activism, and ideologies. *Journal of Consumer Research, 31*(December), 691–704.
Luchs, M. G., & Mooradian, T. A. (2012). Sex, personality and sustainable consumer behaviour: Elucidating the gender effect. *Journal of Consumer Policy, 35*(1), 127–144.
Michalos, A. C., Creech, H., Swayze, N., Maurine Kahlke, P., Buckler, C., & Rempel, K. (2012). Measuring knowledge, attitudes and behaviours concerning sustainable development among tenth grade students in Manitoba. *Social Indicators Research, 106*(2), 213–238.
Okonkwo, U. (2009). Sustaining the luxury brand on the internet. *Journal of Brand Management, 16*(5/6), 302–310.
Osgood, C. E., & Tannenbaum, P. H. (1955). The principle of congruity in the prediction of attitude change. *Psychological Review, 62*(1), 42–55.
Porter, M., & Kramer, M. (2006). Strategy and society: The link between competitive advantage and corporate social responsibility. *Harvard Business Review, 84*(12), 78–92.
Shrum, L. J., McCarty, J., & Lowrey, T. (1995). Buyer characteristics of the green consumer and their implications for advertising strategy. *Journal of Advertising, 24*(2), 71–82.
Strong, C. (1997). The problems of translating fair trade principles into consumer purchase behaviour. *Marketing Intelligence & Planning, 15*(1), 32–37.
Vigneron, F., & Johnson, L. (2004). Measuring perceptions of brand luxury. *Journal of Brand Management, 11*(6), 484–506.

Weller, I., & Walter, S. (2008). Ecology and fashion: Development lines and prospects. www.inter-disciplinary.net/wp-content/uploads/2010/08/sabwalterpaper.pdf. Accessed June 2013.

**Jean-Noël Kapferer** is a worldly renowned authority on luxury. HEC Paris Graduate and Emeritus Professor, PhD Kellogg Business School (USA), he conducts his research at INSEEC Luxury on the mutations of luxury and luxury brand management. Honorary editor of the *Luxury Research Journal*, he has widely published his articles in international journals. Co-author of the reference book *The Luxury Strategy: Break the Rules of Marketing to Build Luxury Brands*, author of *How Luxury Brands Can Grow Yet Remain Rare*, he leads executive seminars on luxury all around the world (USA, China, Korea, and Europe) and is advisor to the president of INSEEC business school. JN Kapferer enjoys travelling, skiing, and windsurfing.

**Anne Michaut-Denizeau** is an Affiliate Professor at HEC Paris. Her research expertise is on new product management and more recently on sustainable development. She manages many luxury programmes at HEC Paris.

# Probing Brand Luxury: A Multiple Lens Approach

Karen W. Miller and Michael K. Mills

## Introduction

Despite a growing body of literature, there is no definitive answer to the question, 'What is brand luxury?' Take, for example, the brand Calvin Klein, ranked by Forbes as the third most desirable luxury brand (Miller 2010) – and also called a status brand (O'Cass and Choy 2008) and a premium brand (Quelch 2004). Luxury brand

---

This chapter was Reprinted from Miller, K. and Mills, M. (2012) 'Probing Brand Luxury: A Multiple Lens Approach', *Journal of Brand Management*, 20, pp. 41-51. With kind permission from the *Journal of Brand Management*. All rights reserved.

K.W. Miller (✉)
School of Management and Marketing, Faculty of Business, University of Southern Queensland, Toowoomba, Queensland 4350, Australia
e-mail: karen.miller@usq.edu.au

M.K. Mills
University of Southern California, Los Angeles, USA

© The Author(s) 2017
J.-N. Kapferer et al. (eds.), *Advances in Luxury Brand Management*,
Journal of Brand Management: Advanced Collections,
DOI 10.1007/978-3-319-51127-6_8

managers could rightly ask, 'Which is it?' Calvin Klein's perfume meets Atwal and Williams' (2009) definition of brand luxury, but Calvin Klein's jeans do not. Because Calvin Klein's underwear is inconspicuous it fails to meet Berthon et al.'s (2009) brand luxury definition. Calvin Klein fails on the criterion of exclusivity using Fionda and Moore's (2009) notion of brand luxury. Yet, in the market place (e.g., Nielsen; Forbes) and according to some branding scholars (e.g., Van Kempen 2004), Calvin Klein continues to be referred to as a luxury brand.

The issue here is the competing definitions of brand luxury (see Table 8), and a lack of clear parameters that delineate brand luxury from other similar terms (e.g., status and prestige) which create confusion about brand luxury. As such, current worldwide estimates of the brand luxury market remain contradictory, and include US$263 billion (Tynan et al. 2010), US$220 billion (Keller 2009), US$130 billion (Fionda and Moore 2009) and US$80 billion (Christodoulides et al. 2009). Brand managers are unable to precisely quantify the percentage of luxury that makes up their brand, or determine with accuracy whether the brand is luxurious or the net worth of the brand luxury market (Vickers and Renand 2003). This lack of consensus about brand luxury, what it is and how it should be operationalised (see Atwal and Williams 2009; Fionda and Moore 2009) needs to be addressed.

This chapter seeks to make a contribution through a multiple lens approach (Batada and Chandra 2003; Moreno et al. 2006). We do this by appraising the current literature looking for patterns and inconsistencies to uncover the truth about brand luxury. The intent is to harness a better understanding of brand luxury; provide parameters that sufficiently delineate brand luxury from prestigious and status brands; and provide clarity about brand luxury.

## Method

Using the multiple lens approach, the authors conducted a literature and secondary data search to identify published and unpublished brand luxury studies occurring between 1990 and 2010. This period

Table 8 Competing definitions, depictions of brand luxury

| Focus | Definitions and depictions of brand luxury | Authors |
|---|---|---|
| Individual meaning | • A matter of degree as judged by consumers, a celebration of personal creativity, expressiveness, intelligence, fluidity and above all meaning.<br>• Material + psychological levels of representation influenced by our social environmental and brand values.<br>• Indulging in one's pleasures and a demonstration of success.<br>• Experiential, encapsulating what a brand does (functional) and what a brand means to the individual (experiential). | Atwal and Williams (2009), Berthon et al. (2009), Dumoulin (2007), Gutsatz (2001), Kapferer and Bastien (2009) and Tynan et al. (2010) |
| Social meaning | • A conspicuous possession that is aesthetically pleasing offering status to the individual and that may be enjoyed.<br>• Scoring high on symbolic interactionism designed to associate the owner with a desired group, role or self-image.<br>• A desire to impress others, with the ability to pay particularly high prices and an ostentatious display of wealth.<br>• Social meaning (symbolic). | Berthon et al. (2009), Dubois and Duquesne (1993), Kapferer and Bastien (2009) and Vickers and Renand (2003) |
| Affordability | • Products and services that are not so expensive as to be out of reach.<br>• Being more affordable, more assessable and by targeting new consumers. | Silverstein and Fiske (2007) and Truong et al (2009) |

(*continued*)

**Table 8** (continued)

| Focus | Definitions and depictions of brand luxury | Authors |
|---|---|---|
| Prestige | • Used with prestige, holds considerable intangible worth.<br>• The highest level of prestige brands.<br>• A form of a prestige brand, with three levels: upmarket, premium and luxury. | Juggessur and Cohen (2009), Kim and Sohn (2009) and Vigneron and Johnson (1999, 2004) |
| Exclusivity | Exclusivity • Has some degree of exclusivity or rarity and a social mystique.<br>• Synonymous with selectivity if not exclusivity.<br>• Designed for an exclusive market and is derived from the Latin word *luxus*, which means indulgence of the senses regardless of cost. | Berthon et al. (2009), Godey et al. (2009), and Nueno and Quelch (1998) |
| Quality | • Good quality and design are associated with luxury.<br>• Products and services that possess higher levels of quality, taste and aspiration than other goods in the category | Husic and Cicic (2009), Prendergast and Wong (2003) and Silverstein and Fiske (2007) |

reflects considerable development in brand luxury research, and as prestige and status have been used interchangeably with brand luxury, these were also included in the search.

To search the relevant literature, first, a computer search of the Science Direct, Ebsco and Emerald databases and dissertation abstracts was performed to find references to brand luxury, luxury brands, prestigious/ premium brands and/or status brand articles. Second, a manual search consisted of reviewing and analysing the sources cited in the reference section of the literature reviews, articles and books on this topic. Finally, an Internet search was undertaken using Google, Google Scholar and Dogpile to locate articles, books, blogs and websites.

# Findings

Each of the seven lenses presents a different perspective on brand luxury. Our first lens is 'old luxe and the functional utility of brand luxury' and discusses the traditional and often contradictory and controversial perspective of brand luxury.

## Lens 1: Old Luxe and the Functional Utility of Brand Luxury

Old luxe, derived from the Latin word *luxus* meaning indulgence of the senses regardless of cost (Nueno and Quelch 1998), seems to be more product-centric (Chevalier and Mazzalovo 2008) and associated with rare or hard to obtain products, hand-crafted products of excellent quality and craftsmanship, offering performance longevity and excellence where high prices, aesthetics and ancestral history are important to the discernable consumer (Berry 1994; Kemp 1998; Phau and Prendergast 2000; Beverland 2004; Wetlaufer 2004; Kapferer and Bastien 2010). This consumer is a connoisseur, a person of good taste, savvy and does not need to look at the label to recognise the brand or designer, and is willing to be put on a waiting list to receive a limited edition, and purchases luxury for himself and/or to share with a selected few (Kapferer and Bastien 2009; Han et al. 2010).

Associated with old luxe are a number of *intangible* brand elements such as a careful brand management, corporate identity, culture and spirit, how visionary, trendy and up-to-date the brand is in the market (Dubois and Paternault 1995; Cailleux et al. 2009; Fionda and Moore 2009; Keller 2009), a brand that is a leader, successful (Kapferer and Bastien 2009), remarkably resilient (Beverland 2004) with a global reputation (Dubois and Duquesne 1993; Nueno and Quelch 1998; Aiello et al. 2009). To remain luxurious and not to be confused with premium brands, Kapferer and Bastien (2010) argue that luxury brands must stay true to their country-of-origin roots and keep manufacturing on home soil.

Uniqueness is an intangible brand element associated with old luxe and linked with originality, scarcity, creative excellence, creative imagination, innovative design, and creative quality and unique symbols, logos and package design (Vigneron and Johnson 1999; Keller 2009). Uniqueness, argues Nueno and Quelch (1998), refers to the individual imperfections on the hand-made luxury product that make it unique, original and difficult to copy or counterfeit. Alternatively, Dubois et al. (2001) and Dubois and Paternault (1995) classify uniqueness and scarcity jointly as having similar meanings, whereas Catry (2003) suggests that uniqueness may also mean one-off, limited edition or technorarity enabled by innovation. Juggessur and Cohen (2009) argue that these unique elements – one-off or limited editions – could also describe the fashion market and are, therefore, not limited to luxury *per se*.

Other authors agree uniqueness is not limited to luxury. Prahalad and Ramaswamy (2004) and Vargo and Lusch (2008) argue that uniqueness occurs through interaction and dialogue creating unique customer experiences. Cailleux et al. (2009) suggest that in luxury service markets an individual may feel like 'a prince' with extra special treatment creating a unique experience.

Our findings suggest that intangible elements such as uniqueness, country-of-origin, culture, success and leadership are not limited to luxury brands. These intangible elements are associated with brands in general (i.e., national brands) and are more likely to be antecedents to brand luxury.

## Lens 2: New Luxury and Brand Symbolism

New luxe differed to old luxe as trademarks moved from the inside (hidden) to be conspicuously displayed for all to see, and there is tangible evidence of the brand, its trademark, logo, name or initials. Some refer to this process as luxurification (Twitchell 2002). With new luxe, luxury is more accessible (Nobbs et al. 2008) and symbolism is more important than aesthetic beauty (Berry 1994; Dubois and Laurent 1996). The new luxury consumer makes money sooner, is younger, more upwardly mobile, flexible with finance options, and willing to trade-up and sacrifice in order to obtain and conspicuously display luxury brands (Dubois et al. 2005; Chadha and Husband 2006; Okonkwo 2007). The aspirational consumer and the nouveau rich are brand luxury's largest purchasers, while increasingly the connoisseur dissociates from the nouveau rich by paying exorbitant prices for inconspicuous (hidden) trade-marks, since only those 'in the know' can discern from the subtle signals that the brand is luxurious (Han et al. 2010). Predominantly, luxury brands are communicated to the masses through the media and the Internet – and *who* you are wearing is more important than *what* you are wearing.

To the new luxury consumer the tangible elements of brand luxury are a badge, a measure of social stratification by which consumers measure their own self-worth and the worth of others by the luxury brands worn and/or conspicuously displayed (Gao et al. 2008; Park et al. 2008). The visible symbols and markings ensure observers recognise the brand (Han et al. 2010), which is important to the *haves* (Nuevo rich; Parvenu) and the *have nots* (counterfeit purchasers or Poseur) (Han et al. 2010) who exhibit a bandwagon effect following others in their reference groups that have already purchased (Juggessur and Cohen 2009). Importantly, Kapferer and Bastien (2009, p. 315) assert that 'no luxury brand can hope to survive if it relies purely on clients who are only interested in reputed signs and recognition, the symbol rather than the substance; these people, those who are only interested in symbols, will drift from one symbol to another, from one logo to another'.

With new luxury, the product is less important than the symbolism (Atwal and Williams 2009; Cailleux et al. 2009) and trading up (Silverstein and Fiske 2007), mass luxury (Solomon and Buchanan 1991; Okonkwo 2007) and masstige brands (Truong et al. 2009) are terms describing this phenomena, developing into a billion dollar global industry (Keller 2009).

The increasing demand for luxury has brand managers experiencing a conundrum – to keep the traditions of old luxe and focus on the connoisseur, or 'cash in' on new luxe and focus on the aspirational consumer (Kapferer and Bastien 2009). This conundrum is causing some confusion about the term 'brand luxury' – that is, whether luxury is associated with prestige and the masses, or whether luxury is associated with extravagance and opulence for a few discernable consumers. As the appeal for luxury brands strengthens there is another added challenge for luxury brand managers, that of counterfeits (Juggessur and Cohen 2009), causing an increase in studies on how to deal with counterfeiters or the effects of counterfeiting (e.g., Clarke and Owens 2000; Gistri et al. 2009; Phau and Min 2009; Hieke 2010) or how far a luxury brand can be extended (Chen and Liu 2004; Hagtvedt and Patrick 2009).

## Lens 3: Levels of Brand Luxury

The higher levels of brand luxury are claimed to be the best or superior (Vigneron and Johnson 2004; Fernie et al. 2008) with higher levels of brand awareness, quality, taste and aspiration (Phau and Prendergast 2000) in a position of superiority with respect to its clients (Kapferer and Bastien 2009). These connotations of luxury levels are similar in conceptualisation to the term 'brand status' (O 'Cass and Choy 2008) or 'prestigious brand' (Vigneron and Johnson 2004).

The contention is that consumers seek conspicuous luxury to signal 'status' to others – the symbolic desire to belong to a superior class chosen according to individual dreams (Kapferer and Bastien 2010) – and that a consequence of brand luxury ownership is the apparent social elevation bestowed on an individual where she/he is perceived to be in a higher position of social class, or signifies a higher station in life (Shipman 2004). Status is an evaluative judgement and may be acquired through possessions (Eastman et al. 1999) and loud signalling (Han et al. 2010). Status, we assert, is a reason to buy brand luxury and is a consequence of brand luxury use and/or owner-ship and should not be confused with the term 'brand luxury'.

## Lens 4: Confusion about Luxury, Status and Prestige

Our findings indicate there is no real debate about how different brand luxury is to prestige and status, with two exceptions – Kapferer and Bastien (2010) and Vigneron and Johnson (1999). Kapferer and Bastien (2010) equate brand luxury with social stratification and being priceless (no price/quality ratio, no sales or discounts), timeless and associated with desires and dreams – which they allege differs to premium brands which are 'realistic', more serious, known for their functionality, performance, investment benefits and for having a price/quality ratio. Fundamentally, Kapferer and Bastien's (2010) distinction is based on what luxury and/or premium brands will *do* for the consumer, rather than the objective difference between luxury and premium (or prestige).

Contrastingly, Vigneron and Johnson (1999) argued that a luxury brand is a form of prestige and that prestigious brands have three levels: up-market, premium and luxury. In their latter study Vigneron and Johnson (2004) changed the term *premium* to *luxury* and developed the brand luxury index (BLI). After Vigneron and Johnson's (2004) study, a plethora of brand luxury typologies followed – adding to the confusion, rather than clarifying the term brand luxury and its proposed levels of distinction.

## Lens 5: Brand Luxury Typologies

Table 9 shows the inconsistencies in the brand luxury typologies in terms of dimensions and number of dimensions which range from 2 (Kapferer and Bastien 2009) to 10 dimensions (Keller 2009). More recently, Christodoulides et al. (2009) found it difficult to support Vigneron and Johnson (2004) study – finding Cronbach's alphas, factor loadings and AVEs were below the minimum threshold. Further, discriminant validity could not be supported reducing any clarity about what brand luxury is and how it is delineated from other similar concepts (e.g., prestige and status), or how brand luxury could be operationalised and what and how many dimensions brand luxury contains.

## Lens 6: The Co-Creation of Brand Luxury

These more recent brand typologies exposed an emergence of a new factor – the idea of brand luxury being co-created by the consumer and the brand owner through experiential consumption. Here, consumers are involved in the processes of both defining and creating value, and co-create their experience (Tsai 2005; Tynan et al. 2010). The *lived moment* within

**Table 9** Competing typologies and depictions of brand luxury

| Dimensions | Authors | Brand luxury typologies and depictions |
|---|---|---|
| 11 | Okonkwo (2007) | Are highly visible, have a distinct identity, a global reputation, emotional appeal, are innovative, creative, unique, appealing, constantly deliver premium quality, premium price with a tightly controlled distribution. |
| 10 | Keller (2009) | Maintaining a premium image, creation of intangible brand associations, aligned with quality, tangible elements like logos, symbols and packaging design, secondary associations with linked personalities or endorsers, controlled distribution, premium pricing, careful management, broad definition and legal protection of trademarks. |
| 9 | Fionda and Moore (2009) | Clear brand identity, luxury communications strategy, product integrity, brand signature, prestige price, exclusivity, history or a story, globally controlled distribution and a luxury organisational culture. |
| 7 | Kapferer (1997) | Include the attributes of quality, beauty, sensuality, exclusivity, history, high price and uniqueness. |
| 6 | Dubois et al. (2001) and Dubois and Paternault (1995) | Excellent quality, high price, scarcity and uniqueness, aesthetics and polysensuality, ancestral heritage and personal history, and superfluousness. |
| 6 | Alleres (2003) | The creators of the brand, the locations, the creations, recognition symbols, history and the brand name. |

*(continued)*

Table 9 (continued)

| Dimensions | Authors | Brand luxury typologies and depictions |
|---|---|---|
| 6 | Beverland (2005) | Attributes of authenticity such as heritage and pedigree, stylistic consistency, quality commitments, relationship to place, method of production and downplaying commercial considerations may be transferred to luxury brands. |
| 5 | Kim et al. (2009) | Encompassing several physical and psychological values, such as perceived conspicuous value, unique value, social value, hedonic value and quality value. |
| 5 | Phau and Prendergast (2000) | Evoke exclusivity, have a well-known brand identity, enjoy a high brand awareness and perceived quality and retain sales levels and customer loyalty. |
| 4 | Atwal and Williams (2009) | Moved beyond the traditional to be experiential and includes the dimensions of entertainment, education, escapist and aesthetic which will vary in levels of consumer participation and connection with the brand. |
| 4 | Wetlaufer (2004) | The significance of corporate identity, culture and spirit, as well as creative excellence is necessary in luxury brand development. |
| 3 | Moore and Birtwistle (2004) | Have iconic product and design with integrity, where the manufacturer has tight control over the product, endorsement, distribution and premium pricing. |
| 3 | Jackson (2004) | Is characterised by exclusivity, premium prices, image and status, which combine to make them desirable for reasons other than function. |

which brand luxury is experienced, the look and the sound of luxury, or how the consumer feels consuming luxury is paramount and forms part of the brand luxury image, as luxury is valued for its *lived* experience (Lageat et al. 2003; Tynan et al. 2010). Recent literature includes the services aspect of brand luxury, with Atwal and Williams (2009) and others advancing the proposition that the experience – whether *Entertainment, Education, Escapist or Aesthetic* – is everything!

## Lens 7: Experiential Consumption of Brand Luxury

Dumoulin (2007) suggests that experiencing luxury involves personal meaning, a celebration of personal creativity, expressiveness, intelligence and fluidity. There is some commonality in the literature that experiencing luxury is based on hedonism and aesthetics, desires realised and/or dreams fulfilled (Dubois et al. 2001; Lageat et al. 2003; Husic and Cicic 2009; Christodoulides et al. 2009; Kapferer and Bastien 2010). Hedonistic consumption (Hirschman and Holbrook 1982) is associated with multi-sensory pleasure, fantasy and fun dominating the utilitarian value of the consumption, where a consumer may generate internal imagery containing sights, sounds and tactile impressions. Kapferer and Bastien (2010) argue luxury should have a strong personal and hedonistic component – otherwise it is no longer luxury, but simply snobbery. However, consumers can and do experience hedonism without it being luxury (Hirschman and Holbrook 1982) – a visit to a theme park is hedonistic but not luxurious; sex is also hedonistic but not luxurious.

Clearly, there is an apparent change in what brand luxury is doing for the consumer. Experiential brand luxury consumption appears to be more about luxury for one's self or a limited shared experience with peers (e.g., a yacht trip to an exotic island), rather than the display of luxury for others. This suggests brand luxury may have moved full circle – beginning with being more for one's self than for others (old luxe) to becoming more about the display of luxury for others than one's self (symbolism) to experiential luxury, luxury for self-gratification or self-reward.

In summary, it seems that brand luxury can be functional (product-centric), symbolic (brand-centric) or experiential (experience-centric), valued for self-indulgent and hedonic purposes, or shared with others and valued for esteem maintenance or esteem building purposes. Consumers are willing to pay more for a brand on the basis of its apparent luxury. This behaviour is not limited to the basis of a person's income, as Van Kempen (2004) found even the poor are willing to pay more for the status associated with a luxury brand name (Calvin Klein).

## Discussion

From the findings, we conclude many of the terms associated with brand luxury are erroneous as they are shared with many brands (luxury or otherwise). We assert these elements are not part of the construct of brand luxury and should not be confused with the construct of brand luxury. In Table 10, we have listed these elements and classified them as antecedents or consequences. While some have argued that the degree to which these antecedents occur are a measure of the demarcation between luxury and the ordinary (Kemp 1998; Tynan et al. 2010) or luxury and prestige (Vigneron and Johnson 2004); (Kapferer and Bastien 2009,

Table 10 Antecedents and consequences of brand luxury

| Antecedents | Consequences |
|---|---|
| Unique or distinct identity | Extend, maintain or enhance self-image |
| Design of the brand, its name, logo, packaging and / or other tangible evidence | Functional, symbolic and/or experiential value; conspicuous value, unique value, social value or hedonic value |
| Personal creativity and expressive style | Association with the desired group |
| Quality of product or service delivery | Sensory pleasure or hedonism |
| Aesthetics and social mystique | Ostentatious display of wealth |
| Heritage, spirit, personal history, pedigree, a story or relationship with a place | To act as a status or success symbol |
| Positive brand images | To pay high or premium prices |

2010); (Kim et al. 2009), we disagree. We argue antecedents shown in Table 10 contribute to the notion of a brand, as well as prestigious or luxury brands. Similarly, the benefits derived from owning or using a luxury brand – privately or conspicuously – are related to the term 'brand luxury', but are not part of its conceptualisation. Clearly, what a luxury brand will do for a consumer is a benefit or a reason to buy and a consequence of brand ownership or brand usage.

Similarly, just as consumer benefits are not part of brand luxury, nor are managerial benefits or strategy decisions. These are mostly ongoing. The double vortex model of De Chernatony and Dall'olmo Riley (1998) is a useful framework to explain brand luxury market orientation and this idea of co-creation – which we argue is distinct from the concept of brand luxury. Management decisions and benefits listed in Table 11 may occur in brand luxury markets, prestige brand markets and national brand markets. These managerial strategy decisions and benefits are not exclusive to the brand luxury market but, rather, make a contribution to the perception of luxury and are a consequence of good brand management.

Ambiguity in the literature and the marketplace has contributed to the difficulty in differentiating luxury brands from prestige brands and status. Status is a consequence of conspicuous brand consumption and assiduous brand management, and is a benefit (consequence) of brand luxury and prestigious brands.

Prestigious brands are also conceptually different to brand luxury as prestigious brands are based on (positive) reputation, (high) honour, (high) esteem, (high) kudos and (high) regard associated with hierarchy and levels (see lens 3), where one brand appears better than another. Where the confusion seems to lie is with the overlap between prestige and luxury as, generally, luxury brands also have positive reputations, high

Table 11 Management strategy and/or benefits of brand luxury

| Management strategy | Management benefits of brand luxury |
| --- | --- |
| Exclusive or controlled distribution | Commanding of high or premium prices |
| Careful management | Retaining sales level |
| Legal protection of trademarks | Achievement of brand loyalty |
| Corporate culture | Well-known or global reputation |

**Table 12** Lexical items delineating brand luxury from prestigious (premium) brands

| Brand luxury | Prestigious brand |
|---|---|
| Magnificent | Reputation |
| Extravagance | Honour |
| Opulence | Esteem |
| Sumptuous | Kudos |
| Lavishness | High regard |

kudos and regard. However, Table 12 shows that brand luxury does differ to prestigious brands as magnificence, extravagance, opulence, sumptuousness and lavishness sufficiently capture the true essence of brand luxury.

# Conclusions

Our contribution to the literature is the clear distinction regarding the parameters of brand luxury. This chapter began with a confusing array of definitions, depictions, typologies and operationalisations of brand luxury (see Tables 8 and 9). By thoroughly researching the literature (using multiple lenses) we conclude that luxury has not really changed its meaning from 'old luxe'. Rather, what has changed is brand luxury's conspicuousness, the number of people who have access to luxury brands and their social stratification (old money versus new money), as well as the prominence and dominance of services over products in the marketplace (Vargo and Lusch 2008) – which has created an intangible brand luxury experience. Tables 10–12 provide new knowledge on the gap concerning the indistinctiveness of brand luxury.

# Brand Academic and Brand Managerial Implications

Tables 10–12 add value to both branding academics and managers by delineating brand luxury from its antecedents and consequences (Table 10), brand management strategy, or benefits of good brand management (Table 11) and prestige (see Table 12). One of the limitations with Table 10 and Table 11 is not all brand luxury antecedents, consequences and brand management strategies/benefits are included, only those items that cloud the conceptualisation of brand luxury were included. Antecedents such as dreams, desires and income have been excluded and would need to be added if future branding academics or managers are to better understand the drivers (or antecedents) of brand luxury consumption.

Tables 10–12 provide branding academics and branding managers with a place to begin, as they provide information on what is brand luxury and what is not. Further, the lexical items in Tables 12 provide academics and managers with a basis for how brand luxury can be operationalised, measured and compared against prestigious brands. This is important as, increasingly, brand luxury managers face a conundrum whether to reduce their brand portfolio or increase their brand portfolio. Brand managers may use this information to measure the effects of their decision (extend or reduce) to discover if any changes have occurred to perceptions of brand luxury. Another area in which this chapter provides value is to the brand luxury industry, as it provides clarity about what is brand luxury and how brand luxury differs from prestigious brands, enabling consistent and accurate measurement of the net worth of the brand luxury market.

# References

Aiello, G. E. A. (2009). An international perspective on brand luxury and country-of-origin effect. *Journal of Brand Management*, 16(5/6), 323–337.

Alleres, D. (2003). *Competing Marketing Strategies of Luxury Fashion Companies*. Adapted, translated and cited M. Bruce & C. Kratz. New York: Elsevier Butterworth-Heinemann.

Atwal, G., & Williams, A. (2009). Luxury brand marketing – The experience is everything. *Journal of Brand Management*, 16(5/6), 338–346.

Batada, A., & Chandra, A. (2003). *Shifting the Lens: Utilizing a Multiple Method Approach to Explore Perceptions of Stress and Coping among Urban African American Adolescents*. Baltimore, MD: Bloomberg School of Public Health, Johns Hopkins University, November.

Berry, C. J. (1994). *The Idea of Luxury: A Conceptual and Historical Investigation*. Cambridge, MA: Cambridge University Press.

Berthon, P., Pitt, L., Parent, M., & Berthon, J.-P. (2009). Aesthetics and ephemerality: Observing and preserving the luxury brand. *California Management Review*, *52*(1), 45–66.

Beverland, M. (2004). Uncovering 'theories-in-use': Building luxury wine brands. *European Journal of Marketing*, *38*(4), 446–466.

Beverland, M. B. (2005). Crafting brand authenticity: The case of luxury wines. *Journal of Management Studies*, *42*, 1003–1029.

Cailleux, H., Mignot, C., & Kapferer, J. N. (2009). Is CRM for luxury brands. *Journal of Brand Management*, *16*(5/6), 406–412.

Catry, B. (2003). The great pretenders: The magic of luxury goods. *Business Strategy Review*, *14*(3), 7–11.

Chadha, R., & Husband, P. (2006). *The Cult of the Luxury Brand: Inside Asia's Love Affair with Luxury*. London: Nicholas Brealey International.

Chen, K. J., & Liu, C. M. (2004). Positive brand extension trial and choice of parent brand. *Journal of Product and Brand Management*, *13*(1), 25–36.

Chevalier, M., & Mazzalovo, G. (2008). *Luxury Brand Management: A World of Privilege*. Singapore: Wiley and Sons.

Christodoulides, G., Michaelidou, N., & Li, C. H. (2009). Measuring perceived brand luxury: An evaluation of the BLI scale. *Journal of Brand Management*, *16*(5/6), 395–405.

Clarke, I., & Owens, M. (2000). Trademark rights in gray markets. *International Marketing Review*, *17*(3), 272–288.

De Chernatony, L., & Dall'olmo Riley, F. (1998). Modelling the components of the brand. *European Journal of Marketing*, *32*(11/12), 1076–1090.

Dubois, B., & Duquesne, P. (1993). The market for luxury goods: Income versus culture. *European Journal of Marketing*, *27*(1), 35–44.

Dubois, B., & Laurent, G. (1996). The functions of luxury: A situational approach to excursionism. In K. P. Corfman & J. G. Lynch Jr. (Eds.), *Advances in Consumer Research Provo* (Vol. 23, pp. 470–477). UT: Association for Consumer Research.

Dubois, B., & Paternault, C. (1995). Observations: Understanding the world of international luxury brands: The 'dream formula. *Journal of Advertising Research*, *35*(4), 69–76.

Dubois, B., Laurent, G., & Czellar, S. (2001). Consumer rapport to luxury: Analysing complex and ambivalent attitudes. Working paper 736, HEC School of Management, Jouy-en-Josas, France.

Dubois, B., Czellar, S., & Laurent, G. (2005). Consumer segments based on attitudes towards luxury: Empirical evidence from twenty countries. *Marketing Letters, 16*(2), 115–128.

Dumoulin, D. (2007, March). What is today's definition of luxury? *Admap*, 27–30.

Eastman, J. K., Goldsmith, R. E., & Flynn, L. R. (1999). Status consumption in consumer behaviour: Scale development and validation. *Journal of Marketing Theory and Practice, 7*(3), 41–51.

Fernie, J., Moore, C., Lawrie, A., & Hallsworth, A. (2008). The internationalisation of the high fashion brand: The case of central London. *Journal of Product and Brand Management, 6*(3), 151–162.

Fionda, A. M., & Moore, C. M. (2009). The anatomy of the luxury fashion brand. *Journal of Brand Management, 16*(5/6), 347–363.

Gao, L., Norton, M. J. T., Zhang, Z.-M., & To, C. K.-M. (2008). Potential niche markets for luxury fashion goods in China. *Journal of Fashion Marketing and Management, 13*(4), 514–526.

Gistri, G., Romani, S., Pace, S., Gabrielli, V., & Grappi, S. (2009). Consumption practices of counterfeit luxury goods in the Italian context. *Journal of Brand Management, 16*(5/6), 364–374.

Godey, B., Lagier, J., & Pederzoli, D. A. (2009). A measurement scale of 'Aesthetic style' applied to luxury goods stores. *International Journal of Retail and Distribution Management, 37*, 527–537.

Gutsatz, M. (2001). Le sage et le createur: Elements pour une analyse des strategies des marquees de luxe. *Decisions Marketing, 23*, 23–33.

Hagtvedt, H., & Patrick, V. M. (2009). The broad embrace of luxury: Hedonic potential as a driver of brand extendibility. *Journal of Consumer Psychology, 19*(4), 608–618.

Han, Y. J., Nunes, J. C., & Dreze, X. (2010). Signalling status with luxury goods: The role of brand prominence. *Journal of Marketing, 74*(July), 15–30.

Hieke, S. (2010). Effects of counterfeits on the image of luxury brands: An empirical study from the customer perspective. *Journal of Brand Management, 18*, 159–173.

Hirschman, E. C., & Holbrook, M. B. (1982). Hedonic consumption: Emerging concepts, methods and propositions. *Journal of Marketing, 46*(Summer), 92–101.

Husic, M., & Cicic, M. (2009) Luxury consumption factors. *Journal of Fashion Marketing Management, 13*(2), 231–245.

Jackson, T. (2004). *International Retail Marketing.* Oxford: Elsevier Butterworth-Heinemann.

Juggessur, J., & Cohen, G. (2009). Is fashion promoting counterfeit brands? *Journal of Brand Management, 16*(5/6), 383–394.

Kapferer, J.-N. (1997). Managing luxury brands. *Journal of Brand Management, 4,* 251–260.

Kapferer, J. N., & Bastien, V. (2009). The specificity of luxury management: Turning marketing upside down. *Journal of Brand Management, 16*(5/6), 311–322.

Kapferer, J. N., & Bastien, V. (2010). *The Luxury Strategy: Break the Rules of Marketing to Build Luxury Brands.* London: Kogan-Page.

Keller, K. L. (2009). Managing the growth trade-off: Challenges and opportunities in luxury branding. *Journal of Brand Management, 16*(5/6), 290–301.

Kemp, S. (1998). Perceiving luxury and necessity. *Journal of Economic Psychology, 19*(5), 591–606.

Kim, G., Kim, A., & Sohn, S. Y. (2009). Conjoint analysis for luxury brand outlet malls in Korea with consideration of customer lifetime value. *Expert Systems with Applications, 36,* 922–932.

Lageat, T., Czellar, S., & Laurent, G. (2003). Engineering hedonic attributes to generate perceptions of luxury: Consumer perception of an everyday sound. *Marketing Letters, 14*(2), 97–109.

Miller, R. K. (2010). *Most desirable luxury brands (section 36.1) cited in in Retail Business Market Research Handbook,* 12th edn. MarketResearch.com, pp. 182–183.

Moore, C. M., & Birtwistle, G. (2004). The Burberry business model: Creating an international luxury fashion brand. *International Journal of Retail & Distribution Management, 32*(8), 412–422.

Moreno, J. F., Smith, D. G., Parker, S., Clayton-Pederson, A. R., & Teraguchi, D. H. (2006). *Using Multiple Lenses: An Examination of the Economic and Racial/ethnic Diversity of College Students.* San Francisco, CA: The James Irvine Foundation.

Nobbs, K., Birtwistle, G., & Fiorito, S. (2008). *Burberry; The Accessible Luxury Brand, 8th European Association for Education and Research in Consumer Distribution Conference.* London: EAERCD.

Nueno, J. L., & Quelch, J. A. (1998). The mass marketing of luxury. *Business Horizons, 41*(6), 61–68.

O'Cass, A., & Choy, E. (2008). Studying Chinese generation Y consumers' involvement in fashion clothing and perceived brand status. *Journal of Product and Brand Management, 17*(5), 341–352.

Okonkwo, U. (2007). *Luxury Fashion Branding: Trends, Tactics, Techniques.* Basingstoke, Hampshire, UK: Palgrave Macmillan

Park, H. J., Rabolt, N. J., & Kyung, S. J. (2008). Purchasing global luxury brands among young Korean consumers. *Journal of Fashion Marketing and Management, 12*(2), 244–259.

Phau, I., & Min, T. (2009). Devil wears (counterfeit) Prada: A study of antecedents and outcomes of attitudes towards counterfeits of luxury brands. *Journal of Consumer Marketing, 26*(1), 15–27.

Phau, I., & Prendergast, G. (2000). Conceptualizing the country of origin of brand. *Journal of Marketing Communications, 6*(3), 159–170.

Prahalad, C. K., & Ramaswamy, V. (2004). Co-creation experiences: The next practice in value creation. *Journal of Interactive Marketing, 18*(3), 5–14.

Prendergast, G., & Wong, C. (2003). Parental influence on the purchase of luxury brands of infant apparel: An exploratory study in Hong Kong. *Journal of Consumer Marketing, 20*, 157–169.

Quelch, J. A. (2004). Marketing the premium product. *Business Horizons, 30*(3), 38–45.

Shipman, A. (2004). Lauding the leisure class: Symbolic content and conspicuous consumption. *Review of Social Economy, 62*(3), 277–289.

Silverstein, M., & Fiske, N. (2007). *Trading up: Why consumers want new luxury goods and how companies create them.* New York: Portfolio.

Solomon, M. R., & Buchanan, B. (1991). A role-theoretic approach to product symbolism: Mapping a consumption constellation. *Journal of Business Research, 22*(2), 95–109.

Truong, Y., McColl, R., & Kitchen, P. J. (2009). New luxury brand positioning and the emergence of masstige brands. *Journal of Brand Management, 16*(5/6), 375–382.

Tsai, S. P. (2005). Impact of personal orientation on luxury-brand purchase value: An international investigation, International. *Journal of Marketing Research, 47*(4), 429–454.

Twitchell, J. B. (2002) *Living it up: America's love affair with luxury.* New York: Columbia University Press.

Tynan, C., McKechnie, S., & Chhuon, C. (2010). Co-creating value for luxury brands. *Journal of Business Research, 63*(11), 1156–1163.

Van Kempen, L. (2004). Are the poor willing to pay a premium for designer labels? A field experiment in Bolivia. *Oxford Development Studies, 32*(2), 205–223.

Vargo, S. L., & Lusch, R. F. (2008). Service-dominant logic: Continuing the evolution. *Journal of Academy of Marketing Science, 36*(1), 1–10.

Vickers, J. S., & Renand, F. (2003). The marketing of luxury goods: An exploratory study – Three conceptual dimensions. *Journal of Marketing Review, 3*(4), 459–478.

Vigneron, F., & Johnson, L. W. (1999). A review and a conceptual framework of prestige seeking consumer behaviour. *Academy of Marketing Science Review, 1*, 1–15.

Vigneron, F., & Johnson, L. W. (2004). Measuring perceptions of brand luxury. *Journal of Brand Management, 11*(6), 484–506.

Wetlaufer, S. (2004). The perfect paradox of star brands: An interview with Bernard Arnault of LVMH. *Harvard Business Review, 79*(9), 117.


**Karen W. Miller** spent many years as a practising marketer before moving into academia and studying brands. Most of Karen's work is in the area of brand image, brand value and brand luxury and much of it from a consumer's perspective. Aside from branding research, Karen also has a keen interest in market research and multiple methods of data collection. Karen is still active in industry research conducting studies about branding in the wine industry, event management and marketing communications.

**Michael K. Mills** career spans some 30 years in senior positions in industry, academia and as a consultant to major multinational firms. He has published more than 70 professional and trade articles in such publications as the *Journal of Advertising Research, Journal of Public Policy and Marketing, Journal of the Academy of Marketing Science, Journal of Consumer Affairs, Journal of Retailing,* and *Contemporary Psychology,* among others.

# Managing the Growth Tradeoff: Challenges and Opportunities in Luxury Branding

### Kevin Lane Keller

## Introduction

Luxury brands are perhaps one of the purest examples of branding, as the brand and its image are often key competitive advantages that create enormous value and wealth for organisations. Pegged as a 220 billion US$ industry at retail by some observers, marketers for luxury brands such as Prada, Gucci, Cartier and Louis Vuitton manage lucrative franchises that have endured for decades.[1]

---

This chapter was Reprinted from Keller, K. (2009) 'Managing the Growth Trade-off: Challenges and Opportunities in Luxury Branding', *Journal of Brand Management*, 16, pp. 290–301. With kind permission from the *Journal of Brand Management*. All rights reserved.

[1] For a number of practical perspectives, see the September 17, 2007 special issue of *Fortune* on luxury branding.

K.L. Keller (✉)
Department of Marketing, Tuck School of Business, Dartmouth College, Hanover, USA
e-mail: Kevin.L.Keller@tuck.dartmouth.edu

**Table 13** Ten defining characteristics of luxury brands

(1) Maintaining a premium image for luxury brands is crucial; controlling that image is thus a priority.
(2) Luxury branding typically involves the creation of many intangible brand associations and an aspirational image.
(3) All aspects of the marketing program for luxury brands must be aligned to ensure quality products and services and pleasurable purchase and consumption experiences.
(4) Brand elements besides brand names – logos, symbols, packaging, signage and so on – can be important drivers of brand equity for luxury brands.
(5) Secondary associations from linked personalities, events, countries and other entities can be important drivers of brand equity for luxury brands.
(6) Luxury brands must carefully control distribution via a selective channel strategy.
(7) Luxury brands must employ a premium pricing strategy with strong quality cues and few discounts and mark downs.
(8) Brand architecture for luxury brands must be managed very carefully.
(9) Competition for luxury brands must be defined broadly as they often compete with other luxury brands from other categories for discretionary consumer dollars.
(10) Luxury brands must legally protect all trademarks and aggressively combat counterfeits.

Just like marketers in less expensive and more 'down-to-earth' categories, however, marketers guiding the fortunes of luxury brands must do so in a constantly evolving – and sometimes rapidly changing – marketing environment. Globalisation, new technologies, shifting consumer cultures and other forces necessitate that marketers of luxury brands be skilful and adept at their brand stewardship. Marketers of luxury brands face continual challenges, and being a skilled marketer is becoming a vital prerequisite for success.

This chapter begins by briefly outlining 10 characteristics that help to define luxury branding (see Table 13). Although these 10 characteristics suggest some strategic and tactical guidelines, we offer more detailed discussion of one particularly difficult challenge for luxury branding – the need to manage growth tradeoffs.[2] We place emphasis on two key

---
[2] For an excellent prescriptive review of luxury branding in the fashion sector, see Okonkwo, U. (2007). *Luxury fashion branding: Trends, tactics, and techniques*. New York, NY: Palgrave Macmillan.

areas – brand equity measurement and brand architecture – that can help luxury brand marketers design marketing strategies and tactics to address these tradeoffs.

## Ten Defining Characteristics of Luxury Brands

(1) *Maintaining a premium image for luxury brands is crucial; controlling that image is thus a priority.* It goes without saying that the success of a luxury brand is predicated on establishing a premium image that can justify a luxury price. This premium image often revolves in some way, extrinsically, around prestige and, intrinsically, around novel, unique product or service features. Given that the target market for luxury brands is often the affluent or near-affluent, this premium image typically needs to be designed to be globally relevant. Obviously, given its importance, marketers of luxury brands must be diligent in ensuring that the brand's image, especially its more intangible aspects, is strong, consistent and cohesive over time.

(2) *Luxury branding typically involves the creation of many intangible brand associations and an aspirational image.* Part of the appeal of a luxury brand is that the brand takes on so much meaning. Many luxury brands have storied histories and rich heritages. They also carry symbolic value in their status and achievement. As such, there is a strong aspirational component to their image that creates a 'trickle down' effect to a broader audience via public relations, word-of-mouth and so on. Non-users become prospects, in part, by virtue of a desire to emulate or at least enjoy the same rewards as current luxury brand users. Much of the transfer of this brand affiliation from current users to prospects is carried out via non-paid media channels and interpersonal influences of various kinds. Through these social influence mechanisms, many prospects add the luxury brand to their consideration set of possible discretionary purchases.

(3) *All aspects of the marketing programme for luxury brands must be aligned to ensure quality products and services, and pleasurable purchase and consumption experiences.* Although luxury brands, compared with many other types of brands, gain their value in their intangibles, it is

also imperative that the more direct performance considerations are of sufficiently high quality to match or exceed customer expectations (Silverstein and Fiske 2003). Premium prices necessitate this to some extent anyway, but luxury brands must be sure to not raise any doubts in customers' minds as to the merits of their purchase. Because of these high expectations, all aspects of the purchase and consumption experience matters, putting pressure on marketers of luxury brands to achieve flawless value delivery every step of the way.

(4) *Brand elements aside from brand names – logos, symbols, packaging, signage and so on – can be important drivers of brand equity for luxury brands.* Given the fundamental importance of the brand to the value proposition for luxury brands, brand elements themselves are very important. Brand names, logos, symbols, packaging, signage or any other trademarkable information for luxury brands may help to convey a premium, prestige image. They can facilitate brand awareness, and can serve as important signals of quality and prestige to customers themselves or to people who customers care about.

(5) *Secondary associations from linked personalities, events, countries and other entities can be important drivers of brand equity for luxury brands.* Another way that marketers of luxury brands can reinforce the inherent value they place in their products and services is to link them to other entities – people, places and things – that have their own positive images and associations. These associations can then become indirectly linked to the luxury brand as a result. The use of popular celebrities, prestigious events or a desirable country-of-origin is common in luxury branding, as these entities often have valuable associations that help to reinforce those of the luxury brand.

(6) *Luxury brands must carefully control distribution via a selective channel strategy.* Because of the highly targeted market segments involved and the need for exclusivity and prestige, retail distribution is usually highly selective and controlled, to ensure that it closely aligns with the brand promise. For maximum control, many luxury brands have their own retail outlets and company stores. Online experiences are challenging for luxury brands, which usually have a strong inter-personal component, although some brands are making progress along that score.

(7) *Luxury brands often employ a premium pricing strategy with strong quality cues and few discounts and markdowns.* To justify a premium price, luxury brands must create strong intrinsic and extrinsic value for their customers. In addition, they must also reinforce that value with well-chosen quality cues, for example, attractive packaging, personalised customer service and generous warranties. Perhaps the strongest quality cue of them all, however, is the price itself, and for this reason alone luxury brands use discounts and any other form of price markdowns very selectively. Excessive price movement or volatility could send the wrong signal as to the worth of the brand.

(8) *Brand architecture for luxury brands must be managed very carefully.* Because of the competing needs, on the one hand, to be selective, discerning and exclusive in all aspects of the marketing for luxury brands and, on the other hand, to continue to grow revenue and profitability, brand architecture becomes crucial. Brand architecture reflects the number and nature of common or distinctive brand elements applied to the different products sold by the firm. In other words, which brand elements can be applied to which products and what is the nature of new and existing brand elements to be applied to new products? Because there is often a vertical dimension to a luxury brand's growth strategies in that lower-priced offerings are developed to attract new customers, brand architecture becomes even more critical, as discussed in more detail below.

(9) *Competition for luxury brands must be defined broadly, as they often compete with other luxury brands from other categories for discretionary consumer dollars.* In developing the positioning of luxury brands and their associated marketing programmes and activities, it is important to recognise that luxury brands do not just compete with other brands in their category as much potentially as with other luxury brands in other categories. Given that luxury brands by definition go beyond the basic necessities offered by other brands in their category, their purchase is more discretionary. In this regard, luxury brands may compete to gain access to consumers' consideration sets with vacations, home remodelling projects or any other potentially discretionary purchase in any other category.

(10) *Luxury brands must legally protect all trademarks and aggressively combat counterfeits.* Finally, because of their significant price margins and premiums, luxury brands are vulnerable to much illegal activity in the form of counterfeiting and so on. Marketers must proactively protect their brand in as many ways as possible, as well as vigorously enforce any infractions.

## Managing Growth Tradeoffs with Luxury Brands

The 10 observations on the defining characteristics of luxury brands and their branding practices provide a basic foundation as to how luxury brands can be marketed. Of course, the actual strategies and tactics will vary somewhat by the specific nature of the luxury brand and the categories in which it is sold.

In many ways, the most fundamental challenge of marketing and brand management for all brands – including luxury brands – is how to reconcile or address the many potential tradeoffs that exist in making marketing decisions (Keller and Webster 2008). Table 14 lists a number of the different possible tradeoffs or conflicts that can occur in making strategic, tactical, financial or organisational decisions for a brand. Clearly, tradeoffs in brand marketing are pervasive, and must be made in the context of constrained – and often fairly limited – resources.

Marketers of luxury brands face some very challenging tradeoffs in their marketing that can often mean the difference between success and failure. Three of the more notable tradeoffs are as follows:

(1) *Exclusivity vs accessibility.* Luxury brands have to be aspirational, and to be seen as something special and out of the ordinary, but, at the same time, may need to be seen as relevant to an expanded customer base in order to maintain sufficient growth in sales and profits over time.
(2) *Classic vs contemporary images.* In a related sense, luxury brands may have much history, heritage and experiences that long-time customers cherish, but this may not be seen as so relevant to younger, prospective customers adopting a more contemporary lens by which to judge brands.

**Table 14** Some brand marketing tradeoffs

| Strategic | Financial |
|---|---|
| Retaining customers vs acquiring customers | Short-run vs long-run objectives |
| Brand expansion vs brand fortification | Sales-generating vs brand-building activities |
| Product performance vs brand image | Accountable or measurable tactics vs non-measurable tactics |
| Points of parity vs points of difference | Quality maximisation vs cost minimisation |
| *Tactical* | *Organisational* |
| Push vs pull | Global vs local |
| Continuity vs change | Customisation vs standardisation |
| Classic vs contemporary image | Top down vs bottom Up |
| Independent vs universal image | Internal vs external |

(3) *Acquisition vs retention.* Finally, marketers of luxury brands must determine the optimal allocation of marketing resources and efforts towards profitable existing customers in the short run vs potentially profitable prospective customers in the long run.

Note that these tradeoffs are actually closely related, and reflect the challenge in managing the growth of a luxury brand over time. In a broad sense, marketers of luxury brands face a dilemma, in that the marketing strategies that reinforce exclusivity, heritage and retention may not be so useful in terms of accessibility, contemporariness and acquisition.

There are a number of areas that luxury brand marketers must consider to address this 'growth tradeoff', but two potentially critical areas deal with brand equity measurement and brand architecture, developed in detail below.

## Brand Equity Measurement

The first important area in successfully managing the growth of luxury brands over time deals with brand equity measurement. To understand the nature of the growth tradeoff and any problems it may pose, marketers of luxury brands must be extremely close to both existing and prospective customers. Only in this way can they assess how relevant their brand equity is across diverse market segments. Although there is a vast variety of different kinds of metrics that can be employed to measure brand equity,[3] the challenge for luxury brands is that metrics are less well developed in several areas for which luxury brands are most distinctive. In this section, we highlight a set of measures that tap into brand strength, stature, imagery, feelings and expectations.

## Brand Strength and Stature

The advertising agency Young and Rubicam (Y&R) has developed a comprehensive model of brand equity called BrandAsset Valuator (BAV). On the basis of research involving approximately 500,000 consumers in 44 countries, BAV provides comparative measures of the brand equity of thousands of brands across hundreds of different categories. According to BAV, there are five key components — or pillars — of brand equity[4]:

- *Differentiation* measures the degree to which a brand is seen as different from others.
- *Energy* measures the brand's sense of momentum.
- *Relevance* measures the breadth of a brand's appeal.
- *Esteem* measures how well the brand is regarded and respected.
- *Knowledge* measures how familiar and intimate consumers are with the brand.

Differentiation, energy and relevance combine to determine *Energised brand strength*. These three pillars point to the brand's future value. Esteem and knowledge together create *Brand stature*, which is more of a 'report card' on past performance.

---

[3] For a review of brand equity measurement issues, see Keller, K. L. (2006). Measuring Brand Equity. In R. Grover and M. Vriens (Eds.), *Handbook of Marketing Research – Do's and Don'ts* (pp. 546–568). Thousand Oaks, London and New Delhi: Sage Publications.

[4] For more information on BAV, see Gerzema, J. and Lebar, E. *The Brand Bubble*, forthcoming.

The relationships among these dimensions – a brand's 'pillar pattern' – reveal much about its current and future status. Energised brand strength and brand stature combined form the *PowerGrid*, depicting the stages in the cycle of brand development – each with characteristic pillar patterns – in successive quadrants. Strong new brands show higher levels of differentiation and energy than relevance, although both esteem and knowledge are lower still. Leadership brands show high levels on all pillars. Finally, declining brands show high knowledge – evidence of past performance – a lower level of esteem, and even lower relevance, energy and differentiation.

Traditional luxury brands are rated very highly by consumers on differentiation and esteem, although due to their aspirational nature and mystique, they may not score nearly as high on relevance and knowledge. Marketers of these goods should monitor these perceptions closely to ensure that the luxury brand maintains its special status.

Interestingly, Y&R researchers have identified the emergence of many 'new luxury brands' in their BAV database (Young & Rubicam Brand Asset Consulting 2005). As has also been observed by other researchers, these new luxury brands are characterised by products and services that, because of their higher levels of quality, taste and aspiration, sell at much higher prices than conventional goods, but at much higher volumes than traditional luxury goods. Y&R emphasises the importance of consumer engagement with these new luxury brands, more so than is the case with traditional luxury goods and their emphasis on status. They cite as examples Coach leatherwear, Bath & Body Works body lotion, Starbucks coffee and Grey Goose vodka.

## Brand Imagery

Brand strength and stature measures provide useful macro-perspectives. More micro-perspectives are useful as well. Much of the equity with luxury brands is intangible, and resides in its brand imagery. Brand imagery deals with the extrinsic properties of a product or service, including the ways in which the brand attempts to meet customers' psychological or social needs. Brand imagery is how people think about a brand abstractly, rather than what they think the brand actually does. Thus, imagery refers to more intangible aspects of the brand. Imagery associations can be formed directly (from a consumer's own experiences and contact with the product, brand, target market or usage situation) or indirectly (through the depiction of these same considerations as communicated in brand advertising or by some other source of information, such as word of mouth).

Many kinds of intangibles can be linked to a brand, but four categories can be highlighted:

1. *User profiles* is the type of person or organisation who uses the brand. This imagery may result in a profile or mental image held by customers of actual users or more aspirational, idealised users. Associations of a typical or idealised brand user may be based on descriptive demographic factors or more abstract psychographic factors. Democratic factors include gender, age, race and income; psychographic factors might include attitudes toward life, careers, possessions, social issues or political institutions (e.g. a brand user might be seen as iconoclastic or as more traditional and conservative). Clearly, with luxury brands, more idealised user images often come into play.
2. *Purchase and usage situations* are under what conditions or situations the brand could or should be bought and used. Associations of a typical purchase situation may be based on a number of different considerations, such as type of channel (e.g. seen as sold through department stores, specialty stores or through the Internet or some other means), specific stores (e.g. Macy's, Foot Locker, or Bluefly.com) and ease of purchase and associated rewards (if any). Similarly, associations of a typical usage situation may be based on a number of different considerations, such as particular time of the day, week, month or year to use the brand; location to use the brand (e.g. inside or outside the home) and type of activity in which the brand is used (e.g. formal or informal). Luxury brands often have strong usage associations, although one challenge for some luxury brands is that if they are seen as too 'precious' or special, they may not be used frequently enough. Chivas Regal ran the ad campaign 'What Are You Saving the Chivas For?' for this very reason.
3. *Personality and values* reflect the fact that a brand, like a person, can be characterised as being 'modern', 'old-fashioned', 'lively' or 'exotic.'

Brand personality reflects how people feel about a brand as a result of what they think the brand is or does, the manner by which the brand is marketed and so on. Brands may also take on values. Brand personality is often related to the descriptive usage imagery, but also involves much richer, more contextual information. Five dimensions of brand personality (with corresponding sub-dimensions) that have been identified are sincerity (e.g. down-to-earth, honest, wholesome and cheerful), excitement (e.g. daring, spirited, imaginative and up-to-date), competence (e.g. reliable, intelligent and successful), sophistication (e.g. upper class and charming) and ruggedness (e. g. outdoorsy and tough).[5] Many luxury brands have associations of sophistication as part of their positioning, but also often competence or even excitement.

4. *History, heritage and experiences* are associations with a brand's past and certain noteworthy events in its history. These types of associations may involve distinctly personal experiences and episodes, or may be related to past behaviours and experiences of friends, family or others. Consequently, these types of associations may be fairly idiosyncratic across people, although sometimes they may exhibit certain commonalties. Alternatively, these associations may be more public and broad-based and may therefore be shared to a larger degree across people. In either case, associations to history, heritage and experiences involve more specific, concrete examples that transcend the generalisations that make up the usage imagery. In the extreme case, brands become iconic by combining all these types of associations into what is in effect a myth, tapping into enduring consumer hopes and dreams (Holt 2004). Luxury brands often have an abundance of strong associations in this imagery category.

Brand associations in each of these four categories may serve as important sources of equity for luxury brands. Understanding exactly how different consumer segments see the brands along these lines is crucial. Luxury

---

[5] See Aaker, J. (1997). Dimensions of brand personality. *Journal of Marketing Research*, *34* (August), 347–357.

brand marketers must evaluate the strength, favourability and uniqueness of imagery associations both over market segments and over time to make sure that sources of equity stay strong.

## Brand Feelings

Another specific area where luxury brands stand out is with brand feelings. *Brand feelings* are customers' emotional responses and reactions with respect to the brand. Brand feelings also relate to the social currency evoked by the brand. What feelings are evoked by the marketing programme for the brand, or by other means? How does the brand affect customers' feelings about themselves and their relationship with others? These feelings can be mild or intense, and can be positive or negative. With luxury brands, feelings are often of paramount importance, but they may come in different forms and may vary across target market segments.

The following are six important types of brand-building feelings (illustrated with a notable brand example in each case) (Kahle et al. 1988).

1. *Warmth*: Soothing types of feelings; the brand makes consumers feel a sense of calm or peacefulness. Consumers may feel sentimental, warm-hearted or affectionate about the brand. Hallmark is a brand typically associated with warmth.
2. *Fun*: Upbeat types of feelings; the brand makes consumers feel amused, light-hearted, joyous, playful, cheerful and so on. Disney is a brand often associated with fun.
3. *Excitement*: A different form of upbeat feeling; the brand makes consumers feel energised, and that they are experiencing something special. Brands that evoke feelings of excitement may result in consumers feeling a sense of elation, of 'being alive', or being cool, sexy and so on. MTV is a brand seen by many teens and young adults as exciting.
4. *Security*: The brand produces a feeling of safety, comfort and self-assurance. As a result of the brand, consumers do not experience worry or concerns that they might have otherwise felt. AIG insurance is a brand that communicates security to many.

5. *Social approval*: The brand results in consumers having positive feelings about the reactions of others; that is, consumers feel that others look favourably on their appearance, behaviour and so on. This approval may be a result of direct acknowledgment of the consumer's use of the brand by others, or may be less overt, and a result of attribution of product use to consumers. Mercedes is a brand that may signal social approval to consumers.
6. *Self-respect*: The brand makes consumers feel better about themselves; consumers feel a sense of pride, accomplishment or fulfilment. A brand such as Tide (or Ariel) laundry detergent is able to link its brand to 'doing the best things for the family' for many homemakers.

The first three types of feelings are experiential and immediate, increasing in level of intensity. The latter three types of feelings are private and enduring, increasing in level of gravity.

Luxury brands can certainly create and become more associated with experiential feelings, but they are more likely to tap into the more enduring feelings. An important distinction can be made within enduring feelings among inner-directed feelings such as a sense of security, comfort or self-assurance, outer-directed feelings such as social approval, or a combination of inner-directed and outer-directed feelings such as self-respect. Importantly, the relative importance or value of inner-directed vs outer-directed feelings may vary across generations, cohorts and other market segments. Understanding the role of inner-directed vs outer-directed feelings is critical for luxury brand marketers, as they have profoundly different implications for their marketing programmes.

## Brand Expectations

Finally, another area that is especially crucial for luxury brand marketers to measure deals with expectations. As many marketing experts agree, a strong brand can be viewed as a 'promise' to consumers. If this is the case, a luxury brand is a 'big promise', as the expectations are typically very high.

But there are different types of expectations, and it is important for marketers of luxury brands to understand each of them. The following are three notable types of expectations (Boulding et al. 1993):

(1) *Could expectations* – what could the makers of the luxury brand choose to do if they wanted to?
(2) *Should expectations* – all things considered, what should the makers of the luxury brand do?
(3) *Will expectations* – what do consumers think the luxury brand maker will actually do?

The three sets of expectations do not necessarily have to agree. Understanding the gaps is thus crucial. Of particular concern is when the 'will' expectations lag too far behind the 'could' and especially the 'should' expectations.

Positive 'will' expectations are especially useful, as they can favourably colour perceptions of what the brand actually does. In other words, because consumers are more likely to expect a brand to do something, they tend to see things that way. 'Should' expectations, however, are more challenging, as they invoke a more rigorous standard of comparison by which brand performance will be judged. 'Should' expectations are also formed as a result of what other brands do, and other external factors, and are less under the control of the luxury brand marketer as a result. Because of the positioning of luxury brands, they will typically have high 'should' expectations, setting a high bar for their marketing in the process. One of the implications of having such high 'should' expectations is that brand failures of any kind are likely to have significant consequences, and take the brand longer to recover from.

Finally, a somewhat related measurement area to 'should' brand expectations concerns brand momentum. In particular, to what extent do customers feel that the brand is doing the 'right things' and is headed the 'right way'? Because luxury brands have so much history and such well-formed expectations, consumers are more likely to have opinions as to whether the firm and marketers of the luxury brand are making good decisions. These perceptions may especially vary between existing and prospective customers. Measuring any gaps is thus a priority.

## Brand Architecture

The optimal brand architecture helps to organise the offerings of the luxury brand in the best possible way to maximise growth in sales and equity across multiple market segments and, possibly, price points. As noted above, as a general rule, luxury brands must be very selective and strategic in any licensing or brand extensions, especially in terms of any downward stretches. Unfortunately, growth initiatives often mandate that luxury brands find new customers. The Gucci experience clearly reinforces the importance of adapting the right brand architecture to brand products and services with luxury brands.

## The Gucci Story

In its prime, the Gucci brand symbolised luxury, status, elegance and quality. By the 1980s, however, the label had become tarnished from sloppy manufacturing, countless knock-offs and even a family feud among the managing Gucci brothers. The product line consisted of 22,000 items, distributed extensively across all types of department stores. Not only were there too many items, but some items did not even fit the Gucci image, for example, a cheap canvas pocketbook with the double-G logo that was easily copied and sold on a counterfeit basis on the street for 35 US$. Sales only recovered when Gucci refocused the brand, paring the product line to 7000 high-end items and selling them through its own company-owned outlets. The strategy helped to propel Gucci to the height of the fashion business. With revenue of 7.7 billion US$ in 2007, Gucci is now the second highest-selling fashion brand in the world (Galloni 2005).

As suggested by the Gucci example, vertical extensions can be especially tricky for luxury brands. One research study found dilution effects with owners of prestige-image automobiles when low-priced extensions were introduced, but not with owners of non-prestige automobiles or with non-owners of either automobile (Kirmani et al. 1999). In such cases, brand portfolios and brand hierarchies with appropriate sub-brands can be employed to minimise cannibalisation and dilution, and to optimise equity flows.

## Vertical Extensions

Despite the problems inherent with vertical extensions, some luxury brand marketers have succeeded in extending their brands to enter new markets across a range of price points. For example, the Armani brand has extended from high-end Giorgio Armani and Giorgio Armani Privé to mid-range luxury with Emporio Armani, to affordable luxury with Armani Jeans and Armani Exchange. In this case, clear differentiation exists between brands, minimising the potential for brand overlap and any resulting consumer confusion and brand cannibalisation. In addition, each of these extensions lives up to the core promise of the parent brand, thus reducing the possibility that they would hurt the parent's image.

Developing a brand portfolio with plainly distinct and unrelated brands is clearly the simplest and 'cleanest' way for marketers of luxury brands to seek new sales at different price points with minimal chances of dilution. The goal of a brand portfolio is to position each of the different brands in such a way as to maximise coverage and minimise overlap of the target market. But introducing and supporting distinct new brands clearly involves a much greater investment and commitment of finances and other resources. It also makes it more difficult to migrate customers within a brand family. Part of the appeal and beauty of a brand architecture such as that of BMW is that their BMW 3, 5 and 7 series hierarchy makes the potential entry point and migration path transparent to customers across the different BMW offerings.

## Sub-branding

Developing a brand hierarchy with appropriate sub-brands can be an effective and efficient way to expand market coverage. *Sub-branding* introduces a new element into the brand hierarchy below the level of the parent or master brand to refine or modify its meaning. Sub-branding with luxury branding can combine the parent brand name with an individual brand or model type (as with BMW) or with various derivations and adaptations of the parent brand (as with Armani).

A sub-brand, or hybrid branding, strategy offers two potential benefits in that it can facilitate access to associations and attitudes regarding the parent brand as a whole and, at the same time, can allow for the creation of specific brand beliefs. Sub-branding thus creates a stronger connection to the parent brand and all the associations that come along with that. At the same time, creating brand-specific beliefs can help customers better understand how products vary, and which particular product may be the right one for them. Sub-brands also help to organise selling efforts so that salespeople and retailers have a clear picture as to how the product line is organised and how it might best be sold.

## Linking Brand Elements

When multiple brands are combined to form a sub-brand, each brand element can vary in the relative emphasis it receives in the combined brand. The *prominence* of a brand element refers to its relative visibility compared with other brand elements. For example, the prominence of a brand name element depends on several factors such as its order, size and appearance, as well as its semantic associations.

The *principle of prominence* states that the relative prominence of brand elements affects perceptions of product distance and the type of image created for new products. That is, the relative prominence of the brand elements determines which element or elements become the primary one(s) and which element or elements become the secondary one(s). In general, primary brand elements should be chosen to convey the main product positioning and points of difference.

Secondary brand elements, on the other hand, are often chosen for a supporting role to convey a more restricted set of associations. A secondary brand element may also facilitate awareness. Thus, with the Motorola Razr cellular phone handset, the primary brand element – reinforced through the slender, hinged design – is the Razr name, which reinforces the sleek, cutting-edge style that makes up the desired user and usage imagery for the phone. The Motorola name, on the other hand, is a secondary brand element that ideally conveys credibility, quality and professionalism.

The relative prominence of the individual brand compared with the parent brand affects perceptions of product distance and the type of image created for the new product. If the parent brand is made more prominent, then its associations are more likely to dominate. If the individual brand is made more prominent, on the other hand, then it should be easier to create a more distinctive brand image. In this case, the parent brand is signalling to consumers that the new product is not as closely related to its other products that share that name. As a result, consumers should be less likely to transfer parent brand associations. At the same time, the success or failure of the new product should, because of the greater perceived distance involved, be less likely to affect the image of the corporate or family brand. With a more prominent parent brand, however, feedback effects are probably more likely to be evident.

Luxury brands can thus use brand design elements to 'dial up' or 'dial down' the parent or master brand with any offering in an attempt to create the right distance among and between products. The products themselves and how they are marketed in terms of price, distribution and communications will have to align with the intended positioning. In particular, if a luxury brand goes down market to a lower price point, it can choose to introduce the offering as a sub-brand. The more distinct the new offering is in the minds of customers though, the more the luxury brand would need to be downplayed as part of the sub-brand.

Brand equity measurement can help to guide this decision, and plays a number of other useful roles in the development and implementation of the brand architecture. Understanding the reactions of existing and potential customers to different branding strategies is critical.

## Conclusion

This chapter first outlined 10 defining characteristics of luxury brands that provide a foundation as to how they can be marketed. The chapter next focused on a particular challenge faced by many marketers of luxury brands – how to attract new customers without alienating existing customers in order to grow. Brand equity measurement and brand architecture were identified as two areas crucial to properly addressing this growth tradeoff. Emphasis in brand equity measurement was placed on how to measure brand strength, stature, imagery, feelings and expectations. Identifying gaps in these different measurement areas across market segments or over time was seen as important in understanding the extent and nature of the growth tradeoff, and in helping to design the proper brand architecture. Brand architecture requires understanding how to build the optimal brand portfolios and hierarchies. Appropriately constructed sub-brands were identified as one potentially useful way to address the growth tradeoff.

# References

Boulding, W., Kalra, A., Staelin, R. & Zenithal, V. (1993). A dynamic model of service quality: From expectations to behavioral intentions. *Journal of Marketing Research*, *30*(February), 7–27.
Galloni, A. (2005, August 9). Inside out: At Gucci, Mr. Polet's new design upends rules for high fashion. *Wall Street Journal*, p. A1.
Holt, D. B. (2004). *How Brands Become Icons*. Cambridge, MA: Harvard Business School Press.
Kahle, L. R., Poulos, B. & Sukhdial, A. (1988). Changes in social values in the United States during the past decade. *Journal of Advertising Research*, *28* (February/March), 35–41.
Keller, K. L. & Webster Jr, F. E. (2008). Marketing balance: Finessing marketing trade-offs. Working Paper, Tuck School of Business, Dartmouth College.
Kirmani, A., Sood, S. & Bridges, S. (1999). The ownership effect in consumer responses to brand line stretches. *Journal of Marketing*, *63*(1), 88–101.
Silverstein, M. J. & Fiske, N. (2003). *Trading Up: The New American Luxury*. USA: Penguin Group.
Young & Rubicam Brand Asset Consulting. (2005). Consumers trade up while marketers trade off. Unpublished presentation.

**Kevin Lane Keller** is the E. B. Osborn Professor of Marketing at the Tuck School of Business at Dartmouth College. Keller's academic resumé includes degrees from Cornell, Duke and Carnegie-Mellon universities, award-winning research, and faculty positions at Berkeley, Stanford and UNC. Over the years, he has served as brand confidant to marketers for some of the world's most successful brands, including Accenture, American Express, Disney, Ford, Intel, Levi Strauss, Procter & Gamble and Starbucks. His textbook, *Strategic Brand Management*, in its third edition, has been adopted at top business schools and leading firms around the world, and has been heralded as the 'bible of branding'. He is also the co-author, with Philip Kotler, of the all-time best selling introductory MBA marketing textbook *Marketing Management*, now in its 13th edition.

# Measuring Perceptions of Brand Luxury

Franck Vigneron and Lester W. Johnson

## Introduction

Considerable research has been conducted to identify and conceptualise the dimensions of various brands, and much of that has been on the symbolic use of brands (Aaker 1991; Keller 1991; Aaker 1997). Yet the measurement of the perceived luxuriousness of a brand has received

---

This chapter was Reprinted from Vigneron, F. and Johnson, L. (2004) 'Measuring perceptions of brand luxury', *Journal of Brand Management*, 11, pp. 484-506. With kind permission from the *Journal of Brand Management*. All rights reserved.

F. Vigneron (✉)
Department of Marketing, California State University,
California, Northridge, USA
e-mail: franck.vigneron@csun.edu

L.W. Johnson
Faculty of Business and Law, Swinburne Business School, Department of Management and Marketing, Melbourne, Australia

© The Author(s) 2017
J.-N. Kapferer et al. (eds.), *Advances in Luxury Brand Management*,
Journal of Brand Management: Advanced Collections,
DOI 10.1007/978-3-319-51127-6_10

comparatively limited empirical attention. This study is focused on understanding what is meant by 'luxury brand', and on the development of a scale to measure the dimensions of perceived luxury.

Despite the importance of luxury brands in consumers' lives and the fact that the luxury market contributes a large amount of economic activity in the industrialised world (McKinsey Corporation 1990; Silverstein and Fiske 2003), little is known about the influence of luxury on the perception of brands once they enter the marketplace. As emphasised by Dubois and Duquesne (Dubois and Duquesne 1993a, p. 115), 'We believe that an analysis of the direct relationship between consumers and brands is the key to an improved understanding of such a market.' Consequently, the development of an instrument measuring the perception of luxury in the form of a scale is of particular interest. This scale could be used not only in the creation of a luxury brand but also in the continuous monitoring of existing luxury brands and in basic research in consumer behaviour.

Researchers have focused on how the supposed luxury of a brand enables a consumer to express his or her own self, an ideal self, or specific dimensions of the self through the use of a brand (Roux 1991; Lichtenstein et al. 1993).

Practitioners view luxury as a main factor to differentiate a brand in a product category (Alle´re's 1991; Kapferer 1997), as a central driver of consumer preference and usage (Dubois and Duquesne 1993b), and as a common denominator that can be used to define consumption across cultures (Bourdieu 1984; Dubois and Paternault 1997). Finally, luxury products offer a different brand category to measure the suitability of the Internet as a communication tool (Nyeck and Roux 1997).

This chapter examines the concept of a luxury brand, with the goals of designing a conceptual framework and developing a scale to measure differences in the luxury of brands. At present there is no scale measuring the perceived luxury of a brand, or even a clear definition of what constitutes a luxury brand compared to a non-luxury brand. Work by Kapferer (1998) and Dubois et al. (2001) goes part way in developing such a measurement scale, but stops well short of full development of a scale.

Although a brand may be perceived as luxurious, consumers and researchers have recognised that not all luxury brands are deemed equally luxurious. 'Luxury is particularly slippery to define. A strong element of human involvement, very limited supply and the recognition of value by others are key components ... So between premium and luxury, in marketing terms, is a difference of degree' (Cornell 2002). For instance, a Cadillac and a Rolls-Royce may be both perceived as luxury cars, but one compared with the other would be considered more luxurious. In this case, the Rolls-Royce could be assumed to be more luxurious than the Cadillac. Kemp (1998) demonstrated that some goods such as water could be viewed by different observers as either a luxury or as a necessity depending on who wants the goods or why. Even more surprising, he showed that these goods could also be either a luxury or a necessity for the same person in different situations. Consequently, the perception of what is and is not a luxury brand, as well as the amount of luxury contained in a brand, may be dependent on the context and the people concerned.

Thus the degree of luxury associated with a brand is conceptualised to be measured on a continuum within the luxury range and in agreement with previous research (Allérès 1991; Roux 1991; Dubois and Duquesne 1993b). This chapter agrees with authors such as Kapferer (1997) who argue that a luxury brand is a discontinuity *vis-à-vis* other types of brands and make a further conceptual distinction between the different degree of 'luxury' in these brands. A scale to measure this degree of luxuriousness (and the degree of each of the sub-dimensions of luxury that are discussed later) would allow an estimate to be made of the amount of perceived luxury of a luxury brand. Cadillac and Lincoln may be perceived overall as having the same level of luxury, but the scale may reveal that their overall brand-luxury perceptions are combinations of different evaluations of the same dimensions of luxury.

The main contribution of the present chapter is to develop an instrument for the researcher and marketer of luxury products who may wish to measure the amount of luxury contained in a given brand. The brand-luxury scale treats luxury as a matter of degree, residing on a continuum from 'very little' to 'a great deal'.

Before presenting the detailed results of this study, a brief review will be made of the luxury construct and its potential relevance to issues pertaining to the analysis of luxury-seeking consumer behaviour. Then the major steps are discussed in the development of the scale, including detailed tests of the reliability and validity of the scale. Finally, key findings of the research are reviewed and discussed.

## Defining the Luxury Construct

The luxury brand market has been growing steadily for the past 20 years, growing by up to 25 percent in 1989, with a minimum of 10 percent per year, although it grew more slowly during the mid-1990s (Roux 2002). There are many reasons why this growth has been maintained, from a growing aspirational affluence (Prendergast and Wong 2003) and growing population of young upwardly mobile consumers (Roux 2002) to an ageing wealthier population (Frances 2002) or a greater relative number of people with high income (Gardyn 2002).

In 1997 Kapferer (1997) presented the semiotics of the word 'luxury', its sociological references and the pragmatics of luxury-brand management:

> Luxury defines beauty; it is art applied to functional items. Like light, luxury is en-lightening. [...] They offer more than mere objects: they provide reference of good taste. That is why luxury management should not only depend on customer expectations: luxury brands are animated by their internal programme, their global vision, the specific taste which they promote as well as the pursuit of their own standards... Luxury items provide extra pleasure and flatter all senses at once... Luxury is the appendage of the ruling classes. (p. 253)

Thus there is an agreement in the literature to define luxury goods as goods for which the simple use or display of a particular branded product brings esteem on the owner, apart from any functional utility. Hence, luxury products enable consumers to satisfy psychological and functional needs, and it seems that these psychological benefits are the main factor distinguishing them from non-luxury products or counterfeits (Arghavan and Zaichkowsky 2000). Nueno and Quelch (1998, p. 61) define luxury brands as 'those whose ratio of functionality to price is low, while the ratio of intangible and situational utility to price is high'. This definition is comparable to the definition made by economists or marketing consultants (McKinsey Corporation 1990) who define luxury brands as those whose price and quality ratios are the highest of the market; that is, their price is significantly greater than the price of products with similar tangible features.

This definition suggests, however, that brands are of two kinds: either luxurious or not luxurious. In effect, there are brands that may be a luxury brand in a certain product category and not a luxury brand in another product category (Dubois and Laurent 1996). Rolls-Royce is considered a luxury brand of car but not a luxury brand of aeroplane engines.

In addition, there is a distinction between luxury brands associated with the upper range of luxury and those associated with the lower range of luxury. A brand may be defined as a luxury brand, but all brands considered luxury brands may not be deemed equal, and one brand having a higher perceived luxury in one product category may have a lower perceived luxury in another product category. Cartier for instance may have a greater luxury image in the jewellery market than in the apparel or fragrance market. The luxury brand Armani may be placed in the upper range of luxury brands (also named 'griffe', see Kapferer (1997) for a discussion). Emporio Armani is the more popular Armani brand, crafted to satisfy the need of a larger target luxury market. It may be ranked in a lower level of luxury, but still considered luxury.

Phau and Prendergast (2000) point out that while luxury is a subjective concept, 'luxury brands compete on the ability to evoke exclusivity, a well-known brand identity... brand awareness and perceived quality'. This concept of exclusivity or rarity is well documented in the literature on luxury (Pantzalis 1995). The contradiction that luxury brands face when increasing exposure and sales while maintaining a fragile perception of limited supply is putting a great deal of pressure on luxury brands (Roux and Floch 1996).

Over the past 20 years, brands that were once traditionally targeting the wealthiest consumers have launched new product lines, new brands or product extensions to market their products to middle-class consumers. In fact some people have called this trend the 'democratisation of luxury' (Anonymous 1993; Gardyn 2002; Lipovetsky and Roux 2003). Rémaury (2002) examines the cultural differences that shape this trend and describes the impact of a greater democratic process influencing luxury-product marketing in the USA compared to Europe (Fig. 7).

In an earlier review article, Vigneron and Johnson (1999) developed a framework of 'prestige-seeking consumer behavior'. This prestige-seeking

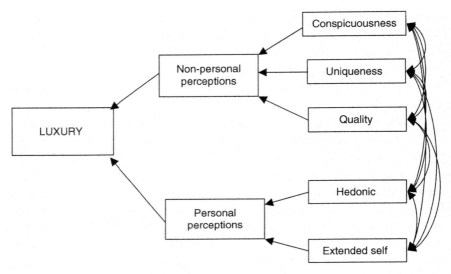

Fig. 7 Proposed framework of brand luxury index

framework was originally inspired by the conceptual work of Mason (1992) who developed a framework of status-seeking behaviour to explain consumers' behaviour in relation to luxury brands. His conceptual framework mostly focused on the interpersonal effects associated with this behaviour.

In contrast, Vigneron and Johnson's framework included personal aspects such as hedonist and perfectionist motives inspired from the work of Dubois and Laurent (1994) as well as the more usual interpersonal aspects (snobbery, conspicuousness, and bandwagon motives) inherited from Leibenstein (1950) and Mason (1992). In doing so, they attempted to establish a balance between personal and interpersonal motives for consumption of luxury brands. This model is also consistent with previous research on luxury that demonstrated that behaviour varies between different people depending on their susceptibility to interpersonal influence (Bourne 1957; Mason 1981; Bearden and Etzel 1982; Horiuchi 1984; Bushman 1993; Pantzalis 1995).

Although Vigneron and Johnson use the terminology 'prestige-seeking behavior', in the present chapter, the term 'luxury' is preferred to 'prestige'. Therefore, this chapter refers to 'luxury-seeking consumer behaviour' and 'luxury brands' when discussing the brand category, whereas 'prestige' is used when relating to the extreme end of the luxury-brand category. The term 'luxury' in this context is more inclusive in the sense that it includes both personal and interpersonal aspects. While prestige or status consumption involves purchasing a higher-priced product to embellish one's ego (Eastman et al. 1999), luxury consumption involves purchasing a product that represents value to both the individual and *vis-à-vis* significant others.

As early as 1986, Andrus et al. (1986, p. 5) noted the need for literature pertaining to the study of luxury brands: 'Status brand strategies are intuitively recognised by marketing professionals and practitioners. However, there is little literature on the topic reported.' A review of the literature since then suggests a growing interest in the topic of luxury (Dubois and Paternault 1995; Kapferer 1997; Kapferer 1998; Nueno and Quelch 1998; Bernstein 1999; Arghavan and Zaichkowsky 2000), but there is still little work on the evaluation of luxury brands (exceptions are Kapferer 1998; Eastman et al. 1999; Phau and Prendergast 2000 and Dubois et al. 2001).

The psychometric work undertaken in the measurement of luxury offers evidence of multiple dimensionalities in defining the concept (Dubois and Laurent 1994; Kapferer 1998; Dubois et al. 2001). Vigneron and Johnson (1999) proposed that the luxury-seeking consumer's decision-making process is explained by five main factors that form a semantic network. They reviewed the latent structure of, and the interrelations among, the primary meanings of the prestige (luxury) concept that underlie the decision-making process undertaken when assessing luxury brands. For comparison (Table 15) presents a review of the factors and communalities between the Vigneron and Johnson five-dimension framework, the Brand Luxury Index items that are derived later in this chapter, and the items developed by Kapferer (1998) and Dubois et al. (2001).

The definition of what separates luxury brands and non-luxury brands has been operationally defined in this study through five perceived dimensions of a luxury brand. Hence the conceptual framework used (Fig. 7), which was derived from the literature, demonstrates the

Table 15 Review of factors describing luxury brands across three studies

| | Vigneron & Johnson (1999) | Items developed in this study | Kapferer (1998) | Dubois, Laurent and Czellar (2001) |
|---|---|---|---|---|
| Non-personal-oriented perceptions | Conspicuousness | Conspicuous<br>Elitist<br>Extremely expensive<br>For wealthy | Belonging to a minority<br>Its price | Conspicuous<br>Elitist<br>Very high price<br>Differentiate from others |
| | Uniqueness | Very exclusive<br>Precious<br>Rare | Exclusiveness | Scarcity |
| | Quality | Unique<br>Crafted<br>Luxurious<br>Best quality<br>Sophisticated<br>Superior | Its uniqueness<br>Craftsman<br>Its quality<br>Beauty of object<br>Excellence of product | Uniqueness<br>Not mass-produced<br>Rather like luxury<br>Excellent quality<br>Good taste |
| Personal-oriented perceptions | Hedonism | Exquisite<br>Glamorous<br>Stunning | Its great creativity<br>Its sensuality<br>Its magic | Pleasure<br>Aesthetics and polysensuality<br>Makes life beautiful |
| | Extended self | Leading<br>Very powerful<br>Rewarding<br>Successful | | Refined people<br>Reveal who you are<br>Pleasing |
| Items without apparent communalities | | | Knowing that few have one<br>Savoir faire and tradition<br>International reputation<br>Long history<br>Grown out of a creative genius<br>Never out of fashion<br>Forefront of fashion | Few people own<br>Ancestral heritage and personal history<br>Superfluous and non-functional<br>Makes dream |

existence of three latent luxury dimensions reflecting non-personal-oriented perceptions: perceived conspicuousness, perceived uniqueness, and perceived quality. It also shows two personal-oriented perceptions: perceived extended self and perceived hedonism. Each one of these dimensions is strongly correlated but not identical as constructed in the formative framework (Diamantopoulos and Winklhoffer 2001).

These are the five key luxury dimensions that must be established or monitored for creating a lasting luxury brand. It is expected that different sets of consumers would have different perceptions of the level of luxury for the same brands, and that the overall luxury level of a brand would integrate these perceptions from different perspectives.

## Perceived Conspicuousness

The early work on conspicuous consumption (Veblen 1899; Bearden and Etzel 1982) suggested that a consumer considered reference group influences when publicly consuming luxury products. The consumption of luxury brands may be important to individuals in search of social representation and position. This means that social status associated with a brand is an important factor in conspicuous consumption. Furthermore, consumers who perceive price as a proxy for quality often perceive high price as an indicator of luxury (Lichtenstein et al. 1993). Hence the measure of conspicuousness includes items such as 'extremely expensive' or 'for wealthy' that tap into perceptions of price and social status associated with the brand. As pointed out by Vigneron and Johnson (1999) 'This argument is further supported by the marketing literature which recommends the use of "prestige-pricing strategy" when appealing to status-conscious consumers' (Berkowitz et al. 1992; Groth and McDaniel 1993).

## Perceived Uniqueness

Research reveals that scarcity or limited supply of products enhances consumers' preferences for a brand (Lynn 1991; Pantzalis 1995). Individuals express a 'need for uniqueness' (Snyder and Fromkin 1977) when they are searching for something that is difficult to obtain (e.g. a Louis Vuitton handbag). The consumer behaviour literature conceptualised consumers' need for uniqueness as subsuming three behavioural dimensions (see, for review, Tian et al. 2001). Uniqueness is sought to enhance one's self-image and social image by adhering to one's personal taste, or breaking the rules, or avoiding similar consumption. The uniqueness dimension is based on the assumptions that perceptions of exclusivity and rarity enhance the desire for a brand, and that this desirability is increased when the brand is also perceived as expensive (Groth and McDaniel 1993; Verhallen and Robben 1994). A luxury brand that would be difficult to find because of its uniqueness (such as a limited edition), and which would be expensive compared to normal standards (e.g. a Jaguar car), would be even more valuable.

## Perceived Extended Self

Consumers may use luxury brands to classify or distinguish themselves in relation to relevant others, but they may also try to integrate the symbolic meaning into their own identity (Holt 1995). Social referencing and the construction of one's self appears to be determinant in luxury consumption. Multiple reference groups refer to the problem of being influenced by pressures and demands from one's own membership group, and being attracted by the standard dictated by another reference group. People's desire to conform to affluent lifestyles and/or to be distinguished from non-affluent lifestyles affects their luxury-seeking behaviour (French et al. 1959; Solomon 1983; Mick 1986; McCracken 1986). Belk's (1988) concept of 'extended self' suggests that people regard their possessions as part of identity. Thus 'luxury imitators' may use the perceived extended-self dimension transferred from luxury brands to enhance their self-concept and replicate stereotypes of affluence by consuming similar luxury items (Douglas and Isherwood 1979; Hirschman 1988; Dittmar 1994).

The possession of luxury brands may be more appreciated by consumers who are highly materialistic and susceptible to interpersonal influence (Bearden et al. 1989; Richins 1994a). Richins (1994b, p. 522) wrote: 'Materialism is a value that represents the individual's perspective regarding the role possessions should play in his/her life.' Materialistic consumers may regard luxury brands as a means to reach happiness, and may use these brands to evaluate personal or others' success. People who are concerned with social acceptance and conformity with affluent reference groups may value possessions that are more socially visible and expensive. Belk (1995, p. 487) stated 'as an essential materialistic activity collecting is a lens viewing all luxury consumption more clearly', and further explained that a person's collections may represent personal success in comparison with other people's collections.

## Perceived Hedonism

Luxury-seekers are considered hedonic consumers when they are looking for personal rewards and fulfilment acquired through the purchase and consumption of products evaluated for their subjective emotional benefits and intrinsically pleasing properties, rather than functional benefits (Sheth et al. 1991; Westbrook and Oliver 1991). 'Hedonic dimension' is used to refer to the luxury dimension reflected by sensory gratification (Rossiter and Percy 1997) and sensory pleasure (Hirschman and Holbrook 1982) expected from the consumption. Therefore, people who rely on their own personal opinion (e.g. role-relaxed consumers (Kahle 1995), or inner-directed consumers (Kassarjian 1965)), and who are not susceptible to interpersonal influence when considering luxury brands, may represent the hedonic type of consumer.

## Perceived Quality

It is expected that luxury brands offer superior product qualities and performance compared with non-luxury brands. Perfectionist consumers may perceive more value from a luxury brand because they may assume that it will have a greater brand quality and reassurance (Aaker 1991). The literature on luxury consumption emphasises the importance of leadership in quality to ensure the perception of luxury (Quelch 1987; Garfein 1989; Roux 1995). It seems rather difficult to develop a luxury brand image without developing a long-term commitment to quality. Accordingly, people influenced by the quality dimension of luxury may perceive that luxury brands have superior characteristics compared with non-luxury brands. These characteristics may include, but are not restricted to: technology, engineering, design, sophistication, and craftsmanship. For instance, speed and acceleration for a luxury car or precision for a luxury watch are elements reflecting the perceptions of quality. In addition, 'high prices may even make certain products or services more desirable' (Groth and McDaniel 1993, p. 10) because consumers perceive higher prices as an indication of greater quality (Rao and Monroe 1989).

Although the five dimensions of luxury are likely to be correlated, they all contribute to an index of luxury. The Brand Luxury Index (BLI) that is developed in this chapter is a multidimensional scale that aggregates five sub-scales to form an overall compensatory index of luxury. While consumers may choose to maximise all five dimensions, in practice, consumers would trade off less salient dimensions for more salient ones. This chapter attempts to crystallise the conceptual framework defined above by developing a scale to measure the multidimensional concept of luxury. Thus a seven-point semantic differential scale, the Brand Luxury Index (BLI), is developed following recommended scaling procedures, as explained in the following section.

# Scale Development

## Methodology

For the purpose of this research, a semantic differential scale was developed (Osgood et al. 1957; Mindak 1961). The scale-development process (see Table 16) employed in this study followed the paradigm and refinements suggested by the American Psychology Association guidelines (Nunnally 1978; Gerbing and Anderson 1988; DeVellis 1991). Data for developing the scale were mostly collected by university faculties using responses obtained from samples of undergraduate

**Table 16** Summary of the scale development process

| Stage of scale development | Sample | Analysis procedure | Results |
|---|---|---|---|
| Item generation | Expert judges ($n = 77$) | Personal rating:<br>• 3 phases | 157 items reduced to 30 items |
| Reliability | Business students ($n = 1060$) | • Internal reliability ($n = 884$)<br>• Reliability over time ($n = 176$) | 30 items reduced to 22 items |
| Validity | Business students ($n = 1322$) | Standard validity procedures:<br>• Content validity ($n = 186$)<br>• Predictive validity ($n = 463$)<br>• Nomological validity ($n = 331$)<br>• Construct validity: convergent and discriminant ($n = 342$) | Significant level of validity: 22 items reduced to 20 items |
| Brands used to develop the scale | David Jones; Hilton; Levi's; Mercedes-Benz; Nike Air shoes; Porsche 911 turbo; Ralph Lauren shirt; Ray Ban; Rolex; house in Sydney. | | |
| Brands used to test the scale | Bally leather shoes; BMW 750i; Hugo Boss; Grace Brothers; Cartier; Chanel No5; Christian Dior; Ferrari F355; Gucci sunglasses; Guerlain; Yves-Saint-Laurent shirt; Herme's; Hilton; David Jones; Moët & Chandon; Nike Air; Bang & Olufsen; Revlon; Sony; Louis Vuitton. | | |

and postgraduate business students at the beginning of lectures in a large Australian university (university students have been used as subjects in several previous empirical studies of luxury (Kapferer 1998; Eastman et al. 1999; Dubois et al. 2001). Several pre-tests were carried out to select a pool of brands that would be perceived as having a subsequent degree of luxury for the samples used. For instance, Levi's in Australia is perceived as an upmarket brand of jeans, but it may not have been acceptable if this study was carried out in the USA for instance.

## Item Generation and First Content Validity

First, a set of word pairs was generated, customised for the specific measurement of luxury. A review of the literature on luxury brands (both academic and commercial, such as advertising material), qualitative interviews with 12 managers of international luxury brands in Australia, and focus groups with 25 postgraduate students (MBA in luxury brand management, taught in English in France), led to the generation of 157 bipolar adjectives. These items were then examined by a panel of reviewers ($n = 77$). These reviewers were composed of managers of luxury brands, marketing academics, or consumers having bought several established luxury brands within the past few months. The reviewers were asked to indicate their agreement or disagreement as to whether they felt that the word pair could be used to evaluate the luxury of a brand. This initial content analysis resulted in reducing the original 157 items to 30.

## Internal Scale Reliability

All the brands that were used in this study were selected in compliance with a certain number of criteria. For instance, brands were tested and selected that had sufficient brand awareness and a potential luxury image with the target respondents. The results from the initial analysis ($n = 418$ business students) indicated that for each brand (Levi's, Ray Ban, Rolex, and Porsche) the Cronbach's alpha coefficients were greater than 0.86, suggesting significant internal reliability for the scale. Cronbach's alpha was also calculated for each one of the five dimensions. It ranged from 0.69 to 0.90 with the hedonic dimension for the Levi's sample being the lowest (see Table 17).

To extend the reliability analysis, the item-to-total correlations were examined for each item within all samples, with significant values ranging from 0.30 to 0.80. No items were dropped based on this criterion, but offending items were identified and flagged for further investigation.

Table 17 Reliability coefficients for each brand and each dimension

| Results | Conspicuous | Unique | Quality | Extended self | Hedonic | Scale alpha |
|---|---|---|---|---|---|---|
| Levi's (n = 106) | 0.87 | 0.84 | 0.73 | 0.78 | 0.69 | 0.86 |
| Ray Ban (n = 104) | 0.85 | 0.90 | 0.87 | 0.80 | 0.86 | 0.89 |
| Rolex (n = 106) | 0.88 | 0.90 | 0.88 | 0.87 | 0.80 | 0.88 |
| Porsche (n = 102) | 0.89 | 0.90 | 0.88 | 0.88 | 0.88 | 0.89 |
| Total data set (n = 418) | 0.91 | 0.93 | 0.87 | 0.88 | 0.86 | 0.95 |

## Exploratory Factor Analysis

Although the authors made a theoretical assumption about a five-dimensional structure, an exploratory factor analysis was performed on the initial 30-item scale to check item loadings and to allow the number of dimensions in the initial exploratory phase to be driven by the data. Separate principle component analyses with varimax rotation were used to evaluate and identify the component factors (Table 18). Varimax rotation was preferred to oblimin rotation, even though factor correlation was anticipated. Oblimin rotation was performed and resulted in a less satisfactory solution from the factor pattern loadings and rational factor structure. These results were also confirmed across the study.

In interpreting the factors, a decision was made (*a priori*) to discard the factor loadings of less than 0.60. The average factor correlations between the sub-scales were calculated and ranged from 0.91 to 0.96. The congruence correlation coefficients were higher than 0.90, showing that the factor structure is invariant (Everett 1983).

For each of the four brands, the first factor accounted for most of the variation in the data, explaining an average of 50 percent of the common variance. Two brands had a number of items that did not load on any factors. Levi's had seven items that did not reach the cut-off of 0.60, and Ray Ban had three items that also did not load on any factor. These items were also registered as offending items, and were further examined in the next analysis. Exploratory factor analysis is useful for data-reduction purposes, but it does not provide evidence of the dimensionality of

Table 18 Varimax rotated factor structure: full data set. Original 30 items used for scale development

| Factors | Factor one | Factor two | Factor three | Factor four | Factor five |
|---|---|---|---|---|---|
| Eigen value | 12.84 | 2.37 | 2.13 | 2.01 | 1.50 |
| % of common variance | 42.8% | 7.9% | 7.1% | 6.7% | 5.0% |
| Items | | | | | |
| 1. Classic | 0.05 | 0.15 | 0.12 | (0.67) | 0.19 |
| 2. Concern | 0.23 | (0.61) | 0.15 | 0.12 | 0.02 |
| 3. Conspicuous | 0.29 | 0.20 | (0.72) | 0.21 | 0.21 |
| 4. Crafted | 0.20 | 0.17 | 0.21 | (0.74) | 0.11 |
| 5. Distinctive | 0.67 | 0.11 | 0.06 | 0.22 | 0.05 |
| 6. Elitist | 0.24 | 0.18 | (0.74) | 0.17 | 0.21 |
| 7. Emotional | 0.18 | (0.81) | 0.18 | 0.13 | 0.27 |
| 8. Exceptional | (0.75) | 0.21 | 0.22 | 0.16 | 0.10 |
| 9. Exclusive | (0.77) | 0.26 | 0.25 | 0.15 | 0.12 |
| 10. Expensive | 0.24 | 0.28 | (0.76) | 0.13 | 0.17 |
| 11. Exquisite | 0.12 | 0.17 | 0.24 | 0.12 | (0.67) |
| 12. Fascinating | 0.30 | 0.25 | 0.23 | 0.13 | (0.72) |
| 13. Glamorous | 0.13 | 0.20 | 0.06 | 0.09 | (0.82) |
| 14. Impressive | 0.19 | (0.73) | 0.11 | 0.14 | 0.16 |
| 15. Leading | 0.14 | (0.77) | 0.15 | 0.19 | 0.10 |
| 16. Luxurious | (0.77) | 0.21 | 0.24 | 0.14 | 0.19 |
| 17. Powerful | 0.22 | (0.74) | 0.17 | 0.16 | 0.22 |
| 18. Precious | (0.77) | 0.18 | 0.17 | 0.17 | 0.16 |
| 19. Quality | 0.23 | 0.15 | 0.16 | (0.78) | 0.14 |
| 20. Rare | (0.76) | 0.22 | 0.19 | 0.19 | 0.18 |
| 21. Rewarding | 0.16 | (0.82) | 0.17 | 0.13 | 0.23 |
| 22. Sophisticated | 0.18 | 0.19 | 0.16 | (0.74) | 0.18 |
| 23. Status | 0.21 | 0.18 | (0.76) | 0.21 | 0.08 |
| 24. Stunning | 0.28 | 0.26 | 0.18 | 0.19 | (0.74) |
| 25. Stylish | 0.17 | 0.08 | 0.08 | (0.70) | −0.004 |
| 26. Successful | 0.20 | (0.76) | 0.08 | 0.19 | 0.12 |
| 27. Superior | 0.16 | 0.19 | 0.16 | (0.72) | −0.01 |
| 28. Symbolic | 0.05 | 0.02 | (0.75) | 0.10 | 0.01 |
| 29. Unique | (0.79) | 0.22 | 0.18 | 0.14 | 0.20 |
| 30. Wealthy | 0.23 | 0.20 | (0.74) | 0.18 | 0.23 |

Italics indicate significant factor loadings (>0.60).

measures, essential in scale development (Gerbing and Anderson 1988). In the present study, confirmatory factor analysis was used to test the reliability of the items (Table 18).

## Confirmatory Factor Analysis

The objective of the next step was to model the proposed structural solution and measure its overall fit using confirmatory factor analysis (CFA) of the 30 items. The proposed framework hypothesised, first, that the factors identified by the exploratory factor analysis would be substantially related to the dimensions indicated by the structural model. Secondly, the conceptual model hypothesised that scores on the five latent variables would measure related, but distinguishable, constructs. The covariance matrix for the 30 items was used, and parameter estimates were computed using the maximum-likelihood method (Arbuckle 2003). The fit of the five-factor solution was assessed by examining factor loadings, goodness-of-fit indicators, factor inter-correlations, and by comparing it to several available alternatives (the null model, one-factor model, and five-factor model). Several alternative indices were used to assess goodness-of-fit (Hair et al. 1995) such as the chi-square statistic and the goodness-of-fit index (GFI).

The five-factor model for every sample, with all 30 items each loading on its appropriate construct, yielded significant chi-square statistics (Table 19). The other indices for measuring the goodness-of-fit also indicated a moderate fit to the data, as evidenced by the findings, for instance relatively small GFI values of 0.70 (Levi's jeans), 0.75 (Ray Ban), 0.71 (Rolex), 0.73 (Porsche 911), and 0.78 (combined data). All of this suggested only a moderately acceptable fit for the five-factor model (Hair et al. 1995).

The measurement models were examined, and the offending items reviewed (Table 20). Items that did not contribute to the scale's internal consistency were removed (8 items out of 30). A revised CFA model was computed with the revised solution (i.e. 22 items) for each one of the brands and for a combined data set. The fit for the revised five-factor model was significantly improved without the eight offending items compared with findings from the initial model (i.e. 30 items). This model, however, still produced a significant chi-square demonstrating a moderate fit. The five-factor solution

**Table 19** Dimensions of original 30-item scale

| Conspicuous | Unique | Quality | Extended self | Hedonic |
|---|---|---|---|---|
| Conspicuous and inconspicuous | Distinctive* and neutral | Classic* and novel | Leading and influential | Emotional* and unemotional |
| Elitist and popular | Exceptional* and normal | Crafted and mass produced | Powerful and powerless | Exquisite and tasteful |
| Expensive and inexpensive | Exclusive and unexclusive | Higher quality and lower quality | Rewarding and unrewarding | Fascinating* and indifferent |
| For wealthy and for well-off | Precious and not precious | Luxurious and upmarket | Successful and average | Glamorous and attractive |
| Imposing* and unimposing | Rare and not rare | Sophisticated and unadorned | | Stunning and memorable |
| Impressive* and unimpressive | Unique and common | Stylish* and standard | | |
| High status symbol* and medium status symbol | | Superior | | |
| High standing* and medium standing | | | | |

*Indicates items that were deleted during the study

**Table 20** Results from the different models

| Results | 30-item model | 22-item model | 20-item model |
|---|---|---|---|
| Chi-square | 1428.21 | 255.30 | 240.74 |
| Degree of F | 395.00 | 160.00 | 160.00 |
| P value | 0.000 | 0.000 | 0.000 |
| Chi-square/df | 3.61 | 1.59 | 1.50 |
| GFI | 0.78 | 0.94 | 0.96 |
| AGFI | 0.74 | 0.93 | 0.95 |
| NFI | 0.85 | 0.96 | 0.97 |
| TLI | 0.87 | 0.98 | 0.99 |
| RMSEA | 0.07 | 0.04 | 0.02 |

This table shows the CFA results from the combined brands (i.e. Levi's, Ray Ban, Rolex, and Porsche) needed further refinement to attain non-significant chi-square statistics for each brand.

## Test-Retest Reliability

The consistency of measurement was determined by collecting data on two occasions separated by two weeks using the same subject population (Bearden et al. 2001). A new set of respondents ($n = 176$ business students) initially rated three new brands: a house in Double-Bay (an affluent area in Sydney, Australia), a Mercedes-Benz 600SEL, and a Ralph Lauren polo shirt. As before an analysis was conducted for each brand and another analysis for the combined set of data.

The average correlation between time one and time two on total scores was 0.84 (two items were removed). Test-retest Pearson correlations for each brand were as follows: house, $r = 0.83$; Mercedes, $r = 0.86$; and Ralph Lauren, $r = 0.82$. These brands were also tested for internal scale reliability over the two periods. The Cronbach's alpha coefficient ranged from 0.89 to 0.91, and the item-to-total correlations were from 0.35 to 0.65. Altogether, these results demonstrated a significant improvement in terms of reliability when compared to the reliability indices originally computed (i.e. with 30- and 22-item scales). In addition, four measurement models were computed, one for each brand (using the 20 items remaining). The revised model sensibly improved the goodness-of-fit and substantially enhanced the chi-square non-significance of the five-factor model. For instance, Mercedes-Benz 600SEL indicated a better fit ($\chi^2 = 170.31$, $p < 0.274$) compared with the model using the previous 22 items ($\chi^2 = 229.35$, $p < 0.069$).

Analysis of the results indicates a satisfactory level of reliability over time for the scale. In addition, it enabled the goodness-of-fit of the structural model to be improved. The items repeatedly affecting the reliability of the scale – i.e. at least three times during the study – were removed from the model. The next study assessed the validity of the scale, using methods such as content validity, predictive validity, and discriminant and convergent validity.

# Scale Validity

## Second Content Validity

This step was an attempt to substantiate and extend the findings of the initial content validity check. Three new brands were used to test the revised 20-item scale: David Jones, an up market department store ($n = 63$), Hilton Hotels ($n = 51$), and Nike Air shoes ($n = 72$). After the respondents (undergraduate students at a large university in Australia) had completed the questionnaire, they were then asked to answer the following open-ended question: 'Please, we would be grateful if you could write in your own words and as simply as possible, the reason why you rated this brand that way.' This method was similar to the procedure outlined by Zaichkowsky (1985). Each subject was classified into one of three groups according to their BLI mean score (high, medium, and low). Then three judges independently assessed the open-ended responses, classifying respondents into groups with attitudes describing a low, medium, or high level of perception of luxury towards the brand. Finally, each subject's BLI classification was correlated with their open-attitude rating to measure an overall agreement between a subject's rating using the scale and the open attitude towards the brand.

The results revealed a significant association between the open-ended answers from the respondents and their scores, providing further evidence to support the validity of the scale. This agreement was as follows: 78 percent agreement for the David Jones department store, 83 percent agreement for Hilton hotels, and 86 percent agreement for Nike Air shoes.

## Predictive Validity

To test validity, a single-item attitude scale (measuring only luxury) was used as a criterion to obtain a score classified into two distinct categories (high and low luxury). A new set of respondents ($n = 132$ students) classified three brands into these two categories. Then 331 students rated the BLI scale with the three following brands: David Jones department stores, Hilton hotels, and Nike Air shoes, respectively. Based on Nunnally (1978) and DeVellis (1991) accuracy was defined as the proportion of

Table 21 Correlations between BLI scale and criterion-related scale

|  | BLI David Jones | BLI Hilton Hotel | BLI Nike Air | Mean score |
|---|---|---|---|---|
| Criterion David Jones | 0.34 |  |  | 5.91 |
| Criterion Hilton Hotel |  | 0.32 |  | 6.58 |
| Criterion Nike Air |  |  | 0.42 | 4.20 |
| Percentage of correct classifications | 88% | 81% | 72% | n/a |
| Mean score | 0.90 | 0.29 | −0.29 | n/a |

This table shows the CFA results from the combined brands (i.e. Levi's, Ray Ban, Rolex, and Porsche)

correct classifications (i.e. the higher the correlation between the high or low luxury scores obtained with the BLI scale and the criterion, the greater the validity of the BLI scale as a predictor of luxury for brands).

The predictive validity study suggested that the brand luxury index scale was sensitive in measuring luxury, and provided further evidence for accuracy. The scores predicted with the criterion-related scale were correlated to a satisfactory degree with the BLI overall luxury scores (correlations ranging from 0.32 to 0.42) (Table 21).

## Nomological Validity

This step consisted of examining the nomological validity between five luxury-related scales and the BLI scale using 331 respondents (business students) and three brands (David Jones department stores, Hilton Hotels, and Nike Air shoes). It was hypothesised that a materialistic person (a measure of materialistic attitudes was used, from Moschis and Churchill (1978)) would be involved with fashion brands (a fashion involvement factor was used, from Tigert et al. (1976)) and brands that contribute to personal image and pleasure (an enduring involvement scale was used, from Higie and Feick (1988)). Such a person would have a positive attitude towards money (a money-prestige scale was used, from Yamauchi and Templer (1982)), would assign luxury to high prices (a price-based prestige sensitivity scale was used, from Lichtenstein et al. (1993)), and would be classified among the higher raters of the BLI scale (Table 22).

**Table 22** Correlations between BLI scale and related attitude scales

| | BLI (n = 331) | Material (n = 168) | Money prestige (n = 168) | Fashion (n = 163) | Price-prestige (n = 163) | Enduring involvement (n = 163) | SDS (n = 168) |
|---|---|---|---|---|---|---|---|
| BLI | (0.82) | | | | | | |
| Material | 0.52 | (0.81) | | | | | |
| Money-prestige | 0.44 | 0.92 | (0.76) | | | | |
| Fashion | 0.69 | n/a | n/a | (0.80) | | | |
| Price-prestige | 0.59 | n/a | n/a | 0.54 | (0.86) | | |
| Enduring involvement | 0.47 | n/a | n/a | 0.77 | 0.48 | (0.83) | |
| SDS | 0.15 | 0.07 | 0.14 | n/a | n/a | n/a | (0.78) |

Correlations are significant at the 0.01 level (2-tailed); n/a data not applicable because these scales were not addressed on the same questionnaires; figures in parentheses on diagonals – Cronbach's alpha

The correlations among the luxury-related scales were strong, providing evidence of related construct measurement among the five scales. The BLI scores were positively related to the five criteria associated with the luxury-related scales (Table 23). For example, 79 percent of the higher BLI raters were materialistic respondents, and 76 percent of the lower BLI raters assumed that high prices were negatively related to the luxury level of brands. In addition, the results from the BLI scale were correlated with the revised social desirability scale from Strahan and Gerbasi (1972) to examine potential external bias. The correlations were either low or not significant, which suggested that the BLI scales were not likely to be influenced by social-desirability bias.

Additional analyses of the construct interrelationships were required to further substantiate evidence of the scale validity. The next step was to assess the construct validity of the scale using classical statistical methods such as Campbell and Fiske's (1959) multitrait-multimethod (MTMM) matrix.

## Assessing Construct Validity Using the Campbell and Fiske Criteria

The MTMM matrix approach to construct validation is expressed in terms of convergent validity (agreement among scores obtained from one procedure with scores from another procedure) and discriminant validity (no correlation with other unintended measures). The Likert and Staple scale was used, as recommended in previous research (Menezes and Elbert 1979), for the two other measurement procedures ($n = 342$ students). The adjectives from the BLI scale indicating a greater level of luxury became the unipolar adjectives of the Staple and Likert scale.

The average reliability coefficient (Cronbach's alpha) was 0.82, with values ranging from 0.71 to 0.90, suggesting values ranging from respectable to very good (DeVellis 1991). Based on the recommendation from Marsh and Hocevar (1983) the heterotrait-monomethod triangles were compared with their respective reliability values to identify any evidence of halo effects. This review did not show any indication between both values,

Table 23 Percentage of respondents sorted among each scale category

| Scale | Materialism | | Power-prestige of money | | Fashion involvement | | Price-based prestige | | Enduring involvement | |
|---|---|---|---|---|---|---|---|---|---|---|
| Respondents | (1) | (2) | (1) | (2) | (1) | (2) | (1) | (2) | (1) | (2) |
| (a) High BLI raters | 79% | 21% | 76% | 24% | 82% | 18% | 77% | 23% | 72% | 28% |
| (b) Low BLI raters | 28% | 72% | 34% | 66% | 12% | 88% | 24% | 76% | 24% | 76% |

High BLI score – respondents with BLI score above the overall mean score; Low BLI score – respondents with BLI score below the overall mean score; (1) Respondents positively related to the rated concept; (2) Respondents negatively related to the rated concept; (a) Cases with mean scores higher than the overall mean BLI score; (b) Cases with mean scores lower than the overall mean BLI score

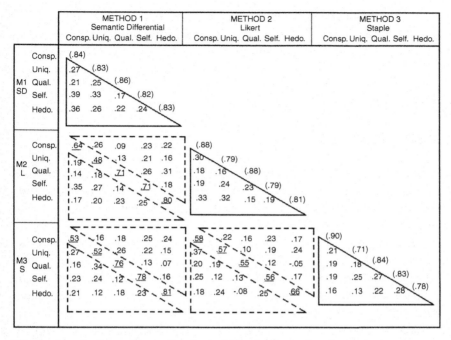

Fig. 8 Results from the mulitrait-multimethod matrix of correlations

and subsequently supported the proposal of non-method biases. Following Campbell and Fiske's requirements, it can be identified that: first, between the three methods, the validation is excellent; secondly, all the validity diagonals exceed the heterotrait values of both the monomethod and heteromethod; and, finally, the pattern of correlation among the traits is relatively illustrated in every heterotrait triangle. Note that the actual validity coefficients of these five traits ranged from 0.48 to 0.81 with a degree of validity significant at the 0.01 level. The Campbell-Fiske criteria performed well in the present study (Fig. 8).

Each of the conditions regarded as necessary for assessing convergent and discriminant validity were met. This method initiated a substantial assessment regarding the construct validity as well as the method/halo bias. Research has encouraged the use of this approach to provide initial information on the analysis of variance of MTMM data.

The present study yielded encouraging evidence concerning the construct validity of the BLI scale and its multi-dimensionality (i.e. conspicuousness, uniqueness, quality, self-perception, and hedonism).

# Discussion

## Implications

This research offers several potential contributions, but particularly, extends the studies carried out by Kapferer (1998), Vigneron and Johnson (1999) and Dubois et al. (2001) on the attitudes towards the concept of luxury and brand luxury.

Vigneron and Johnson's luxury-seeking consumer behaviour framework was used to derive the five dimensions of the scale. Dubois and Laurent's (1994) luxury scale measures perceptions of luxury as a general concept. In comparison, researchers may use the BLI scale to measure consumers' perceptions of the luxury of specific brands or products. The present research revealed that the concept of luxury is multi-dimensional and substantiated by a five-factor model. In developing a scale measuring the luxury of a brand, evidence was established for aspects of reliability and validity.

The implications of this research are of significance for marketers and scholars in the field of luxury brands. It establishes a structural analysis of brand luxury and proposes a managerial instrument capable of creating and evaluating luxury brands. As noted, the results of this research could serve various purposes, but perhaps be specifically applied to create and build brand luxury, or address issues such as how to maintain brand luxury once it is established. The value of the BLI scale is to measure the amount of luxury contained in a luxury brand (i.e. from its high to its low range). One of the applications could be to use the scale to help an 'upper-range established' brand build a luxury-brand image.

In summary, these findings contribute to new explanations of luxury brands beyond those in the economics/analytical literature. These findings support the existence of latent luxury constructs influenced by personal and interpersonal perceptions towards the brands. These findings help explain the key luxury dimensions that managers must establish or monitor for creating a lasting luxury brand. In addition, the BLI scale is particularly useful for comparing several luxury brands and thus for recognising competitive advantages. Relative strengths and weaknesses can be identified in the target market along either each of the 20 items comprising the scale or each of the five underlying dimensions determined by the research.

For instance, Levi's, although considered by Australian students as a luxury brand, received the lowest luxury score among the brands used to develop the scale. Rolex ranked first followed by Mercedes-Benz and Porsche, which indicated that the scale was not measuring the expected monetary value but rather brand luxury. In addition to indicating if a brand is luxurious or not, the scale allows the marketer to rank the brands and also help to discover the factors that support or decrease the luxury dimension. Mercedes-Benz and Porsche had very similar scores for quality and uniqueness, but conspicuousness was much higher for Mercedes, which contributed to make the Mercedes brand luxury greater than that of Porsche.

Hence the BLI scale is helpful to understand how consumers view luxury brands. From a market segmentation point of view, clustering groups according to their different perceptions of brand luxury may reveal salient psychographic characteristics useful in advertising, for instance. From a market positioning point of view, if a manager of a luxury brand witnessed declining brand luxury, the specific weakening dimension could be identified. Thus, taking remedial actions such as changing the advertising message, stressing the luxury attributes, or emphasising the benefits of the brand over competing brands could be undertaken. For example, if the luxury image of a car maker was slowly decreasing due to an increasing number of dealers (i.e. weakening uniqueness), then appeals emphasising the limited number of cars available, or informing the consumer about the precious components used in making the car, would be appropriate to reinforce the overall luxury image.

## Future research

Further replication and extension would be required before the findings could be considered definitive. Hence one suggestion for further research would be to empirically compare the BLI scale with the Kapferer (1998) and Dubois et al. (2001) scales. Potential measures of convergent validity or measures of attitudes towards the concept of luxury and cross-tabulations with particular brands could be examined.

In addition, the replicability of these findings should be tested with additional samples (in particular, with actual consumers of luxury products). The BLI scale could be examined using a second-order confirmatory factor analysis to reduce the number of items to a more parsimonious version. Studies using the BLI in other countries may provide further evidence of nomological validity, where samples could be matched across countries, an important consideration in cross-national research.

## Limitations

A major critique is that there may be a 'demand effect' from 'leading' terms such as 'elitist' (positive connotations) and 'popular' (negative connotations). An individual's motivation is not always obvious and conscious. Indeed, abstract constructs are more difficult to measure, and people may try to give biased answers when dealing with luxury brands.

The MTMM matrix approach used two other types of self-report questionnaire measures, different only in the scale type. It would be an improvement to apply other methods with substantially different validity threats such as observational measures in addition to self-report. Further, more research to determine norms for different brands and categories needs to be carried out to investigate issues of validity. In addition, replication using different data sources other than students and managers from Australia is needed to reinforce the validity of the scale.

In conclusion, the final 20-item scale (Table 24) is sensitive to the luxury image over different socially desirable brands, demonstrating reliable measures and valid results compared to what was anticipated. This scale has potential value for researchers interested in measuring the decision-making process involving the consumer's perceptions of luxury. From a practical standpoint, the more complete measurement of luxury perceptions

**Table 24** Twenty items in the BLI scale

| | | | |
|---|---|---|---|
| **Non-personal-oriented perceptions** | | | |
| Conspicuousness | Conspicuous | ___:___:___:___:___:___:___ | Noticeable |
| | Popular | ___:___:___:___:___:___:___ | Elitist* |
| | Affordable | ___:___:___:___:___:___:___ | Extremely expensive* |
| | For wealthy | ___:___:___:___:___:___:___ | For well-off |
| Uniqueness | Fairly exclusive | ___:___:___:___:___:___:___ | Very exclusive* |
| | Precious | ___:___:___:___:___:___:___ | Valuable |
| | Rare | ___:___:___:___:___:___:___ | Uncommon |
| | Unique | ___:___:___:___:___:___:___ | Unusual |
| Quality | Crafted | ___:___:___:___:___:___:___ | Manufactured |
| | Upmarket | ___:___:___:___:___:___:___ | Luxurious* |
| | Best quality | ___:___:___:___:___:___:___ | Good quality |
| | Sophisticated | ___:___:___:___:___:___:___ | Original |
| | Superior | ___:___:___:___:___:___:___ | Better |
| **Personal-oriented perceptions** | | | |
| Hedonism | Exquisite | ___:___:___:___:___:___:___ | Tasteful |
| | Attractive | ___:___:___:___:___:___:___ | Glamorous* |
| | Stunning | ___:___:___:___:___:___:___ | Memorable |
| Extended self | Leading | ___:___:___:___:___:___:___ | Influential |
| | Very powerful | ___:___:___:___:___:___:___ | Fairly powerful |
| | Rewarding | ___:___:___:___:___:___:___ | Pleasing |
| | Successful | ___:___:___:___:___:___:___ | Well regarded |

*Indicates item is reverse-scored

provides useful information for effective positioning and promotional strategies. This is particularly effective when comparing the luxury image of different brands, and hence for identifying competitive advantage.

**Acknowledgements** The authors would like to thank Bernard Dubois, Harold H. Kassarjian and Judith L. Zaichkowsky for suggestions and comments on earlier drafts of this chapter. The anonymous reviewers are also thanked for their helpful comments.

# References

Aaker, D. (1991). *Managing brand equity: Capitalizing on the value of a brand name*. New York, NY: Free Press.

Aaker, J. L. (1997). Dimensions of brand personality. *Journal of Marketing Research*, *34*(August), 347–356.

AllérèS, D. (1991). Spe´cificite´s et strategies marketing des differents univers du luxe. *Revue Française Du Marketing*, *133*(2/3), 71–97.

Andrus, D. M., Silver, E. & Johnson, D. E. (1986). Status brand management and gift purchase: A discriminant analysis. *Journal of Consumer Marketing*, *3*(March), 5–13.

Anonymous. (1993). The luxury goods trade: Upmarket philosophy. *The Economist*, *325*(December), 95–98.

Arbuckle, J. L. (2003). *AMOS 5.00*. Chicago, IL: Smallwaters Corporation.

Arghavan, N. & Zaichkowsky, J. L. (2000). Do counterfeits devalue the ownership of luxury brands? *Journal of Product and Brand Management*, *9*(7), 485–497.

Bearden, W., Netemeyer, R. G. & Teel, J. E. (1989). Measurement of consumer susceptibility to interpersonal influence. *Journal of Consumer Research*, *15*(March), 473–481.

Bearden, W., Hardesty, D. M. & Rose, R. L. (2001). Consumer self-confidence: Refinements in conceptualization and measurement. *Journal of Consumer Research*, *28*(June), 121–134.

Bearden, W. O. & Etzel, M. J. (1982). Reference group influence on product and brand purchase decisions. *Journal of Consumer Research*, *9*(September), 183–194.

Belk, R. W. (1988). Possessions and the extended self. *Journal of Consumer Research*, *15*(September), 139–168.

Belk, R. W. (1995). Collecting as luxury consumption: Effects on individuals and households. *Journal of Economic Psychology*, *16*(4), 477–490.

Berkowitz, E. N., Kerin, R. A., Hartley, S. & Rudelius, W. (1992). *Marketing* (3rd edn.). Homewood, IL: Irwin.

Bernstein, L. (1999). Luxury and the hotel brand. *Cornell Hotel and Restaurant Administration Quarterly*, February, 47–53.

Bourdieu, P. (1984). *Distinction: A Social Judgment of Taste*. Trans. R. Nice, Cambridge, MA: Harvard University Press.

Bourne, F. S. (1957). Group influence in marketing and public relations. In R. Likert & S. P. Hayes (Eds.), *Some applications of behavioral research*. Paris, France: UNESCO.

Bushman, B. J. (1993). What is in a name? The moderating role of public self-consciousness on the relation between brand label and brand preference. *Journal of Applied Psychology*, 78(5), 857–861.

Campbell, D. & Fiske, D. (1959). Convergent and discriminant validity by the multitrait-multimethod matrix. *Psychological Bulletin*, 56(1), 81–105.

Cornell, A. (2002). Cult of luxury: The new opiate of the masses. *Australian Financial Review*, 27th April, p. 47.

DeVellis, R. F. (1991). *Scale development: Theory and applications*. Newbury Park, CA: Sage Publications Inc.

Diamantopoulos, A. & Winklhoffer, H. M. (2001). Index construction with formative indicators: An alternative to scale development. *Journal of Marketing Research*, 38(May), 269–277.

Dittmar, H. (1994). Material possessions as stereotypes: Material images of different socio-economic groups. *Journal of Economic Psychology*, 15(December), 561–585.

Douglas, M. & Isherwood, B. (1979). *The World of goods*. New York, NY: Basic.

Dubois, B. & Duquesne, P. (1993a). Polarization maps: A new approach to identifying and assessing competitive position — The case of luxury brands. *Marketing and Research Today*, 21(May), 115–123.

Dubois, B. & Duquesne, P. (1993b). The market for luxury goods: Income versus culture. *European Journal of Marketing*, 27(1), 35–44.

Dubois, B. & Laurent, G. (1994). Attitudes toward the concept of luxury: An exploratory analysis. *Asia-Pacific Advances in Consumer Research* (Eds. S. M. Leong & J. A. Cote), *1*, 273–278.

Dubois, B. & Laurent, G. (1996). Le luxe par-dela` les frontie`res: Une etude exploratoire dans douze pays. *De´Cisions Marketing*, 9(September–December), 35–43.

Dubois, B., Laurent, G. & Czellar, S. (2001). 'Consumer rapport to luxury: Analyzing complex and ambivalent attitudes', Consumer Research Working Paper No. 736, HEC, Jouy-en-Josas, France.

Dubois, B. & Paternault, C. (1995). Understanding the world of international luxury brands: The "dream formula". *Journal of Advertising Research*, July/August, 69–76.

Dubois, B. & Paternault, C. (1997). Does luxury have a home country? An investigation of country images in Europe. *Marketing and Research Today*, 25(May), 79–85.

Eastman, J. K., Goldsmith, R. E. & Flynn, L. R. (1999). Status consumption in consumer behavior: Scale development and validation. *Journal of Marketing Theory and Practice*, Summer, 7, 41–52.

Everett, J. E. (1983). Factor comparability as a means of determining the number of factors and their rotation. *Multivariate Behavioral Research*, 18, 197–218.

Frances, P. (2002). Older and wealthier. *American Demographics*, 24(November), 40–42.

French, J. R., Jr, & Raven, B. H. (1959). The bases of social power. In D. Cartwright (Ed.), *Studies in Social Power* (pp. 150–167). Ann Arbor, MI: Institute for Social Research.

Gardyn, R. (2002). Oh, the good life. *American Demographics*, 24(November), 30–36.

Garfein, R. T. (1989). Cross-cultural perspectives on the dynamics of prestige. *Journal of Services Marketing*, 3(Summer), 17–24.

Gerbing, D. W. & Anderson, J. C. (1988). An updated paradigm for scale development incorporating unidimensionality and its assessment. *Journal of Marketing Research*, 25(May), 186–192.

Groth, J. C. & McDaniel, S. W. (1993). The exclusive value principle: The basis for prestige pricing. *Journal of Consumer Marketing*, 10(1), 10–16.

Hair, J. F., Jr, Anderson, R. E., Tatham, R. L. & Black, W. C. (1995). *Multivariate Data Analysis* (4th edn). Englewood Cliffs, NJ: Prentice-Hall Inc.

Higie, R. A. & Feick, L. F. (1988). Enduring involvement: Conceptual and methodological issues. In T. Srull (Ed.), *Advances in Consumer Research* (Vol. 16, pp. 690–696). Provo, UT: Association for Consumer Research.

Hirschman, E. C. (1988). The ideology of consumption: A structural-syntactical analysis of 'Dallas' and 'Dynasty'. *Journal of Consumer Research*, 15(December), 344–359.

Hirschman, E. C. & Holbrook, M. B. (1982). Hedonic consumption: Emerging concepts, methods and propositions. *Journal of Marketing*, 46(Summer), 92–101.

Holt, D. B. (1995). How consumers consume: A typology of consumption practices. *Journal of Consumer Research*, 22(June), 1–16.

Horiuchi, Y. (1984). A systems anomaly: Consumer decision-making process for luxury goods. unpublished doctoral dissertation, University of Pennsylvania, Philadelphia, PA.

Kahle, L. R. (1995). Role-relaxed consumers: Empirical evidence. *Journal of Advertising Research*, 35(2), 59–62.

Kapferer, J.-N. (1997). Managing luxury brands. *Journal of Brand Management*, 4(4), 251–260.

Kapferer, J.-N. (1998). Why are we seduced by luxury brands? *Journal of Brand Management*, 6(1), 44–49.

Kassarjian, H. H. (1965). Riesman revisited. *Journal of Marketing*, 29(April), 54–56.

Keller, K. L. (1991). Conceptualizing, measuring and managing customer-based brand equity. *Journal of Marketing*, 57(1), 1–22.

Kemp, S. (1998). Perceiving luxury and necessity. *Journal of Economic Psychology*, 19(October), 591–606.

Leibenstein, H. (1950). Bandwagon, snob, and Veblen effects in the theory of consumers' demand. *Quarterly Journal of Economics*, 64(May), 183–207.

Lichtenstein, D. R., Ridgway, N. M. & Netemeyer, R. G. (1993). Price perceptions and consumer shopping behavior: A field study. *Journal of Marketing Research*, 30(May), 234–245.

Lipovetsky, G. & Roux, E. (2003). *Le Luxe Eternel: De l'Age du Sacre' au Temps des Marques*. Paris, France: Gallimard.

Lynn, M. (1991). Scarcity effects on value: Quantitative review of the commodity theory literature. *Psychology and Marketing*, 8(1), 45–57.

Marsh, H. W. & Hocevar, D. (1983). Confirmatory factor analysis of multitrait-multimethod matrices. *Journal of Educational Measurement*, 20(Fall), 231–248.

Mason, R. S. (1981). *Conspicuous Consumption*. New York, NY: St Martin's Press.

Mason, R. S. (1992). Modelling the demand for status goods. Working paper, Department of Business and Management Studies, University of Salford, UK.

McCracken, G. (1986). Culture and consumption: A theoretical account of the structure and movement of the cultural meaning of consumer goods. *Journal of Consumer Research*, 13(June), 71–84.

McKinsey Corporation. (1990). *The Luxury Industry: An Asset for France*. Paris, France: McKinsey.

Menezes, D. & Elbert, N. F. (1979). Alternative semantic scaling formats for measuring store image: An evaluation. *Journal of Marketing Research*, 16(February), 80–87.

Mick, D. G. (1986). Consumer research and semiotics: Exploring the morphology of signs, symbols, and significance. *Journal of Consumer Research*, *13*(September), 196–213.

Mindak, W. A. (1961). Fitting the semantic differential to the marketing problem. *Journal of Marketing*, *25*(1), 28–33.

Moschis, G. P. & Churchill, G. A., Jr. (1978). Consumer socialization: A theoretical and empirical analysis. *Journal of Marketing Research*, *15*(November), 599–609.

Nueno, J. L. & Quelch, J. A. (1998). The mass marketing of luxury. *Business Horizons*, November–December, 61–68.

Nunnally, J. C. (1978). *Psychometric Theory* (2nd edn.). New York, NY: McGraw-Hill.

Nyeck, S. & Roux, E. (1997) WWW as communication tool for luxury brands: Compared perceptions of consumers and managers. *24th International Research Seminar in Marketing*, 3–6 June, La Londe les Maures, pp. 296–316.

Osgood, C. E., Suci, G. J. & Tannenbaum, P. H. (1957). *The Measurement of Meaning*. Urbana, IL: University of Illinois Free Press.

Pantzalis, I. (1995). *Exclusivity Strategies in Pricing and Brand Extension*, unpublished doctoral dissertation. University of Arizona, Tucson, AZ.

Phau, I. & Prendergast, G. (2000). Consuming luxury brands: The relevance of the 'rarity principle'. *Journal of Brand Management*, *8*(2), 122–138.

Prendergast, G. & Wong, C. (2003). Parental influence on the purchase of luxury brands of infant apparel: An exploratory study in Hong Kong. *Journal of Consumer Marketing*, *20*(2), 157–169.

Quelch, J. A. (1987). Marketing the premium product. *Business Horizons*, *30*(3), 38–45.

Rao, A. R. & Monroe, K. B. (1989). The effect of price, brand name, and store name on buyers' perceptions of product quality: An integrative review. *Journal of Marketing Research*, *26*(August), 351–357.

Rémaury, B. (2002). Luxe et identité culturelle américaine? *Revue Française Du Marketing*, *187*(2), 49–60.

Richins, M. L. (1994a). Valuing things: The public and private meanings of possessions. *Journal of Consumer Research*, *21*(December), 504–521.

Richins, M. L. (1994b). Special possessions and the expression of material values. *Journal of Consumer Research*, *21*(December), 522–533.

Rossiter, J. R. & Percy, L. (1997). *Advertising Communications and Promotion Management* (2nd edn.). New York, NY: McGraw-Hill.

Roux, E. (1991). Comment se positionnent les marques de luxe. *Revue Française Du Marketing*, *132/133*(2–3), 111–118.

Roux, E. (1995). Consumer evaluation of luxury brand extensions. EMAC Conference, May, ESSEC, Paris, France.

Roux, E. (2002). Le luxe: Au-dela` des chiffres, quelles logiques d'analyse? *Revue Française Du Marketing*, *187*(2), 45–47.

Roux, E. & Floch, J. M. (1996). Ge´rer l'inge´rable: La contradiction interne de toute maison de luxe. *De´Cisions Marketing*, *9*(September–December), 15–23.

Sheth, J. N., Newman, B. I. & Gross, B. L. (1991). Why we buy what we buy: A theory of consumption values. *Journal of Business Research*, *22*(1), 159–170.

Silverstein, M. J. & Fiske, N. (2003). Luxury for the masses. *Harvard Business Review*, *81*(4), 48–57.

Snyder, C. R. & Fromkin, H. L. (1977). Abnormality as a positive characteristic: The development and validation of a scale measuring need for uniqueness. *Journal of Abnormal Psychology*, *86*(5), 518–527.

Solomon, M. R. (1983). The role of products as social stimuli: A symbolic interactionist approach. *Journal of Consumer Research*, *10*(December), 319–329.

Strahan, R. & Gerbasi, K. C. (1972). Short, homogeneous versions of the Marlow-Crowne social desirability scale. *Journal of Clinical Psychology*, *28*(1), 191–193.

Tian, K. T., Bearden, W. O. & Hunter, G. L. (2001). Consumers' need for uniqueness: Scale development and validation. *Journal of Consumer Research*, *28*(June), 50–66.

Tigert, D. J., Ring, L. R. & King, C. W. (1976). Fashion involvement and buying behavior: A methodological study. In B. B. Anderson (Ed.), *Advances in Consumer Research* (Vol. 3, pp. 46–52). Provo, UT: The Association for Consumer Research.

Veblen, T. B. (1899). *The Theory of the Leisure Class*. Boston, MA: Houghton Mifflin.

Verhallen, T. M. & Robben, H. S. (1994). Scarcity and preference: An experiment on unavailability and product evaluation. *Journal of Economic Psychology*, *15*(June), 315–331.

Vigneron, F. & Johnson, L. W. (1999). A review and a conceptual framework of prestige-seeking consumer behavior. *Academy of Marketing Science Review*. Available online at http://www.vancouver.wsu.edu/amsrev/search.htm.

Westbrook, R. A. & Oliver, R. L. (1991). The dimensionality of consumption emotion patterns and consumer satisfaction. *Journal of Consumer Research*, *18*(June), 84–91.

Yamauchi, K. T. & Templer, D. I. (1982). The development of a money attitude scale. *Journal of Personality Assessment*, *46*(5), 522–528.

Zaichkowsky, J. L. (1985). Measuring the involvement construct. *Journal of Consumer Research*, *12*(December), 341–352.

**Franck Vigneron** is an assistant professor of Marketing at California State University, Northridge. His research focuses on measuring the effect of luxury brands on consumer behaviour and evaluating the impact of social taste on consumer judgement and decision making. His work has been published in the *Academy of Marketing Science Review* and the proceedings of the American Psychology Association and the European Marketing Academy, among others.

**Lester W. Johnson** is a professor of Marketing at the Melbourne Business School, Australia. His research focuses on customer satisfaction and consumer behaviour in services. He has published in the *Journal of the Academy of Marketing Science, Academy of Marketing Science Review, Journal of Retailing, Journal of Services Marketing, Journal of Advertising Research, Journal of Business Research,* and the *Journal of International Marketing*, among others.

# Managing Luxury Brands

Jean-Noël Kapferer

## Introduction

Luxury brands are very distinct. And yet, even though not only France, Italy but also Germany, the UK and the USA have created famous luxury brands, there is still some confusion between the concepts of luxury, luxury brand, not to mention the French 'griffe' concept which can neither be translated into English nor into hardly any other language (griffe literally means claw in French). Naturally, everyone is able to sense the differences and to quote a typical example for each of those concepts.

---

This chapter was Reprinted from Kapferer, J. (1997) 'Managing Luxury Brands', *Journal of Brand Management*, 4, pp. 251-9. With kind permission from the *Journal of Brand Management*. All rights reserved.

J.-N. Kapferer (✉)
Inseec Business School, Paris, France
e-mail: jnkapferer@inseec.com

© The Author(s) 2017
J.-N. Kapferer et al. (eds.), *Advances in Luxury Brand Management*,
Journal of Brand Management: Advanced Collections,
DOI 10.1007/978-3-319-51127-6_11

However, when pressed for an exact definition, most people, even luxury specialists, hesitate to give a straightforward answer (Stanley 1989).

This issue is much more than just a search for some definitions and for the minimum requirements to be met in order to quality as a griffe or a luxury brand – or neither of the two. In reality, this nebulous definition of luxury hints at the fact that some essential differences between the management of a luxury brand and that of a brand, say a massmarket brand, are gradually disappearing. At a time when most luxury makers are losing their independence, as they are absorbed by big industrial groups with high-performing marketing techniques, it is important to recall the meaning of concepts and categories. This indeed helps people to become aware of the limits and dangers of simply applying classical marketing methods to luxury management. Yet it also reminds them that luxury has indeed become a true industry demanding a high level of profitability.

The luxury brand, more than any other kind, reflects the existence of an internal project. Its purpose is not just to meet some requirement, but to convey a creative intent. What this entails for luxury brand management is important; it is detailed hereafter.

## What Is Luxury?

The problem with the word 'luxury' is that it is at once a concept (a category), a subjective impression and a polemical term, often subjected to moral criticism. Thus, what is luxury for some is just ordinary for others: while some brands are qualified as luxury brands by one-half of public opinion, others are simply considered as 'major brands' by the other half. Likewise, given the economic crisis, it has become indecent to say 'to like luxury' or 'to pursue luxury'. Real luxury brands remain attractive, but the word itself has lost its spunk and sparkle because of the dull morosity brooding over the industrialised countries. This erosion of the word luxury is a hindrance to market researchers who wish to measure their customers' sensitivity to luxury.

In economic terms, luxury objects are those whose price/quality relationship is the highest of the market. By quality, economists mean 'what they know how to measure', that is, tangible functions. Thus, the McKinsey report (McKinsey Corp 1990) on luxury brands defines luxury brands as those which 'have constantly been able to justify a high price, ie significantly higher than the price of products with comparable tangible functions'. This strictly economic definition of the luxury brand does not include the notion of an absolute minimum threshold. What counts indeed is not the absolute price, but the price differential between luxury products and products with comparable functions. This price can vary from £100 for a cologne brand to hundreds of thousands of pounds. (See Fig. 9.)

As will be seen, this strictly economic perspective does not help dissociate the upper-range brand from the luxury brand and a fortiori from the 'griffe'. Furthermore, even though a Jaguar has always been cheaper than a Porsche, in terms of comparable tangible functions, Jaguar still has a stronger luxury image than Porsche, which is more often perceived as a very technical sport brand. Finally, the economic approach does not help clear the confusion because it is based on the following dichotomy: a brand either is, or is not, a luxury brand. Yet, later on, it will be seen that is time to recognise that Dior is a 'griffe' for one part of its activities, a luxury brand for the second part and an upper-range brand for the third part. By wanting to classify the brand once and for all, it is often forgotten to make the appropriate distinctions according to its various functions and processes. Simultaneously managing the three types of action of a given brand is precisely the challenge that luxury faces today.

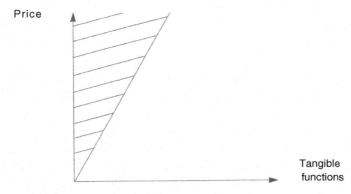

**Fig. 9** The luxury industry according to McKinsey

What does the luxury concept actually encompass? What are the essential attributes of this category of so-called luxury items? Once again, etymology will help to clarify the concepts. Luxury comes from 'lux' which in Latin means light. This explains the typical characteristics of so-called luxury items. Luxury glitters. It fancies gold, gems, brilliants so that, overall, each and every item tends to become a jewel in itself. The fact that luxury is visible is also essential: luxury must be seen, by oneself and by others. That is why luxury brands externalise all of their signs: the brand signature must be seen and recognised on the person wearing the brand. It is their halo which also makes them glow, and, like the beams from a light house, their power depends how visible they are. The geographic expansion of luxury is programmed in its genetic code. If they wish to shine all the way from Ginza to New York, so be it: it is their prerogative. Finally, it is what emerges that shines: made to ultimate perfection, luxury items stand out and embody the ideals contemplated from afar. Luxury defines beauty; it is art applied to functional items.

Like light, luxury is enlightening (critics would rather say blinding). Luxury brands make tangible references for the most sophisticated fashions of a given time. As such, these brands all implicitly convey their own culture and way of life: hence, Saint Laurent is not Chanel. They offer more than mere objects: they provide references of good taste. That is why luxury management should not only depend on customer expectations: luxury brands are animated by their internal programme, their global vision, the specific taste which they promote as well as by the pursuit of their own standards.

Upper-range products are tangibles associated with a specific product category, while luxury ones are intangibles associated with values and ethics.

On a symbolical level, light means life and fertility. Luxury is thus both creation and the vital source of inspiration. In effect, most luxury institutions were founded by a creative genius, whose constantly renewed inspiration rhythmed the attention (and interest) of the ruling classes and the elite. Relating to luxury indeed requires two things: the monetary capacity (for the price of quality) and a propensity to appreciate the object's artistic, creative and sensuous dimensions, that is, anything beyond mere practicality. Luxury items provide extra pleasure and flatter all senses at once.

Etymology is not the only means of deciphering the mystery of the luxury concept. Sociology and history can also help. Luxury is the appanage of the ruling classes. It is indeed widely acknowledged that luxury plays a classifying role according to which a restricted group bonds and outdistances the rest of society in terms of price and preferences (taste). In this respect, luxury brands are just perpetuating and exemplifying the signs and attitudes of former aristocracy. Is it not paradoxical that luxury has blossomed precisely in a society which eradicated aristocracy, yet has preserved the aristocrats' social ideal? Luxury ennobles both the object and its owner. Coats of arms have disappeared, but blazons and brand seals are today's ostentatious adornments. Not many luxury symbols exist: they represent the past privileges of European aristocracy (in the meaning of T. Veblen 1989), living a life of leisure, free from all work, money, time or space obligations. That is why the horse, Hermes' founding myth, works so well: anything even remotely connected to a horse conveys elegance. That is also why modern luxury has produced cars such as Jaguars and Rolls Royces. Everything is made to conceal mere practical utility: leather, wooden fascia, quietness, the multiplicity of detail which make the vehicle itself seem like a drawing room. In this respect, Ferrari and Porsche are prestigious sport brands rather than typical examples of luxury. Created by a talented engineer, they certainly do convey the mythical quest for speed, but they nonetheless embody above all the basic automobile function: mobility.

Likewise, luxury would constantly seek to escape time constraints: focusing on leisure, concealing the effects of time with wigs and face make-up. As for perfume, it also helped to distinguish aristocrats from the common folk. As is seen, it is significant that modern luxury brands have fallen for the cosmetics and perfume industry, not to mention the other essential class attributes: clothing and jewels.

## Luxury Brands and Griffes

A good deal of confusion surrounds the meaning and relationship of these two terms. Many people use the term 'griffe' if a prestigious brand is applied to many different products. Others claim that brands can become griffes.

In reality, brands and griffes must be distinguished in terms of the ground they cover and the way they work. Confusion has been caused by the fact that some famous names, for example, Dior, are griffes for one part of their production and brands for another. Hence, a griffe can become a brand, but the reverse is not true.

The law scarcely clarifies the differences between brands and griffes: in its eyes, a griffe is the fixed image of a signature, set down to be used as a trade-mark. Fortunately, the griffe concept can be understood by examining the word itself. A griffe (French for claw) has something to do with instinct, violence and lightning: it conveys something unpredictable, that leaps out powerfully and leaves its poignant mark. The griffe is the mark of an inspired and instinctive creator. Last, but not least, griffe has the same root as the word 'graphic', thus refers back to the hand. The griffe's specific territory is clearly that of pure creation. Its world of reference is art, its production is hand-made and its obsession is to create a work of unsurpassable, striking, perfection, which hits you in the face. The term 'work' is crucial: the ideal behind a griffe is a unique work of art which can never be reproduced. YSL is a griffe when he signs his haute couture gowns in his boutique on the Rue St Honore: they are one of a kind, luxury brand items. Nina Ricci, on the contrary, is no longer a griffe since her visibility in the small circle of haute couture has faded.

This explains why Dunhill, Dupont, Montblanc, or Boss is not griffe in this sense, but luxury brands. These products were not born in a workshop but in a factory, and they are not intended to be unique pieces, but products made in series – limited series, granted, yet not even in all cases. Their manufacture is not based on instinct but on streamlined production. Workshops can become industrialised and move into series, then mass production but the opposite has never happened.

The fact that the luxury industry comprises three levels must be acknowledged (see Fig. 10).

At the top of the pyramid is the griffe – the creator's signature engraved on a unique work. This explains what is feared most: being copied. Brands, on the contrary, particularly fear fakes/counterfeits. The second level is that of luxury brands produced in small series within a workshop, that is, a 'manufacture', in its etymological sense, which is the

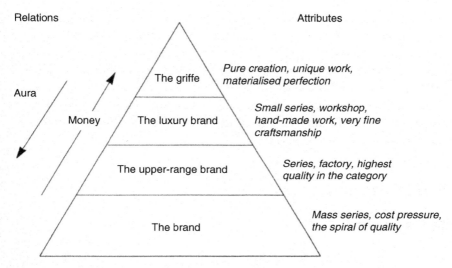

Fig. 10   The luxury and brand system

sole warrant of 'good-facture'. This is the case of Hermes, Rolls Royce or Cartier. The third level is that of streamlined mass production: there are found Dior or YSL, cosmetics and perfumes and SL Diffusion textiles. At this level of real industrialisation, the brand's fame generates added value for expensive and prime quality products, which have, nonetheless, gradually tend to look more and more like the rest.

The whole issue of luxury management hinges on the interactions between those three levels. The perenniality of griffes depends on their integration in industrial conglomerates capable of providing the financial and technical means (R&D) to launch new worldwide products on the third level (Sanofi-Elf for cosmetics, L'Oreal for perfumes). Profit accrues at this level and it is the only means to survive, given the huge investments required for preserving the griffe's potential aura and creativity. If the latter ever disappears, the amount of profit at the bottom of the pyramid will certainly drop, as the brand name will lose its shine. Yet the more brand equity is used, the more it needs to be regenerated: which is why the industrial groups that have invested a lot in luxury brands would be mistaken if they decided to cut the prestige expenses incurred by haute couture and pure creation. These are expenses which help build up new dream and aura capital. What happens is that this capital gradually gets used up by the series process introduced at the third level, that is, the upper-range brand one. Reality consumes dreams: the more a luxury brand is bought, the less it is dreamt about. Hence, somewhat paradoxically, the more a luxury brand is purchased, the more its aura needs protection. It is not only necessary to ensure that its awareness always surpasses its penetration, but also, above all, that its creative potential and prestige are preserved (Dubois and Paternault 1995).

# Principles of Luxury

## Management

Luxury historians and sociologists have pointed out some of the basic principles of luxury brand management: for instance, the necessity to protect clients from non-clients, by creating a distance, a no-mix area, or, as economists would put it, entrance barriers for those who are not invited. This is implemented through prices, selective and exclusive distribution as well as the aesthetic dimension of the products (taste does indeed segment). But for the distinctive sign to work, it must be known by all. Thus, paradoxically, luxury brands must be desired by all but consumed only by the happy few.

This outward/inward dialectics is reflected by a combination of relative visibility in the media with very restricted diffusion, which is why luxury brand awareness must be superior to its penetration. It is indeed the quantitative differential, between those who know the brand and those who buy it, which works as the crucial lever of desire. Consumer product brands function altogether differently: they communicate after having diffused their products. This dialectics also explains the logic behind accessories, such as Chanel's £80 earrings and Hermes' £100 scarves.

Loss of control occurs precisely when luxury brands no longer protect their clients from the non-clients. In our open democratic societies, groups are constantly trying to recreate separations of all kinds. The latter do eventually disappear when, for instance, prestigious brands get distributed in hypermarkets. The infinite multiplication of Vuitton bags (not counting the counterfeits) also hinders the distinctive function of luxury. Likewise, distributed in large quantities, Chanel T-shirts ended up being worn by an excessive amount of women, far beyond the initial target.

Chanel thus became associated with too many women. But above all, such an ordinary T-shirt proved that the marketers had forgotten a crucial element: an object must always be up to par with its brand, and not just serve as a mere prop for the brand name. The genuine luxury brand ensures that both frame and picture, the exterior and interior are worth the same. If the two get disconnected, the luxury brand enters the realm of sham and abdicates in favour of counterfeit. If the luxury brand itself no longer believes in the object itself but only in the fluff around the sign, it encourages people to consciously buy counterfeits. In doing so, they are indeed rather purchasing the brand's lasting halo, and not the object itself as it has been reduced to a mere advertisement prop with no edge to it and no spunk. In the short term, it is highly profitable to multiply licences and to extend the luxury brand to a great deal of ordinary products (pants, socks, belts). But, in doing so, the luxury brand becomes not only democratised but also commoditised. On the contrary, luxury is meant to always be slightly excessive: excess of detail, excess of care, excess of honour, excess of precaution, all reflecting a traditional way of working that practically no longer exists in this age of standardisation and cost minimisation of series. This does not mean that the past is a shrine as some luxury brands unfortunately tend to think: in worshipping tradition so, they might end up disappearing along with their ageing clients. The challenge modern luxury now faces is to please and preserve today's consumers. Explicitly reminiscing about the past can be alienating. Having fully understood that, Cartier introduced steel in its watches, but still coined it like a precious metal. Likewise, Hermes' traditional crocodile or leather suitcase is now also available in carbon fibre, yet its interior is still made of numerous personalising details and of soft, sensual leather.

The modern luxury brand must belong to those who rule the world today. Their reference is no longer land nor castle, but mobility. It is true that excessive practicality can harm the luxury product – in that respect, Seiko and Sony are not luxury brands. Conversely, though, if the products are not practical enough, they gradually start to lag and become obsolete. Luxury brands cannot just ignore the threat of basic brands, strictly focused on practicality: by constantly improving the quality of their products, the latter are indeed continually redefining the ever-increasing standards of 'basic' quality. However prestigious and potentially attractive Jaguar may have been, it was doomed by its deficiencies both in its engine and in its basic components. By relying too heavily on its symbolical added value, Jaguar actually lost some of its global luxury value and attractiveness. Its legend was no longer leading it: it was left behind.

Basic brands are meant to democratise progress, thanks to a virtuous circle mechanism and to competitors: these are indeed continuously raising quality standards at the cheapest price possible, thanks to mass production. Being partly relieved from price constraints, luxury brands, on the contrary, perpetuate an exceptionally high level of quality. For them, indeed, a wide variety of sensations counts just as much as a wide variety of functions. That is why they use the finest materials for their products and extensively customise them in order to prove how customer-focused they are. In doing so, they actually condemn mass production as they make service an integral part of their offer. Anything that is considered optional or added on for 'normal' brands is precisely the norm for luxury brands, because for them what is extra is ordinary. Luxury brands would be wrong, however, to think that they are totally on the safe side. Actually, luxury should not always be exorbitant. In the car industry, for instance, technological improvements have made production more flexible, thus capable of providing greater customisation possibilities, at no extra cost. Therefore, the customisation differential is now being jeopardised by the cost differential, due to the deliberate differences in the two production processes. Neither the rarity of the object nor the potency of the brand image can alone continue to justify the price differential. As can be seen, luxury defines the ideal degree of personalisation and sublimation of a given object, in relation to the more basic brands. In turn, the latter challenge luxury, by their continuous technical improvements and very competitive pricing. Luxury watches, for instance, were meant to perpetuate mechanical movements forever; but quartz technology, developed for the mass market, soon established new standards of precision and reliability, which no mechanical system could possibly meet – within the limits of realistic production costs, that is. Both the economic cost of this quality differential and the negative impact on brand image were all the greater as the renown of luxury watch brands had long been associated with lifetime guarantees.

## Brand Awareness and Desire

It has been mentioned above that the necessary inward/outward dialectics of luxury brands had an implication that was often ignored: the need to always preserve a differential between brand awareness and brand diffusion. The dream of luxury has to be constantly regenerated, as it gradually gets eroded by the real world and consumers buying it. Therefore, there needs to be more people who know and understand the brand than who actually buy it. This outlook was confirmed by RISC (1991), in their recent survey of 12,500 people, aged 15 and above, throughout Europe (Fig. 11). Out of a list of major luxury brands, the latter were asked to say which ones they knew (awareness) of, which ones they had dreamed of (attractiveness) and of which ones, if any, they had purchased (in this instance, buying Cardin cigarettes was enough). As demonstrated in the following graph, there is a strong correlation between the brand's dream potential and the differential – not its awareness per se – between the number of people who just know it and those who have already had some of it. Thus all the brands above the line have a greater dream potential than what they should have had, given their awareness and consumption percentages. All the brands below the line suffer from a dream deficiency.

Those who know a given brand, in the survey, are divided into buyers and dreamers. By analysing each brand, it has thus been possible to identify four different situations, four customer types:

– The buyers who still dream of the brand are the addicts. They are the brand's proselytes. They must be encouraged and rewarded for their loyalty.

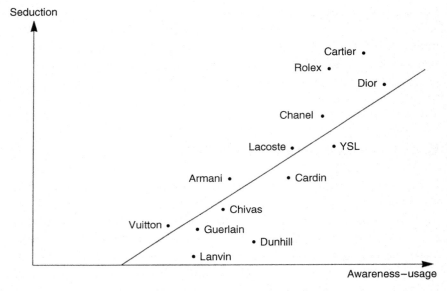

**Fig. 11** Luxury brands' attraction power in Europe (*Source*: RISC)

- The buyers who no longer dream of the brand are 'blase', saturated. Their desire must be revived.
- The non-buyers who dream of the brand do not actually buy, for whatever reason. They must be encouraged either through a more appropriate price/product policy or through wider distribution.
- Finally, the non-buyers who do not dream of the brand are indifferent and off target.

If a brand such as Armani, known by 46 per cent of all Europeans is considered, each customer type respectively represents 6 per cent, 5 per cent, 12 per cent and 23 per cent. Thus, there is an enormous potential of non-buyers who dream of the brand. The Emporio Armani line and its specific stores have been created so that the latter can make their dream come true. However, in Givenchy's case, the figures are, respectively, 2 per cent, 6 per cent, 3 per cent and 30 per cent. The small number of proselytes and the large number of indifferent people show that this brand name is no longer on target.

# From Creator to Brand

Established for the very sake of creation, most luxury institutions quite naturally bear the name of their creator. This is the case for Cardin, Saint Laurent, Ricci, Armani, Chanel, Lanvin, etc. This situation brings about the following paradox: luxury brands only really appear when their creators disappear. As long as the latter lives and continues managing the institution, the name's destiny fully merges with the personal projects of its creator. Thus many people criticise the licensing policy adopted by Cardin, that is, the way in which this name has been over-extended to a wide variety of product categories. This policy actually does nothing but convey Pierre Cardin's personal intellectual curiosity and appetite for adventure. A creator cannot be submitted to managerial directives or self-fulfilment constraints. Creators are in control of two inseparable destinies: their brands' and their own. Hence, the brand stays hidden in the shadow of its creator, until he or she passes away. At this point, there is no need for a charter highlighting a project, positioning, or deep creative urge. The creator's existence is all that is needed: he/she is the living answer to the above, the corporate cement and the proselytiser.

Only when the creator disappears can the brand at last become an actor. It then becomes fully responsible for launching new products, fragrances, events. It rules over those hired to take over the founder's creative function. Previously, the latter was sole commander. Now, however, the new managers must adapt, in part at least, to the project of a brand which has since become sovereign. It is actually quite significant that renowned couturiers, capitalising on their griffe, have kept a boutique in their own name: there, they can express their personal style, freed from any constraints linked to the necessity of adapting to the 'griffe'. This was the case for Claude Montana when he worked for Lanvin and for K. Lagerleld, who was then with Chanel.

The creator's death generally causes immediate problems either to the inheritors of the name or to the managers taking over. From a mere patronymic, the name changes into a full-fledged, decision-maker. But what are its specific projects, its set of values, its ethics and its inner essence? In fact, many luxury brands do not know who they are. Having so far remained implicitly borne by the creator, the brand's programme had not been not clearly stated but rather revealed in the artist's work. Now, it must become explicit if it is to be shared with all and accepted by all actors in the world of brands: staff, new creators, worldwide distribution channels.

Not knowing what to do at the death of Mr Ricci, Nina Ricci's new managers launched a research study on their identity, aiming at revealing the genetic programme of the brand. However, the concept of a brand's intrinsic identity, flesh and corporeal existence should by no means be assimilated to research on brand image, as this only reflects the way in which the brand is perceived by different consumers throughout the world. Moreover, each continent generally perceives the brand in a different way. Much unlike any others, luxury brands are not meant to be managed democratically, for instance by asking the Japanese, the Americans or the Germans how they would like Nina Ricci to be and to develop in the future. As is well known, an image is only a fragmented, heterogeneous reflection of the brand. Brands, on the contrary, are unique: there is not one Balmain for the Asian continent and another for the USA. Balmain is Balmain. The identity concept is crucial to luxury brand management (Kapferer 1997): it alone provides altogether the basis for long-term capitalisation, respect for the brand's specific itinerary and for vital worldwide harmonisation. Everyone is aware of the pressure for change and discontinuity exerted by the numerous parties involved in the brand's international diffusion. The only valid recommendation therefore is to never compromise on the brand's set of values or its deeply rooted identity traits. The brand is a living memory. Thus, it is necessary to know what brains, that is, what genetic programme the brand has, in order to successfully control its future life. The brand's truth lies within itself. The purpose of brand identity research is to try to detect the brand's most striking achievements among all, those which have had a major impact. From past to present, the brand's most symbolical products are thus carefully scanned: from which programme do they seem to emanate?

# References

Dubois, B., & Paternault, C. (1995). Observations: Understanding the world of international luxury brands. *Journal of Advertising Research*, *35*(4), July–August, 69–76.

Kapferer, J.-N. (1997). *Strategic brand management* (2nd Edn.). London: Kogan Page.

Mc Kinsey Corp. (1990). *The Luxury industry*. Paris: McKinsey.

RISC. (1991). *Brand value and management in the luxury industry*. Paris: International Research Institute on Social Change, September.

Stanley, T. (1989). *Selling to the affluent*. Homewood, IL: Irwin.

Veblen, T. (1989). *The theory of the leisure class*. New York: Macmillan.

**Jean-Noël Kapferer** is a world renowned expert on brand management. Professor at INSEEC Business School and at the Luxury Business Institute (Shanghai and Seoul) he is co-author of *The Luxury Strategy*, and author of Kapferer on Luxury. Academic director of executive programmes, he leads seminars on the evolution of luxury management in the USA, China, Japan, Korea.

# Index

**A**
Advertisement, 34, 51, 74, 78, 80, 82, 134, 147, 186, 188, 225, 243
Anti-laws of marketing, 32
Apple, 30, 127
Armani, 126, 194, 203, 246, 247
Artification, 35, 37
Authentic consumers, 101

**B**
Benefits of fame, 30
BMW, 29, 39, 53, 54, 75, 76, 78, 194
Bottom-up relationship, 16, 60
Brand architecture, 181, 183, 185, 193, 194, 196
Brand dream, 35
Brand equity measurement, 181, 185–186
Brand fame, 30, 241
Brand identity, 14, 44, 72–73, 87, 203, 248
Brand name products, 11, 26, 169, 182, 193, 194, 195, 241, 243, 246
Brand value, 3, 49
Bugatti, 29
Burberry, 61, 130

**C**
Cadillac, 201
Calvin Klein, 66, 157, 158, 169
Cartier, 29–31, 60, 67, 81, 179, 203, 241, 243
CEO, 27, 28, 34

## Index

Chanel, 26, 28, 29, 32, 37, 50, 67, 72, 73, 75, 126, 238, 242, 243, 247
China, 16, 26, 29, 33, 35, 38, 45, 50, 60, 77, 128, 130, 136, 147, 148
Chow Tai Fook Jewellery Group Limited, 8
Coach, 28, 130, 187
Coco Chanel, 37, 73
Co-creation, 13–14, 76, 165–168, 170
Collector, 28, 29
Compagnie Financiere Richemont SA, 5
Consumer behaviour, 3, 44, 62, 200, 201, 205, 208, 224
Consumer luxury brand, 3–11, 14
Consumption of luxury, 45–46, 88, 204, 207
Contemporary consumers, 44, 45
COO, 81, 82
Core luxury brands, 28, 29
Corporate brand perspective, 2
Cost of the goods, 28
Counterfeit consumers, 91, 93, 95, 97, 101
Counterfeit goods, 14, 17, 63, 85, 93, 94, 96
Counterfeiting, 15, 17, 60, 85, 86, 88, 93, 94, 97, 99, 100, 102, 164, 184
Counter-intuitive rules, 16, 80
Craftsmanship, 3, 5, 83, 101, 130, 133, 143, 161, 210
CRM, 71, 76
Cult products, 30–31
Culture convergence, 16, 60
Customer value perception, 88–91, 101
Customer values, 54, 80, 147, 183

D
Digital communications, 16, 60
Dimensions of luxury, 17, 89, 201, 210

E
Ecology, 127, 132
E-commerce, 26, 32, 35, 38, 39
Economic crisis, 80–82, 129, 236
Ermenegildo Zegna, 52
Essence of luxury, 31, 68–69, 133
The Estée Lauder Companies Inc., 5
Evolution of capitalism, 26
Exclusivity, 2, 13, 27, 28, 32, 35, 39, 44, 53, 61, 87, 92, 158, 182, 185, 203, 208
Experiential marketing, 16, 43, 44, 46–49, 53, 61, 63

F
Fake, 33, 88, 92, 93, 99, 100, 240
Family brands, 34, 196
Fashion, 2, 33, 37, 44, 50, 52, 60, 63, 66, 67, 72, 92, 95, 128, 130, 162, 193, 238
Fashion brands, 30, 34, 53, 128, 193, 219
Fashion goods, 125, 131
Ferrari, 32, 51, 67, 77, 239
Financial model of fashion, 30
Financial Value, 91

Flagship stores, 26, 30, 33, 35, 52
Ford, 65, 66
Founder, 3, 27, 31, 34, 247
Framework of brand-luxury, 17
France, 33, 62, 126, 135, 148, 202, 212, 235
Functional value, 91–92
Functions of luxury, 16, 68, 147

### G

Genuine Goods, 14, 17, 93, 101
Germany, 33, 48, 148, 235
Globalisation, 16, 59, 69, 141, 180
Google, 11, 39, 160
Growth trade-offs, 17
Gucci, 26, 29, 32, 50, 67, 179, 193

### H

Haute couture, 72, 240, 241
Hedonistic consumption, 168
Hermès, 3, 27, 29, 34, 35, 126, 147, 239, 241, 242, 243
Hermès International SCA, 9
High pricing, 30
High status buyers, 35
Hyper-reality, 46, 47

### I

Iconic products, 30
Identity traits, 18, 248
Importance of space, 33
India, 16, 48, 51, 52, 60, 77, 148
Individual Value, 91, 92–93
Innovative experience design, 16, 55
Intel, 11
Intellectual Property rights, 88, 97
International diffusion, 18, 248
Investor-owned brands, 34
Italy, 33, 62, 126, 130, 235

### J

Jaguar, 45, 65–66, 76, 208, 237, 239, 244
Japan, 61, 74, 148

### K

Kering SA, 7, 31, 38
Kors, Michael, 28, 34

### L

Lacoste, 71, 73, 74
Lamborghini, 26, 29
Land Rover, 65
Lauren, Ralph, 34, 73, 74, 128, 130, 217
Lexus, 73, 74
Lifestyle, 16, 44, 45, 54, 61, 87, 134, 208
Limit distribution, 35
Long-term value, 34
L'Oréal Luxe, 241
Louis Vuitton, 26, 29, 37, 60, 67, 76, 79, 80, 82, 100, 129, 147, 179, 208
Luxottica Group SpA, 6
Luxuries, 27, 32, 33, 36, 38, 39, 40, 92, 96
Luxurification, 45, 162

## 254  Index

Luxury and sustainability, 14–15, 18, 124–125, 131, 132, 134, 135, 144–146, 148
Luxury brand co-creation, 13–14
Luxury brand management, 2, 13–16, 18, 27–32, 34, 39, 40, 59, 62–64, 69, 202, 212, 236, 242, 248
Luxury brand marketing, 16, 43–55
Luxury brand's nature, 17–18
Luxury brand strategy, 16, 59–64
Luxury business, 25, 26, 33, 63
Luxury challenges, 39–40, 63
Luxury concept, 87–88, 238, 239
Luxury consumption, 16, 17, 37, 45, 46, 51, 52, 55, 61, 85, 87, 89, 91, 92, 101, 124, 145, 168, 172, 205, 208, 209
Luxury event, 27
Luxury goods, 11, 15, 16, 33, 43, 44, 46, 47, 49–53, 60, 63, 66–68, 70, 86–88, 93–96, 101, 131, 132, 145, 147, 187, 202
Luxury imitators, 208
Luxury industry, 1, 2–3, 27–29, 38, 53, 130, 139, 145, 172, 240
Luxury industry rankings, 2
Luxury pyramid, 28
Luxury spirits industries, 26
Luxury strategy, 32, 33, 62, 67, 126, 130
Luxury watch brands, 28, 245
Luxury watch industry, 26
LVMH, 3, 27, 29, 38, 59, 61, 147

M

Margins, 27, 29, 32, 34, 184
Marketing strategy, 40, 44, 53, 55, 181, 185
Mass fashion brands, 128
Mass markets, 28, 32, 67, 245
McCartney, Stella, 44, 128, 148
Mega-brand, 29–30, 32, 37
Mercedes, 29, 39, 73, 74, 75, 82, 191, 217, 225
Mikimoto, 77
Millennials, 38, 40
Mission, 3
Multiple lens approach, 17, 157–172

N

New luxury markets, 16, 60
Non-luxury brands, 10, 11, 27, 40, 200, 205, 209, 210

O

Oligopoly, 33
Omni channel, 13
Operating profit, 28

P

P&G, 66, 67, 75, 78
Parameters of luxury, 44–45
Patek Philippe, 74
Perceptions of brand luxury, 17, 172, 199–228
Porsche, 29, 31, 71, 212, 215, 225, 237, 239
Postmodernism, 46–48
Prada, 28, 29, 32, 51, 67, 130, 179

Premiumisation, 10, 32, 33, 39, 61, 67, 68, 71, 74, 77, 125, 127, 157, 160, 161, 165, 181–184, 201
Premium pricing strategy, 183
Premium products, 32, 33, 67, 74
Prestige, 27, 32–36, 66, 77, 81, 88, 89, 91, 93, 158, 160, 163–165, 169, 170, 172, 181, 182, 205, 241, 242

Q
Quality, 12, 13, 14, 27, 30, 32, 44, 45, 61, 63, 66, 67, 74, 86, 87, 89, 91, 92, 94, 99, 133, 134, 161, 162, 164, 165, 182, 183, 193, 195, 202, 207, 209, 210, 224, 225, 236, 241, 244, 245

R
Ralph Lauren Corporation, 2
Rarity, 10, 35, 77, 87, 125, 133, 203, 208, 245
Rarity principle, 35
Retail sector, 38
Richard Mille, 28, 29, 79
Role of retail, 38
Rolex, 3, 29, 32, 60, 212, 215, 225
Rolex SA, 9
Rolls Royce, 201, 203, 239, 241
Russia, 16, 45, 60, 77, 148

S
Scrutiny, 129–131
Seiko, 74, 244

Smith, Adam, 31
Social media, 13–14, 28, 35
Social responsibility, 101, 125
Social status, 45, 207
Social Value, 93
Status brand, 79, 88, 157, 158, 160, 205
Sub-branding, 194–195
Sustainability, 14–15, 17, 37, 123–149
Sustainable development, 17, 26, 37, 124, 126, 130, 131, 133, 135, 136, 139, 141, 144, 145, 147
The Swatch Group Ltd., 7
Switzerland, 33

T
Tag Heuer, 11
Tesla, 39, 131
Three pillars of incomparability, 34
Tiffany, 30, 32
Timelessness, 72
Tod's, 73
Top-down relationship, 16
Trade-Off, 17, 86, 89, 101
Trading-up, 45, 67, 69, 77, 78, 163
Traditional luxury, 67, 132, 187

U
UK, 61, 130, 139, 235
Ultra-luxury segments, 28
Uniqueness, 10, 11, 13, 33, 45, 61, 89, 92, 130, 162, 190, 207, 208, 224, 225
United States, 33, 66, 71, 73, 74, 78, 79, 81, 82, 148

## V

Vertical extension, 193, 194
Visibility, 26, 30, 78, 123, 130, 195, 240, 242
Vision, 3, 59, 74, 75, 76, 148, 238
Volume, 26, 29, 30, 35, 37, 66, 79, 126, 128, 130, 187

## W

Wealth-creation opportunities, 16, 59
Wealth gap, 134, 147

## Y

Yves Saint Laurent, 75

CPSIA information can be obtained
at www.ICGtesting.com
Printed in the USA
LVOW13*1801040218
565253LV00011B/669/P